Practical social work

Published in conjunction with
the British Association of Social Workers

D1332684

Founding editor: Jo Campling

Social Work is a multi-skilled profession, centred on people. Social workers need skills in problem-solving, communication, critical reflection and working with others to be effective in practice.

The British Association of Social Workers (www.basw.co.uk) has always been conscious of its role in setting guidelines for practice and in seeking to raise professional standards. The concept of the Practical Social Work series was developed to fulfil a genuine professional need for a carefully planned, coherent, series of texts that would contribute to practitioners' skills, development and professionalism.

Newly relaunched to meet the ever-changing needs of the social work profession, the series has been reviewed and revised with the help of the BASW Editorial Advisory Board:

Peter Beresford
Jim Campbell
Monica Dowling
Brian Littlechild
Mark Lymbery
Fraser Mitchell
Steve Moore

Under their guidance each book marries practice issues with theory and research in a compact and applied format: perfect for students, practitioners and educators.

A comprehensive list of titles available in the series can be found online at: www.palgrave.com/socialwork/basw

---

Series standing order **ISBN 0–333–80313–2**

You can receive future titles in this series as they are published by placing a standing order. Please contact your bookseller or, in the case of difficulty, contact us at the address below with your name and address, the title of the series and the ISBN quoted above.

Customer Services Department, Macmillan Distribution Ltd, Houndmills, Basingstoke, Hampshire RG21 6XS, England

---

Practical social work series

New titles

Sarah Banks   *Ethics and Values in Social Work* **(4th edition)**

Veronica Coulshed and Joan Orme   *Social Work Practice* **(5th edition)**

Veronica Coulshed, Audrey Mullender and Margaret McClade   *Management in Social Work* **(4th edition) Coming soon!**

Celia Doyle   *Working with Abused Children* **(4th edition)**

Gordon Jack and Helen Donnellan   *Social Work with Children* **Coming soon!**

Paula Nicolson and Rowan Bayne   *Psychology for Social Work Theory and Practice* **(4th edition) Coming soon!**

Michael Oliver, Bob Sapey and Pamela Thomas   *Social Work with Disabled People* **(4th edition)**

Mo Ray and Judith Philips   *Social Work with Older People* **(5th edition)**

Steven Shardlow and Mark Doel   *Practice Learning and Teaching* **(2nd edition) Coming soon!**

Neil Thompson   *Anti-Discriminatory Practice* **(5th edition)**

For further companion resources visit www.palgrave.com/socialwork/basw

Celia Doyle

Working with Abused Children

Focus on the Child

Fourth Edition

THE BRITISH ASSOCIATION OF SOCIAL WORKERS

First edition 1989; reprinted once
Second edition 1997; reprinted three times
Third edition 2006; reprinted four times
Fourth edition 2012

Published by
PALGRAVE MACMILLAN

Palgrave Macmillan in the UK is an imprint of Macmillan Publishers Limited, registered in England, company number 785998, of Houndmills, Basingstoke, Hampshire RG21 6XS.

Palgrave Macmillan in the US is a division of St Martin's Press LLC, 175 Fifth Avenue, New York, NY 10010.

Palgrave Macmillan is the global academic imprint of the above companies and has companies and representatives throughout the world.

Palgrave® and Macmillan® are registered trademarks in the United States, the United Kingdom, Europe and other countries

ISBN 978–0–230–29794–4

This book is printed on paper suitable for recycling and made from fully managed and sustained forest sources. Logging, pulping and manufacturing processes are expected to conform to the environmental regulations of the country of origin.

A catalogue record for this book is available from the British Library.

A catalog record for this book is available from the Library of Congress.

10   9   8   7   6   5   4   3   2   1
21   20   19   18   17   16   15   14   13   12

Printed and bound in Great Britain by
CPI Antony Rowe, Chippenham and Eastbourne

This book is dedicated to Eunice, Denny, Gill and all my Early Years colleagues at the University of Northampton from whom I have learnt so much

Brief contents

Contents

List of figures

Preface to the fourth edition

The focus of this book is the child who is abused particularly by their caregivers or within their own home. The reason for the focus on the domestic and the family is because parents and homes normally represent security and safety for children. If children cannot retreat to the love and protection of their home then the present isolation and agony and the implications for future development are dire.

At the time of the first edition, child protection workers in the UK were coming to terms with the Children Act 1989 and recovering from upheaval and change in the wake of the Cleveland Inquiry. At the time of the second edition, practitioners found themselves 'refocusing' their intervention after the publication of a raft of government-sponsored research. The discourse became one of a 'child in need' rather than 'at risk' and 'assessment' not investigation. By the third edition, child protection workers were reeling from the 2003 Laming Report after the death of Victoria Climbié and the 2004 Bichard Inquiry following the murders of two young girls. The discourse changed again becoming one of 'safeguarding' with the recognition that 'every child matters'.

Despite Laming, Bichard, 'safeguarding', refined and redefined procedures, green papers and revised laws, children continue to be abused, exploited and tortured at the hands of familiar adults. At the time of writing, early years practitioners in England are coming to terms with the sexual abuse of babies by a staff member at 'Little Teds' nursery and the death from starvation and neglect of Khyra Ishaq. Meanwhile Lord Laming has produced a second report after the violent death of two-year-old Peter Connelly.

The headline cases of Victoria, Khyra, Peter and the babies at Little Teds nursery mask all the good protective work undertaken by dedicated professionals making shrewd but compassionate judgements. Although now there is an emphasis on evidence-based or evidence-informed practice, it is often difficult to demonstrate that the actions of practitioners result in benefits. What is clear, however, as highlighted by Munro (2011), is that practitioners know that it is not enough to just assess, file a report, offer some support to the parents, or even remove the children, and then leave the victims to cope unaided until, maybe, they come to the notice of the agencies again. Furthermore, while assessment is important – so is assistance with the healing process given through individual, family or group work. Equally important is prevention, especially at a societal level, by changing the way that children are constructed as objects and possessions rather than fellow citizens with rights to dignity, justice and protection. A book on working with abused children, updated by research and reflection, still seems as valid today as it did when the first edition was published over twenty years ago – in the previous millennium.

Nevertheless, changes arise in learning about practice, and so do books, hence the need to revise *Working with Abused Children* from time to time. One of the major changes in this edition is the provision of a number of features to enhance the accessibility of the ideas and also to appeal to different learning styles. These include:

- Chapter overviews at the start of each chapter to signpost where various topics and debates can be found within the chapter.
- Additional and clearly demarked *case studies* (called Practice Focus) to highlight many of the dilemmas and complexities of work with abused children.
- *Reflective exercises* (called Point for Reflection) to help enhance critical consideration of what has been written.
- *Practice-based exercises* (called Putting it into Practice) to assist in putting the ideas in the book into practice whether in work or placement situations.
- *Messages from research*, identifying key findings from selected research reflecting the importance of evidence-informed practice.
- *Further resources*, which is similar to the further reading of the earlier editions but encompasses resources additional to books.

Some exercises ask you to remember and reflect on a particular situation that applied to yourself. If you are feeling emotionally vulnerable, please choose a relatively superficial memory, unless you feel well supported and have someone to turn to in the event of your memories overpowering your capacity to cope.

One sad change is the withdrawal from this edition of the account given by 'Helen' about her childhood. She has been silenced. She asked for her story to be withdrawn and I have respected this. She felt that her words had been deliberately manipulated and misunderstood by an author of a paper, which appeared in a social work journal. Her daughter, training to be a social worker, found the paper and showed it to her. Helen read it with mounting horror because she felt that the author seemed to blame her father for the fact that her brother was abusing her because he was absent a lot and Helen could not tell him about the abuse. Helen loved her late father and described him as 'a loving, caring man I adored'. He had, like many men in the 1960s and 1970s, to go away a lot representing his business in Europe. Helen also could not tell her father about the abuse because she loved him so much she did not want to hurt or upset him. She felt the writer of the paper for the social work journal had violated both her and her father.

I am concerned not just about the hurt caused to Helen but because this misuse of her words by the author is a symptom of child protection adults who mishear the voices of children in order to focus on the needs of parents.

I have respected Helen's wish to withdraw but have kept the accounts by other survivors from the earlier editions and added one by a brother and sister, Jake and Josie. I ask readers to read the accounts of survivors and the words of children in the book with respect.

To turn to another point, since the first edition, my own research and understanding of emotional abuse and emotional and physical neglect has steadily increased. These forms of abuse, particularly in the early years, can have profoundly adverse effects on the development of children's brain architecture and physiology, which, in turn, can damage the child's physiological, social and emotional growth. This underpins all other forms of abuse. Even when it is the sole or main form of abuse, it is arguably the most corrosive because it is an attack on the persona and sense of self of a vulnerable individual. Yet paradoxically, emotionally abused and neglected children are those least likely to be offered a therapeutic service. My research however also showed that abused children can be remarkably resilient and factors promoting resilience are often ones that can be readily harnessed by helping professionals.

This edition, as with previous ones, has been informed by my own experiences of childhood, with loving parents, but coping with undiagnosed 'dyslexia' and a varied cultural heritage. Added to this are years of practice on the front-line of child protection work.

Although my focus is on the child, I can nevertheless empathise with parents. As one myself, I have gained insights into the challenges of adoption and the demands of a multiple birth. Having being widowed when my youngest child was only seven-years-old, I can also appreciate the pressures of coping as a single parent.

Additionally, this fourth edition has been hugely augmented by my moving into the sphere of 'early years' and working alongside colleagues and students focused exclusively on the welfare of young children. Despite once being dismissed as 'mere' nursery nurses, early years practitioners have always had an exquisite understanding of the developing child and a brilliant natural ability to communicate with small children. Now they are increasingly articulating their skills, extending their roles and deservedly having their professionalism recognised. Their child-centred research and practice has substantially influenced my recent reading, thinking and writing.

As with previous editions, I conclude this preface with a note on terminology. Words have the power to both increase or challenge discrimination and to create positive or negative concepts. I have chosen words and terminology with all due care but recognise that some concepts and terms, which are currently appropriate, will alter subtly in meaning and become unacceptable over the next few years. It is to be hoped that later readers will mentally insert the more appropriate contemporary terminology, which of course I cannot currently anticipate.

CELIA DOYLE

Acknowledgements

Inevitably the greatest thanks go to those who have made a central contribution to this and previous editions but who, for reasons of confidentiality, are simply known as Sarah, Roy, Lloyd, Marie, Josie and Jake, as well as Helen. Their courage and generosity in offering their accounts of childhood adversity should not be under-estimated.

Past colleagues who inspired me, thereby contributing to the content of this book, are too numerous to mention but include Peter Barbor, Maddie Collinge, Judy Fawcett, David Jones, Margaret Oates and Jenny Still. In recent years my thinking has been spurred and clarified by social work colleagues such as Angie Bartoli, Chris Durkin, Sue Kennedy, Sukhwinder Singh and, above all, Prospera Tedam. Another important group of colleagues who have so unstintingly shared their ideas and encouraged me are the wonderful staff and students in the Early Years Division at the University of Northampton and include Gill Handley, Eunice Lumsden, Denise Hevey, Maggie Hunt and, independent consultant, Sally Romain. Considerable assistance has been so patiently and consistently given by the staff at Palgrave Macmillan, especially Kate Llewellyn.

Finally, thanks are due to my family and friends for their patience and understanding. Their willingness to wade over or around piles of books, journals, papers and bits of assorted computers in order to reach their mother, sister or friend is highly valued and their love and tolerance cherished.

CELIA DOYLE

CHAPTER 1

Laying foundations

CHAPTER OVERVIEW
There is an acknowledgement of the challenging nature of working with abused children. Subsequently, the chapter explores:

- definitions of child abuse
- power as an important defining factor
- foundations of good practice
- evidence-informed practice and the need to evaluate research and theory
- obstacles to recognising abuse
- recording and inter-agency working

> Staff across frontline services need appropriate support and training to ensure that as far as possible they put themselves in the place of the child or young person and consider first and foremost how the situation must feel for them. (Laming, 2009, p. 22)

'Putting themselves in the place of the child' is what this book is all about. The first prerequisite for those working with abused children is the ability to empathise and appreciate the child's perspective. No volume can claim to provide sufficient support and guidance to guarantee that practitioners can adequately protect and work with children. However, the purpose of this book is to make at least a modest contribution towards professionals' ability to work with, rather than simply for, abused children.

Front-line practitioners know all too well that working with abused children is extremely demanding. However, the challenges can be eased and the work will be all the more effective if practice is based on sound foundations. This first chapter, therefore, looks at some of the foundations for good practice.

The extract below is from a poem, *No worst, there is none*, by Gerard Manley Hopkins (see Jenkins 2006, p. 151). Although the full poem is a description of depression, the three lines extracted here have an alternative meaning for those who work in the front-line of child protection:

> O the mind, mind has mountains; cliffs of fall
> Frightful, sheer, no-man-fathomed. Hold them cheap
> May who ne'er hung there.

The lines of Hopkins' poem encapsulate the feelings of dread when standing on the doorstep, anticipating the reception when the door is opened by parents who are troubled, defensive, insulted or angry. It expresses the depth of disbelief and supressed disgust as a child hesitantly describes the extreme degradation to which she was subjected. It articulates our despair when our only option is to remove children after all our efforts to help a family have failed. It reflects the agony of practitioners when they see their profession excoriated, knowing that those who condemn have not the faintest understanding of what it is like to battle though exhaustion or disillusionment to try, yet again, to wring out sufficient emotional energy to cope somehow with the unthinkable, the unbelievable, the unimaginable – and the, sometimes, unbearable.

Working with abused children can be particularly demanding because often parents and carers, even abusing ones, can be people who attract our compassion. Often they are struggling with immense pressures, some show great courage and, for many, life simply seems extraordinarily tough and unfair.

On the other hand, in a perceptive paper written after Lord Laming's 2003 inquiry, Cooper (2005, p. 5) recalled a senior social work manager commenting 'many of the adults we have to deal with in child abuse cases are complete bastards'. Cooper added that the child protection social worker's task 'means waking up every day and wondering if today your duty will involve pursuing enquiries with people who will, in Lord Laming's more temperate language, be "devious and menacing"' (p. 5). Trying to work in partnership with parents who raise in us very strong feelings is exhausting enough. Expecting practitioners, on top of this, to fully embrace the perspective of an abused child is well-nigh demanding the impossible. And yet that is precisely what *is* required of child protection professionals. No one who has not been in the front line of child protection can really understand those 'cliffs of fall, fright-ful, sheer no-man-fathomed' and yet the alternative of leaving vulnerable children undefended and exposed to avoidable harm is not an option.

Therefore, working with abused children requires more than a wish to help, an ability to communicate with the very young or a willingness to respect their views – all essential attributes. It also requires emotional resilience plus an appreciation of how, why and when particular forms of assistance and intervention are appropriate. Such an understanding is based partly on reflection upon one's own experiences and observations, partly on professional guidelines, and partly on 'theory', which is, in a sense, other people's reflection on their experiences and observations. However, before proceeding further to look at the recognition of abuse and the foundations of good practice, it is worth clarifying what is meant by the 'abuse' of 'children'.

Defining child abuse: socially constructed concepts

For the purpose of this book, 'child abuse' means the maltreatment of people aged under 18 years by their parents or carers or by other people to whom their parents have knowingly exposed them. Such maltreatment can be by acts of commission such as hitting, poisoning, raping or by acts of omission such as failing to provide food, warmth and affection.

It is impossible to define child abuse to the satisfaction of all people at all times. This is because concepts such as 'child', 'childhood' and 'abuse' are socially constructed; they have different meanings at different times and in different cultures. This does not mean that child abuse does not exist and that children do not suffer. Rather, it means that there are no absolute distinctions between parental behaviour which is deemed acceptable, that which might be less satisfactory but is not a matter of public concern and that which is indisputably socially and publically intolerable. For example, the severe flogging of children by parents has been deemed an essential parental duty during some periods of history. At other times, it has been largely ignored and considered a private matter. More recently in the UK, it is viewed as child maltreatment requiring state intervention. Even within a society or state there may be little consensus. Some sectors of UK society consider sending a child to boarding school to be emotionally abusive whereas others argue that not to send them and to deprive them of the 'best education' would be neglectful.

The socially constructed nature of 'child abuse' also means that it is difficult to determine the boundaries between what is viewed as abuse and other hazards. For example should young people, who are at serious risk of harm located in the community, such as gang violence, be defined as 'abused'? By focusing on maltreatment by parents, or for which parents bear responsibility, this book is not denying the seriousness of physical, sexual or emotional violence and exploitation at the hands of non-parents, non-related children, organised criminals or even the 'state'. To do justice to the full range of abuses to children and young people, several volumes would be required. Therefore, boundaries are drawn to contain ideas into one modest book and the key one is to focus on intra-family maltreatment. Nevertheless, some of the perspectives and ways of helping children outlined in the book may be of relevance to extended or community-based forms of abuse.

An important source of contemporary UK definitions of abuse is the *Working Together* document (Department for Children, Schools and Families (DCSF), 2010). It states that 'somebody may abuse or neglect a child by inflicting harm, or by failing to act to prevent harm' (p. 35). It then gives detailed definitions of the different forms of maltreatment: physical, sexual and emotional abuse, and neglect.

Despite being refined over the years, the *Working Together* (DCFS, 2010) definitions can still all be contested because child abuse is a socially constructed concept. For example, the document's description of physical abuse includes 'hitting, shaking, throwing, poisoning, burning or scalding, drowning, suffocating, or otherwise causing physical harm to a child' (p. 38). However, 'hitting' and 'throwing' could be applied to children involved in contact sports. Those thoroughly enjoying judo may well be thrown quite forcibly and sometimes be hurt. A similar case can be made of all the definitions, for example, in terms of neglect: what is appropriate in one context may be negligent in another. To take one scenario, in a rural village preventing a child from 'playing out' with other children may be deemed abusive over-protection, whereas in a city area beside a busy road a parent who allows a child to wander beyond the garden gate or flat balcony might be seen as neglectfully providing inadequate supervision.

The difficulties described above do not mean that there should be no attempt to define the terms within which we work. Nor does it signify that the *Working Together* (DCFS, 2010) definitions have no value; they are extremely useful as guidelines. However, it demonstrates that working with abused children is no easy task because of the lack of a clear consensus about what a 'child' or 'abuse' is.

Finally, the term 'safeguarding' has been adopted in recent years to indicate a broader approach than protection. The term embraces:

- the general enhancement of children's well-being;
- the prevention of abuse occurring in the first place;
- when abuse occurs, the prevention of further mistreatment;
- the alleviation of the effects of abuse.

To some extent, in this book, 'protection' and 'safeguarding' tend to be used interchangeably although it is acknowledged that safeguarding is a rather broader term applying to the child's total welfare.

Defining child abuse: uses and abuses of power

One way of helping to determine 'abuse' is to examine how power is being used. Power can be a positive force, as Foucault (1980) explains 'it transverses and produces things, it induces pleasure, forms knowledge, produces discourse' (p. 119). But power can be corrupted. Maltreatment and oppression occur if people with power abuse or misuse it. In the macro-environment, wider society or the nation, oppressions (for example, the former South African Apartheid) are officially sanctioned by those 'in power' even if they are the minority. Conversely 'force' of numbers can mean that the majority often oppresses minority groups in society. In the micro-environment, such as small institutions and family homes, abuse occurs when there is a power imbalance and those with the greater power misuse it, illustrated by Figure 1.1.

A number of commentators have recognised that 'power' is not a single entity but rather there are different forms of power. Handy's (1985) analysis is perhaps one of the most useful because it is relatively easy to understand and it readily transfers from the world of business and organisations, for which it was originally devised, into the social and welfare domain. Handy identified six forms of power and here they are adapted to relate to child abuse:

- *Physical power*: this is clearly apparent in the domestic setting, given the larger physique of adults compared to children. Parents constantly use their physical power for their children's benefit by, for example, picking up small children for a cuddle

Abuse of power

Different forms of power:
physical, position, resource, expert, personal, negative

Objectification of victims:
e.g. viewing slaves as property or a child as 'it'

Silent witnesses:
co-perpetrators, co-victims, those who are powerless to intervene or who do not understand what they are witnessing

←—————————————————————————————→

Macro-environment   Micro-environment

Worldwide	**State level**	**Sub-state institutions**	**Families**
Discriminations e.g. sexism, racism, homophobia, paedophile networks	Oppressive political systems and laws, e.g. Apartheid, Nazi 'final solution' holocaust	Maltreatment in residential settings, schools, day care	Child, intimate partner, vulnerable adult and elder abuse

Figure 1.1   Roots of oppression

or lifting them out of danger. But it can be misused to burn, poison, assault, rape or profoundly intimidate less powerful family members.

- *Position power*: this power, invested in those with parental responsibility, is normally used wisely by parents and carers who often have to make judgements about what is in their child's best interests. However, this power can be misused, for example in relation to some types of physical abuse. In England, simply by virtue of their position as parents, adults are allowed to assault a child in way that would be illegal if inflicted on another adult.

- *Resource power*: most parents use their resources such as money, possessions, ability to give love and praise to care well for their children. However, the failure of parents to use this power in terms of material resources is clearest in cases of physical neglect. Resource power in the form of love, valuing and encouragement, all of which are given freely by loving parents, are often denied in cases of emotional abuse.

- *Expert power*: parents use their wisdom and expertise in understanding their children to guide and support them. However, expert power can be misused as demonstrated by sex offenders, who often use their knowledge of what attracts children in order to seduce them into sexual activities.
- *Personal power*: this is personal magnetism, charisma and charm. Children's attachment and admiration are used by most parents to influence their children and provide a valuable role model. But this power can be misused, for example, by sex offenders to beguile and groom children, as well as their parents or other adults who might protect them.
- *Negative power*: this is the ability to be subversive and to stop things happening. Loving parents may be provoked to use this on behalf of their children, for example by campaigning to stop the closure of a valued resource. However, abusers sometimes use this power in order to impede an investigation. They may, for example, repeatedly use the complaints procedure to block progress and ensure that the investigators have to focus on defending their actions rather than concentrating on the investigation.

Therefore, when assessing whether or not abuse has occurred, practitioners could usefully look at the *Working Together* (2010) definitions alongside an analysis of the power that the parents or carers hold and how they are using their power.

Practice focus

Courtney

Courtney is a widower, his wife having died of breast cancer leaving him caring for three young children. Since his teens he had been diagnosed with schizophrenia. At times his behaviour could be reckless or paranoid. For example, he once drove very fast down the wrong carriage of a motorway with all the children in the car. On another occasion he would not allow his children to eat or drink because he believed their food was poisoned. His parents lived nearby and have always been supportive. Courtney realises that when he starts wearing garish clothes or dying his hair he could be heading for a breakdown. When he was well, Courtney and his parents drew up an arrangement, agreed with children's services and the adult mental health team, that when he became ill the children would go to stay with grandparents until he was well again.

Point for reflection

In the case of Courtney and his family above, are the three children being emotionally abused?

Comment: Clearly the children suffered considerable emotional distress, from the death of their mother and the erratic and sometimes frightening behaviour of their father. However, Courtney has been doing all in his power to safeguard their welfare. He has been disempowered by his wife's death and by his illness, therefore he has limited ability to care for his children. Although emotionally distressed, 'in need' and requiring support from their grandparents as well as social and medical services, the children are not being abused by a misuse of Courtney's power as their father. He has put their needs first and has made arrangements with the grandparents and welfare services to take over his parental powers and responsibilities if he cannot exercise them.

Putting it into practice

Now look at another family familiar to you through your work load or placement and similarly work out what powers parents may have. Are they disempowered by another person, illness or environmental pressures? How are they using the power that they have? Are they putting the needs of their children to the forefront?

Comment: By looking at the power parents or carers have and by looking at how it is used, it is possible to determine whether children are emotionally distressed and 'in need' or are 'at risk' of being abused.

Problems in recognising children are being abused

However well-thought out, any policies, procedures or laws are of little value if practitioners cannot recognise when abuse is happening. This was apparent in the cases of, amongst others, Victoria Climbié (Laming, 2003) and Khyra Ishaq (Radford, 2010). The inquiry into the death of Khyra Ishaq revealed a 7-year-old girl, with special educational needs, who was exceptionally malnourished and wasted, and beaten with a cane on several occasions 48 to 72 hours before her death, when she was suffering from bronchial pneumonia, septicaemia and bacterial meningitis. There was little effective protective intervention in the years and months leading to her death despite repeated incidents of concern. In the month before she died, it was recorded that the 'Team Manager discussed case with Social Worker in supervision and agreed case could be closed because home tutoring had been approved' (Radford, 2010, p. 75). They and the other agencies failed to understand and recognise the signs of maltreatment.

Yet another serious case review (Salford Safeguarding Board, 2010, p. 8) in the wake of the murder of an 11-year-old child reported that 'there were 7 separate incidents when Section 47 Enquiries under the Children Act 1989 should have been undertaken'.

It is easy to be judgemental with hindsight. However, there are very many obstacles to recognition and, arguably, what is remarkable is not that cases are missed but that instances of maltreatment so often come to light. In recognising that abuse is occurring, child protection professionals have to overcome substantial difficulties. These include the fact that:

- 'Checklists' are of little use because abuse occurs in all sectors of society and can be present in what might be seen as 'nice' families. There are many instances of apparently advantaged families in which abuse occurs. A recent example is the case where on '14 April 2010 M was charged with 88 counts of child cruelty. F was charged with 14 counts of child cruelty and one of perverting the course of justice' (Brabbs, 2011, p. 4). M and F in this case were two well-respected doctors, one a research scientist and the other a GP.
- Children can show a range of physical, developmental and behavioural problems which can be readily attributed to causes other than maltreatment. This is particularly true of children with special needs and disabilities where, for example, bruising can be dismissed as falls in children with weakened balance. Nevertheless, Goldberg *et al.* (2009) found that patterns and sites of accidental bruising was similar in children whatever their ability.
- Children may be unable to communicate what is happening to them. Again, this is particularly true of children whose disability impairs communication or those too young to have developed language skills.
- Where children and families do not speak the majority language (English in the UK) and interpreters are required,

there are considerable challenges (see Kriz and Skivenes, 2010, below).

- Even children physically capable of clear communication may not give clear messages because of psychological barriers such as features of the Stockholm syndrome and post-traumatic stress disorder.

- Adult perpetrators of abuse are often adept at keeping potential inquiries at bay.

- Some issues are located within the professionals themselves. This includes the 'rule of optimism' which is to take note of all the positive factors, making assumptions that in the absence of clear evidence to the contrary everything is fine. In the serious case review summary of Derby Safeguarding Board (2009, p. 5) it was noted that 'The practitioners involved with this family were over optimistic about the capacity of the adults to prioritise the needs of the children' and there was the assumption 'that the children were safe and that, in the absence of a definitive diagnosis of the injuries, there must be an innocent explanation for the fractures. They ceased to consider the bruising to the chest'.

- Other professionals find child abuse so painful that it is easier to ignore it or focus on adult concerns. Some are so exhausted and burned out that they can no longer work effectively. These last issues are examined further in the final chapter.

Messages from research

Kriz and Skivenes (2010)

The researchers explored the use of interpreters in child welfare work where children and their carers are not proficient in the language of the country. They compared the experiences of 28 social workers in Norway and 23 in England through the use of in-depth, semi-structured interviews.

Kriz and Skivenes found a number of problems faced by both English and Norwegian social workers when using interpreters in child welfare work. These included:

- deficits in information obtained; this was two-way with issues not clearly explained to families and interpreters summarising what children and carers say, so that details are not given to the workers;

- more curtailed relationship-building processes;
- feelings of mistrust, with carers not trusting the interpreter because of worries about confidentiality and workers not trusting either interpreters or carers;
- practical obstacles for ethnic minority carers trying to access social workers.

These concerns in relation to child protection work are that neither children nor other family members will be able to convey any problems occurring in the home.

While Kriz and Skivenes focused on important information being lost in translation of verbal language between practitioners and members of minority ethnic families, the points they made will be relevant in all instances where interpreters are required, as in the case of people who are hearing impaired and use sign language.

Foundations of good practice

There are some basic requirements of helping professionals and many features will be common to those working with adults as well as those in child care. Therefore, although not all are specific to working with abused children, it is worth providing a brief reminder of the essentials.

Power in practice

When working with abused children, helping professionals need to be aware of the power dynamics in the situation. This includes awareness of their own power, which is often considerably less than the literature would suggest, especially for social workers. Holding only a modicum of position and resource power, social workers, health visitors and early years professionals often have to rely substantially on their expert power. However, often this is not recognised and they find themselves over-ruled by other professionals who are seen to be more expert. Some people with whom they work will have very little power indeed, hence the requirement to empower vulnerable 'clients'. On the other hand it would be a mistake to believe that empowerment is the ultimate goal for all. Some perpetrators, for example Carl Manning who beat Victoria Climbié with bicycle chains (Laming, 2003), could usefully have been disempowered while others could be shown how to use their power differently.

Empowering children

Coulshed and Orme (2006) identify components of empowerment as the giving of a 'voice' and conferring rights. Children can be given a voice in several different ways. The first is by recognising how children communicate. The second is by enabling them to communicate in a variety of ways, not just verbally. The third is to listen respectfully to their wishes and feelings. The fourth is by having adults advocate for them. It is a matter of concern that in child protection case conferences, while the parents have a right to be present, the children are usually absent. Yet they should have an inalienable right to be present or to choose a person to advocate for them. The fifth is to listen equally respectfully to adult survivors who can articulate experiences more holistically than children can.

Children can be given a voice by being actively involved in research (Greene and Hogan, 2005; Greig *et al.*, 2007; Christensen and James, 2008; Tisdall *et al.*, 2009). Parental consent requirements should not be used as an excuse to 'gag' children who have a right to express their opinions. Similarly, there is now an emphasis on service users being involved in social work training. This must include the most vulnerable of service users, particularly maltreated children; not to do so further disempowers them. Some universities and placement providers have, for example, devised imaginative ways of embracing the views of children such as the employment of videos or young people preparing their own training materials and Powerpoint presentations.

Putting it into practice

Choose any case of child protection with which you are familiar. Draw a circle to represent the maltreated or 'at risk' child. Around this, draw additional circles to represent the key people or agencies involved with him or her. In each circle identify the types of power held by each person, including the child. For example, the parents or main carers may well have all six forms of power in relation to the child, including substantial physical and personal power. Social workers may have resource, position and expert power but no, or very limited, physical, personal or negative power. How have the various players been using, failing to use or misusing power?

Comment: The purpose of this exercise is to show how important power is to an understanding of child protection issues. Children are protected if parents, family, friends and agencies use power benignly and effectively. Children will be abused if they lack effective power and that held by significant others is misused or not used effectively. Altering the power dynamics can prevent further abuse.

Boundaries

Establishing boundaries is essential to all care professionals but is particularly important in child protection work. A chummy friendship with parents can leave a child exposed to danger. Failure to establish boundaries when exploring sexual abuse with a child can result in the touching of the adult's private parts by the child or vice versa (yes, it does still happen! I was consulted about an instance recently) and this might lead to the worker facing charges of sexual assault and dismissal.

Workers also need to try to be firm about establishing work and private life boundaries. This is easier said than done and employers often fail to recognise the counter-productive nature of forcing their employees to overwork which leads to illness and burnout, a matter that will be explored further in the final chapter.

But workers can also draw too tight a boundary and refuse to see beyond the immediate focus of their work. The Stephen Meurs case (Norfolk County Council, 1975) was one in which helping professionals were visiting children fostered by Stephen's mother. They took little interest in Stephen's welfare and he died of neglect despite their visits.

Values

All helping professionals are required to maintain the values and ethics of their profession. These values are often made explicit by their regulatory bodies and usually embrace areas such as confidentiality, avoiding discrimination, respecting difference and not abusing any power and authority the professional may possess.

However, maintaining professional values may not be conflict-free. When there is a particular 'moral panic' against societal 'folk devils' then legislation against a particular disadvantaged group may become very restrictive and punitive. Professionals then find that their values of respecting people's right to self-determination are undermined by the restrictive legal framework in which they have to work.

Professionals can also find that there are conflicts between one value and another. When clinging to one value it is important to ensure that it is not undermining another. So refusing to share information on the grounds of maintaining confidentiality of one person, may result in failing in one's duty of care to another.

There are times when values are misinterpreted. I have met workers who interpret the value of 'non-judgemental attitudes' to mean making no judgements at all. This means that in child protection cases they just become neighbourly visitors and do nothing about safeguarding the children. Moreover, some have gone further to obstruct the judgements of other professionals who are concerned about the parents' behaviour and the children's condition. Child protection professionals have to make judgements about the child's environments, the family functioning and parents' behaviour. Being 'non-judgemental' means avoiding making judgements without the professional's expertise and remit. There is a world of difference between 'from the palpable smell of alcohol on her breath and the twenty empty bottles of gin evident on my last visit, alcohol consumption might be a factor hampering her care of her baby' and 'she's a drunken sot, a hopeless mother who doesn't deserve her baby and is destined for hell'. The first is a legitimate professional judgement, the second is not.

Lastly, there may be a conflict between a professional's personal values and professional ones. Here reflection and the use of supervision and consultation are important.

Anti-discriminatory practice

This is an essential value, which should be at the heart of the practice of all professionals. In order to practise in a truly anti-discriminatory way and to help those who are abused, social workers and other helping professionals need to understand and analyse power dynamics. Not only do they have to exercise their own power in a way that does not discriminate or oppress but they also have to be aware of other means through which people are being oppressed and disadvantaged.

Anti-racist practice and the challenging of policies and practices which disadvantage black, Asian, dual heritage and other minority ethnic groups is at the forefront of anti-discriminatory practice. However, professionals are aware that there are other discriminations, including ageism, disablism and homophobia. Meanwhile, child protection workers can find themselves torn by opposing claims. For example, many theorists claim mothers are oppressed by child protection procedures while others believe fathers are being treated unfairly. It is the fate of child protection workers that we will never manage to meet the competing claims of all interest groups but we can but reflect on how we are using our power and try to use it wisely and well.

Reflective practice

Thinking theoretically without any form of reflection becomes rigidity of thought, which leads ultimately to unthinking intervention, whereas reflection without any sort of theoretical basis is woolly thinking, which also leads ultimately to unthinking intervention. Unthinking intervention becomes habitual intervention, which in turn leads to ineffective practice. Therefore, one important element of working with abused children is reflective practice. Reflection in particular includes:

- An explicit awareness of personal values, including bias and prejudice plus a recognition that other people will have opposing views or very different values.
- Acknowledging the impact of the self on other people and appreciating power differentials.
- Being aware of feelings aroused by other people or situations. We can helpfully, for example, analyse why we feel threatened when visiting a particular home and how realistic is the perceived threat.
- Evaluating the effectiveness of intervention. For example, if we feel threatened we might avoid raising a necessary but sensitive topic with a particular family. We need to be aware of factors which lead us to unrealistic optimism or to minimise or, indeed, exaggerate potential risks.
- Identifying the theoretical bases for the intervention and questioning how appropriate they are.

Evidence-based practice

Evidence-based practice or 'evidence-informed' practice means ensuring that any intervention is based on the facts and information available. There needs to be a careful factual assessment of the issues in the case as well as other external contextual information including research findings. The importance of this is illustrated by the situation in Britain, in the 1980s, when specialist social workers became aware of the research findings of Abel *et al.* (1987) and Finkelhor (1984) into the repeat offending and grooming behaviour of sex abusers. They often found themselves powerless to influence case conferences and courts which, unaware of the research, accepted the abuser's protestations of the offence being 'a one-off' and 'out-of-character' and left children in the home unprotected.

Theory in practice

Inevitably professionals intervening in the lives of others will be basing their intervention, whether consciously or unconsciously, on 'a set of related propositions that suggest why events occur in the manner that they do', that is, forms of theory (Hoover and Donovan, 1995, p. 38). Well-founded theories, albeit not perfect, will be better than unthinking mechanical input or mindless prejudice, which will fill the vacuum in the absence of theoretical approaches.

Types of theory

One reason why practitioners may struggle with the application of theory is that there are different types and not all have the same weight or application.

Some are *descriptive* theories offering explanations about *what is happening* and metaphorically 'open the eyes' so that practitioners become more aware of phenomena. Often they provide a framework of understanding. Elizabeth Kubler-Ross's (1970) work on loss and mourning has provided invaluable insights for those helping people in a state of grief. More recently the Barker theory (Barker, 1990; Nicoletto and Rinaldi, 2011) has highlighted the importance of maternal nutrition for the unborn child's health in adulthood.

Others are *causal* theories and explain *why things happen*. For example, social learning theory suggests that people learn violent behaviour by watching others who behave violently (Bandura, 1973).

Yet others are *interventive* theories indicating *what should be done* about what has happened. Examples here include theories of crisis intervention (Thompson, 2011; Aguilera, 1998) and again more recently Chambers' PACT (parent-and-child-therapy) theory (Chambers *et al.*, 2006)

Some theories have all three functions. Psychodynamic theory, for example, *describes* human functioning including the role of the unconscious, *explains* why people behave in certain ways and *provides guidance* about how people can be helped.

Integrated models and ecological theory

There are a number of perspectives through which the different approaches and theories are developed or interpreted. One key example is the economic and class interpretations of Marxist philosophy. Another major influence is feminist thinking which offers both a critique and interpretation of theories and fits well with anti-discriminatory practice because 'a feminist stance endorses egalitarianism across all social dimensions' (Dominelli and McLeod, 1989, p. 2).

Increasingly, it is recognised that 'child abuse and neglect cannot be explained by a single factor; it is a consequence of complex interactions between individual, social and environmental influences' (Browne, 2002, p. 57). Theories that locate the cause solely within parental dysfunction fail to account for the fact that abuse is over-represented where there are environmental stressors such as poverty and unemployment. However, purely sociological theories cannot explain why many socio-economically disadvantaged parents do not abuse their children. Recognition of the multi-faceted nature of child protection has led to the increased acceptance of ecological theory, which highlights the complex interplay of psychological and sociological factors

Ecological theory is a systems approach based on concepts advanced by Bronfenbrenner (1979). According to the theory, the child is located within a series of nests. The first, the *micro-system,* comprises the child's immediate family and close contacts. The second nest is the *meso-system*, containing the micro-system and embracing wider contacts such as playgroup, school or immediate neighbours. Next is the *exo-system*, whose components are beyond the child's direct contact but whose influence impacts on the child, such as the parents' workplace and friendship network, the wider neighbourhood or distant extended family. Finally all these systems exist within the all-encompassing *macro-system* comprising the political and cultural context.

Ecological theory underpins the approach and structure of this book. This is because while the focus is on the child at the centre, the impact and influence of the surrounding systems, such as the family, environment and wider societies' attitudes to children cannot be ignored.

Practice focus

Tim

This example shows how when working with abused children the systems around the child cannot be neglected. Tim, who was aged nine years, was hearing impaired. He had been physically and emotionally maltreated by his mother's boyfriend. Among other abuses, the boyfriend had deliberately taunted Tim about his hearing difficulties. Working directly with him, the therapist was sensitive to Tim's impairment but in addition she needed to help him with the emotional consequences of the particular nature of the taunts. This was undertaken not in isolation but with an awareness, first, of society's sometimes discriminatory attitudes to Tim's relatively 'hidden' impairment but also of the potential help that could be given by others in Tim's wider systems. His school head teacher, for example, was knowledgeable and supportive in relation to pupils with hearing impairments.

Evaluating theories

Smith (1998, p. 187) warns that, 'In all areas where there is a fairly structured and extensive body of thought in a particular social science, we can witness a reluctance to question bedrock assumptions'. Because no theory is the absolute 'truth', each will have both strengths and limitations. They may be useful in helping to explain why or how things occur or suggest interventions but there are dangers when they are used uncritically. All theories need to be questioned and appraised.

Attachment theory is a useful example because it is vitally important in the appreciation of the relationship needs of young children and the understanding of the relationship patterns of people in later life (Howe, 1995; Howe *et al.*, 1999; Howe, 2005). The theory emerged from the work of Bowlby (1951; 1969) and hypothesised that on the basis of babies' interactions with their mother they develop 'internal working models' of what might be expected from relationships in general. Young humans need to explore their environment and develop independence but to do so successfully they need a secure base to return to for comfort and reassurance when under stress. This base, essential to future mental health according to Bowlby, is 'a warm, intimate and continuous relationship with his mother (or permanent mother-substitute – one person who steadily 'mothers' him) in which both find satisfaction and enjoyment.' (Bowlby, 1969, p. 13). This has sometimes, led to 'mother blaming'.

Bowlby, however, used his immense intellectual powers to evaluate his own theory. In 1969 he was writing 'fathers have their uses even in infancy... [providing] for their wives to enable them to devote themselves unrestrictedly to the care of the infant and toddler' (p. 15). By 1980, Bowlby had revised this aspect of his theory and he acknowledged the important role of fathers 'by providing an attachment figure for his child, a father may be filling a role closely resembling that filled by a mother' (Bowlby, 1980, p. 12).

Another enigma with which practitioners struggle is that Bowlby's attachment theory fails to explain why poorly attached, abused children do not inevitably go on to be unsatisfactory parents. Practitioners, working for long periods in one area, will be familiar with the families where all the children are mistreated and given little affection, yet while one or more siblings may become abusive, others will prove able and fulfilling parents. An internal working model, based on early abusive relationships would suggest that abuse would inevitably be inter-generational and found in all the family members. This demonstrates that despite its value, attachment theory cannot be the whole 'truth'. Recently, for example, interest has turned to brain architecture and neurobiological development (Gunnar and Quevedo, 2007; Tsujimoto, 2008; Perry 2009; Fox *et al.*, 2010) to explain some of the consequences of early life experiences.

Another issue is the indiscriminate use of theory. Allen (2011a) in a comprehensively researched paper points to some issues in the uncritical use of Bowlby's ideas. Handley and Doyle (2008) explored the theories on which child care social workers drew when ascertaining the wishes and feelings of younger children for the purposes of Family Court proceedings. Of 61 respondents, 36 per cent stated that Bowlby's theory was the most helpful. Although relationship difficulties might help explain why some children find expressing their feelings difficult, when it comes to understanding how to communicate with young children and how to help them express their ideas, arguably more cognitively based theorists such as Vygotsky (1978) would be equally useful. However, only 5 per cent nominated him. This is hardly surprising because compared to 100 per cent given knowledge of Bowlby's ideas whether at qualifying, post-qualifying or in-service training, only 29 per cent had had any introduction to Vygotsky in any form. Munro (2011, p. 89) in her definitive review of child protection noted 'This review has heard that social workers sometimes feel inadequately trained to communicate with children'.

Any theory, if applied uncritically or inappropriately, can become unhelpful. Therefore there is a need to approach the use of theory with a degree of critical evaluation and reflection.

Point for reflection

Choose any theory with which you are familiar. If you are already working in a caring profession it is likely that you can choose one from social science or social work theory. If you are new to child protection or the caring professions you might need to draw on a theory from your other studies. Having chosen a theory, try to list all the helpful, positive features of the theory. Then list all the limitations of the theory that you can identify. Draw a conclusion about whether, on balance, the positive features outweigh the limitations.

Comment: This activity is designed to help you evaluate the theories that you are likely to use in practice. This is preferable to applying a theory in an unquestioning way.

Some theories and principles are elevated to dogma, that is, expressed as incontrovertibly true and often followed without the exercise of critical judgement. Philpot (1995) explained:

> Sacred cows have no place in child protection work. Where practitioners have become inseparably attached to a particular theory or preconception, we have been left with cases where the truth has been pushed out of reach and children's experiences have been shrouded in confusion. (p. 1)

Anti-discriminatory practice might appear to sit uneasily in a section on dogma because it is difficult to see how it can be anything other than beneficial. It is the challenge to discrimination and oppression wherever it is encountered and at all levels, including in professionals themselves and in systems used by them.

The emphasis on anti-discriminatory and anti-racist ideologies has, however, had some negative consequences for intervention. The removal of black children by white workers who condemn child care practices, which they do not understand, has been rightly condemned as discriminatory. Nevertheless, Ahmad (1989) and Owusu-Bempah (2003) both point out that it is equally discriminatory to do nothing to protect children from minority cultures when there is evidence of abuse. For fear of being seen as racist, child protection workers have at times shied away from their duties of protecting the black child from abuse. Similarly, Corby (2000) reminded us of the culturally relative nature of child abuse which means that social workers have an obligation to challenge the imposition of the standards of the majority culture on minority groups. Nevertheless, he warned against the 'extraordinary degree of tolerance' (p. 67), in the name of anti-discriminatory practice and cultural sensitivity, shown by social workers of unequivocally abusive behaviour, which has led to the death of a number of children.

Dogmas are, or were, rooted in theories of good practice. However, in all professions, when promoted from theory to a dogmatically imposed ideology they have been applied inappropriately, insensitively and without proper analysis.

Recording

An extract from Munro (2011, p. 20) provides a timely caution for a section on recording, the 'assumption that records provide an adequate account of a helping profession has led to a distortion of the priorities of practice. The emotional dimensions and intellectual nuances of reasoning are undervalued in comparison with simple data about service processes such as time to complete a form'. Despite the importance of Munro's words, time and again, inquiry reports into the deaths of children have commented upon poor record keeping and communication. While extensive records do not equate with high-quality intervention, good, accurate, recording is essential if information is to be shared with other colleagues, agencies and courts.

It is advisable when writing up records to avoid general terms such as 'the house was dirty' or 'her clothing was inadequate'. First, these convey very little meaning to others because one person's 'dirty' house is another person's 'lived in' one. Second, when parents and children have access to their records, terms like these can be emotive. Far better is to use an accurate description or if a judgement has to be used then concrete examples given. An example is the Malcolm Page case (Denham, 1981, p. 47) where for months the social worker and health visitor had been recording general comments such as 'some improvement', which proved meaningless. The police officer investigating Malcolm's death gave a purely factual, if stomach-turning, description of the state of the house leaving the reader in no doubt that it was unfit for any child. Below is a *short* extract about the children's sleeping conditions from the detective chief inspector's report:

> In the rear bedroom was one double bed and a cot, the bed had a double mattress on it which was very heavily stained and sopping wet with urine. There was a white blanket on the bed and lying on top of this were lumps of excrement and there was excrement ground into the blanket which was again soaked with urine. When the blanket was lifted up there was a lump of excrement lying on the mattress and this had obviously been pressed in by somebody lying on the blanket and pushing it into the mattress. There was a soiled sheet sodden with urine and mixed with excrement lying on the floor under the bed. There were several lumps of excrement all over the floor and at least twelve empty milk bottles lying in different positions on the floor.

Writing records is time-consuming and there are a number of illustrative methods that can prove effective. Methods include:

- *Flow charts:* these are lists and dates of all the injuries or abusive incidents to a child. In a separate column, other important events are recorded in a way that matches dates, incidents and events. It is a simple exercise but can be remarkably effective in demonstrating patterns of abuse. Practitioners on seeing these charts have made comments such as: 'The incidents seem to occur at regular intervals' or 'I didn't realise she had had so many hospital admissions in only sixteen weeks'. Several inquiry reports use flow charts to collate all the known incidents (e.g. Bridge Child Care Consultancy Services, 1991). It might be useful after case conferences for the independent chairs to produce such charts. This would demonstrate clearly to both professionals and parents why there is cause for concern.
- *Ecomaps:* circles are drawn, one each for the child and the main relationships and influences in the child's environment such as parents, siblings, relatives, school, other helping professionals, friends and even pets. The nature and importance of the relationships can be indicated by differences in the lines attaching the circles, e.g., a bold line for a strong positive relationship, a wavy line for an ambiguous one, a dotted line for a weak one.

- *Growth charts:* children who have been abused sometimes fail to put on sufficient weight and height despite the fact that their families are of average build and there is no growth-impairing disease or explanatory physical condition present. A child's physical progress can be monitored through the use of growth charts. Medical staff, who can interpret them correctly, and who have access to the same scales and measuring devices each time, are best placed to maintain them but a copy could usefully be kept on the key worker's file. Jasmine Beckford (Blom-Cooper, 1985) aged four years, was returned from care only to be killed by her stepfather. Her weight rose in care and fell on return home. The inquiry report states: 'The failure of Area 6 to take particular note of Jasmine's weight over the three years of a Care Order is perhaps the most striking, single aspect of child abuse that was fatally neglected' (p. 114).
- *Geneograms or family trees:* rather than attempt to describe in words all members of the family it is useful to draw up a family tree. This does not need to be the detailed, formal creation of the genealogist. However, it is advisable to use symbols others can recognise. Normally a male is a square, and female a circle. If the gender is unknown then a triangle is used and an X is put over the shape for someone who has died. For all living members it is useful to put their present age. As with the ecomap, it is also helpful to indicate, through the connecting lines, the nature of the relationship between the child and members of the family.

Inter-agency working

Child protection work is rather like a jigsaw with different agencies often holding several key pieces and it is only when the pieces are shared and placed together with accuracy that the full picture becomes apparent. It is not, however, easy to work with other organisations and professions. This is evidenced by the fact that time and again public inquiries and serious case reviews highlight the failure of agencies to communicate and share information in a timely fashion. Multi-agency working and case conferences are seen as a panacea for poor practice. However, the obstacles and difficulties faced by child protection practitioners are often overlooked and these are discussed in more detail in the final chapter.

Impossible dreams

Preston-Shoot and Ayre (2010, p. 128) identify the key themes in current UK children's service policy and practice as 'managerialism, the audit culture and over-reliance on quantitative key performance indicators' resulting in loss of contact with children. Forrester (2010, p. 115) refers to the fact that practice 'is now dominated by managerial and bureaucratic approaches'. Meanwhile, Ferguson (2010, p. 32) traces how, prior to the 1990s alongside group and community work, social work could also be delivered through one-to-one relationships requiring theoretical resources that were relational, individualistic and person-centred. Subsequently, social work appeared to move to assessment and then signposting of any therapeutic work to others. In the light of this enforced retreat from direct work with children, some practitioners will read the guidance in this book and wish they could work with abused children but have little doubt that organisational constraints make it impossible.

However, the seemingly impossible may take time but it can be achieved. To illustrate how in a relatively short space of time situations can change dramatically, I can think back to early in my career when I questioned why Down's syndrome children were left under-stimulated, uneducated and unloved in the grim, plain wards of a special hospital. When I inquired why, if their parents could not care for them, could they not be fostered or adopted, my query was greeted with ill-concealed incredulity and contempt, 'Who would ever want to adopt or foster *that* type of children?' A few years later I was visiting a foster home and noted there were two babies with Down's syndrome. The foster carers had adopted them, their new mother explaining, 'the authorities thought we were bonkers to want them, but we won in the end'. Subsequently, what had once seemed impossible became common practice. Before long, when children with Down's syndrome were unable to remain in their birth families, alternative parents, rather than neglected wards of special hospitals, were sought.

Finally

A final reminder: all family members are important and all can suffer in cases of child abuse. Parents in particular warrant our respect and consideration. However, the child victims of abuse, and the term includes siblings who witness abuse, need understanding and appropriate assistance. A significant proportion of the public inquiries following the deaths of children, have highlighted the fact that some social workers and other professionals have become so preoccupied with the needs of the parents that they have overlooked those of the children to the detriment of everyone involved.

The remainder of the book focuses on understanding abused children, appreciating their perspectives and on intervening in ways that will help them both in the short and longer term.

Further resources

Beckett, C. (2007) *Child Protection: An Introduction*, 2nd edn. London: Sage.
This is a good introductory text. It sets current practice within its historical context. It is highly readable and deals with many of the complexities of child protection including children with disabilities.

Ferguson, H. (2005) 'Working with violence, the emotions and the psycho-social dynamics of child protection: reflections on the Victoria Climbié case', *Social Work Education*, 24 (7), pp. 781–95.
This masterful review by Ferguson of the feelings engendered in child protection workers provides perceptive reading. He writes about the often unspoken fears, disgust and paralysing difficulties faced by child protection workers. There are rewards and positive challenges in child protection work but Ferguson eloquently exposes the emotional under-belly of the task of working with abused children.

Hughes, L. and Owen, H. (eds) (2009) *Good Practice in Safeguarding Children*. London: Jessica Kingsley.
This is an intriguing set of collected chapters that covers multi-disciplinary issues with some often-neglected areas, such as working with hostile families or trafficked children.

Lindon, J. (2008) Safeguarding *Children and Young People*. 3rd edn. Abingdon, Oxon: Hodder & Stoughton.
This is a basic guide to safeguarding but Jennie Lindon's work is always thorough, well researched and covers all essential elements. A psychologist, she specialises in the early years and therefore her writing is child-centred.

Stalker, K., Lister, P. G., Lerpiniere, J. and McArthur, K. (2010) *Child protection and the needs and rights of disabled children and young people*: A scoping study. Strathclyde: University of Strathclyde.
This is an abridged report but it highlights important issues relating to practice, particularly some areas of concern: for example, at case conferences, disabled children are rarely present nor do they appear to have advocates to represent their views but good practice is also acknowledged.

Wilson, K. and James, A. (2007) *The Child Protection Handbook*, 3rd edn. London: Ballière Tindall.
This newer edition of authoritative chapters on various aspects of child protection by leading authors provides the same excellent grounding as did the 2002 edition.

NSPCC http://www.nspcc.org.uk/: this is the official website of the NSPCC. From the home page there are links to resources for professionals. The research briefings and information from the NSPCC are well-researched and reliable.

CHAPTER 2

Listening to the voices of the children

CHAPTER OVERVIEW
This details the accounts of six children who were abused:

- Marie's story illustrates how even a child not directly sexually abused can still live in constant fear
- Lloyd explains that being rejected by his parents, he became vulnerable to other abuses
- Sarah's voice is that of a child seemingly living in a world of privilege but whose reality was that of shame and degradation
- Roy's account is that of an isolated child witnessing extreme domestic violence and being subjected to emotional abuse
- Josie and Jake's account is of siblings who lived with neglect and abuse

Anyone who has read the report of Victoria Climbié (Laming, 2003) will be struck by the fact that few professionals bothered to attempt to engage or listen to her. Victoria was aged eight when she died in unimaginable circumstances. She was of an age when she could communicate both verbally and non-verbally. Victoria was the only real expert on her life, feelings and experiences. However, as Laming (2003, p. 65) observed:

> During the nine weeks or so that Victoria had been Ealing's responsibility, none of the social workers who had come into contact with Victoria got beyond saying 'hello' to her.

It is not just in the UK that child protection workers do not attempt to engage the voice of the child sufficiently. In, arguably, the more child-centred Scandinavian context, Hennum (2011, p. 337) found 'as a rule accounts voiced by children about their situations are rarely found in Norwegian child welfare documents'.

This chapter therefore looks at listening to children. A number of abused children can ask for help in a firm, direct manner and are able to describe their experiences clearly and coherently. But these are probably in the minority. Most are inhibited by fear, shame, mistrust or attachment to their abusers. Furthermore, younger children do not have the command of language needed to communicate their distress in a straightforward manner. For these reasons the perspectives of maltreated children are all too often ignored or misunderstood. Yet child-care workers will fail to give effective help to children unless they can appreciate what the experience of abuse means for the victims. They also need to recognise how a child may attempt to communicate their experiences.

Working with diversity

Much of this chapter and the next is about giving a voice to children and the chapters take account of the limitations children have in relation to communication. As noted, few will be able to give a coherent oral account of what has happened to them because of age, the limitations of vocabulary particularly if English is not their first language, emotional constraints and, for some children, their disabilities will limit the number of people with whom they can communicate.

Care also has to be taken not just with the technicalities of how to communicate but also the interpretation and meaning of what is being communicated. An example is given by Lewis (2011) who explains how researchers asked children with learning disabilities to contribute some diaries and artwork for a project. The researchers thought they were behaving ethically in returning each child's contributions to the child at the end of the project. However, the children were upset because they believed their contributions were returned because their writing and artwork were not good enough to be kept and valued by the adults. This type of miscommunication can occur with all children but there needs to be extra sensitivity towards abused children with disabilities because they may already have had too many messages of 'not being good enough' or 'flawed' and so readily make assumptions that what they do will be rejected.

The world of abused children

Insight into the world of the abused child can be provided by adults who have suffered childhood mistreatment and are willing to describe their experiences. This chapter contains six such accounts, which serve as examples to increase our understanding of the predicaments of abused children.

These are real accounts of real children. For reasons of confidentiality names and identifying details have been changed. However, the words are theirs, albeit modified or summarised to make reading easier; exact transcripts of interviews of one to three hours would not have been readily readable.

The cases are not a 'representative sample'. They are accounts given by adults who, with great generosity, have been willing to have their memories appear in print. Their ethnicity has not been identified nor have any special needs or disability of the children concerned been provided. There is a reason for this. Too often professionals, especially social workers, are so concerned about externals or parental dynamics that they fail to listen to the child.

These case examples are not evenly balanced between abuse by mothers or fathers, between white or black families, between wealth and poverty. The voices of the children below should not be used by those with the proverbial 'axe to grind' or distorted to make political judgements about the accounts 'failing to value fathers' or 'mother-blaming' or 'discrimination by including too many black/Asian families or by not including any non-white families' or any other manifestations of the cases. Instead we are likely to fail children if we become so preoccupied with the appearance of the family – just as the professionals in Victoria Climbié's case did not get beyond seeing the labels 'black "mother and daughter" with housing problems'. I ask any readers tempted to do so to stop grinding their axes and listen to the voices below of the experiences of children who are abused – with compassion and without axes.

Marie's account

I lived with my mother, father, brother and sisters. Pauline was the eldest. Barry, my brother was two years younger than me, and Linda was the youngest. My father was violent to my mother and all of his children.

Until I was eight years old our family seemed fairly 'normal'. There were rows but I was not aware of any extreme violence. My father was in the navy and away from home for quite long periods until I was aged about five. Despite the apparent normality of the situation there was already an atmosphere of fear in the house because my father was very strict. At bedtime he would look at the clock and whoever's turn it was to go to bed would scurry away.

After my eighth birthday came a dramatic change. My father had played with us giving us 'twizzles', swinging us around. My eldest sister then went to live with grandma. Us other children were asked a lot of questions by our mother. Father was also away at this time. When he came back there were lots of rows and we were not allowed to play the games with him any longer.

The situation went from bad to worse. I had the impression that something bad had happened. I heard sexual words like 'climax' for the first time but I didn't really understand what they meant. I remember Pauline being withdrawn and unhappy. A cloud descended over our house. We were not encouraged to have any friends. My father always found something wrong with them. Everything became very secretive. When my father went away to sea we became happy as a big weight was lifted but we all knew he would be coming back and the void would return.

Our mother used to work hard. She would often cry. At nights I would go to bed then get up later, creep down, make her a cup of tea and stay up with her until three or four in the morning when my father was away. I was very close to her and I knew this was a comfort to her. I was an eight-year-old comforting my mother.

This pattern continued until I was about eleven. Then we moved house. We hoped this would be a new beginning; things were going to be different and get better. But they weren't and from then on the situation was horrific. At around this time Pauline told me that our father had sexually abused her. He had done nearly everything except penetrate her. She wanted it to stop. He kept saying 'Have you come yet?' to her but she didn't know what he meant. Not long after this conversation Pauline ate a hundred aspirins in front of me. I didn't realise what was happening, I thought she was eating crumbly white cheese. She tried to commit suicide six times after this. I just didn't understand what she was going through. I was totally confused and afraid. When I did realise I felt it was my fault. I should have stopped her. My mother accompanied Pauline in the ambulance and she kept saying, 'Don't tell anyone why you did it. They will ask you but don't tell them'. These incidents seemed to have no effect on my father, he denied abusing Pauline, apart from the one earlier incident when I was eight.

Our father was often very violent. Frequently he had been drinking. On one occasion when I was outside the house and everyone else was inside, my father was on the rampage and had his hands round my mother's throat. A next-door neighbour called me over to her house and told me to listen. Through the walls I could hear someone shouting to get the police. The neighbour gave me a lift to the police station. I felt this was all I could do but I knew how violent my father could be. When the police arrived he tried to pretend it was just a domestic dispute. Us children ran out of the house and hid. The younger two kept singing 'They've come to take him away ha ha, he he!'. Although the police arrested him he did not stay away for long.

On another occasion my father wanted money. He started throwing my mother's perfume and all her possessions about the house in a temper because she would not give him any. At the time I had a paper round, my mother told me to hide my money. My father asked me where it was. When I said that I had lost it he started hitting me. He also hit my mother and wrecked her bedroom, breaking up everything as he looked for money.

One Christmas a row started over something trivial. My father smashed a plant, a present for my mother, on to the kitchen floor. It made a mess with the soil and broken pot. He threw a large box of chocolates on top. He then made the younger children take the baubles off the tree and threw them into the kitchen too. My mother aimed an ashtray at my father. It missed but caused a hole in the wall. He, in retaliation, cut her leg with a broken dinner plate. The other children were crying and he slammed out. I was left picking up the pieces and I helped to bathe my mother's leg.

I always used to calm the others and tried to look after them. Pauline would go to her room and became increasingly withdrawn. Linda would switch off and block out what was happening. Barry never seemed to be around, he managed to 'duck out'. I sometimes used to hide with him in the cellar. It was however usually my mother, Barry and myself who had the good hidings. Our father used to hit us with anything – his belt, his fist or kick us with his boots. When I was bruised I was kept off school until the bruises faded.

The night times were bad. Us girls shared a room. I used to be awake a lot particularly because I would try to comfort my mother by going to her to hold her hand. We would hear my father's key then I would quickly clamber back to bed and pretend I was asleep. My father would creep into our room, ostensibly to tuck us in but he seemed to be trying to see who was in the deepest sleep. Sometimes he would stay by our bedside for two minutes, sometimes for fifteen. At that stage he didn't touch me but there was always the fear, the dread, wondering if it was going to be my turn. If one of the other two woke he would say, 'Shh, you're only dreaming go back to sleep.' Living in fear was the worst thing. One night he dragged me out of bed at one o'clock because I hadn't cleaned his shoes. He started hitting me and made me clean them in the middle of the night. My mother tried to defend me saying, 'I'll do it, she's got to go to school tomorrow.'

I couldn't mix in school; I used to sit alone. From thirteen years onwards I played truant continually. We were cut off from the other children for fear of letting anything slip. I was dying to tell someone who would take me away, someone kind who would understand. But then I used to think, 'How would my mother and the others cope without me?' I felt it was me who held them together. We always appeared clean and tidy. We were not allowed to wear make-up or be fashionable and we felt different from everyone else. We knew too much. I felt so very alone, totally alone.

You can't concentrate at school while wondering what will happen when you get home. I was very wary of all the male teachers. I couldn't learn from them because of the need to put up all the defences. I assumed that underneath they were all like my father and I was hostile to them. I tried to be helpful to the women teachers. I used to sit wondering if they were battered at home too. I also wondered what other children's lives were like at home. I once went to another girl's house and I couldn't believe how nice her mum and dad were and thought why aren't mine like that?

We would swing from a semi-normal life when my father was away and we could have friends including boyfriends, to a state of fear when he came back. It was difficult to have friends because they couldn't understand why I was friendly one moment and suddenly distant the next. It was easier not to have friends, so I became isolated. I couldn't tell people what was happening at home, they wouldn't believe me or they would misunderstand what I was saying. I began to try to predict what my father would do, try to get to know the enemy and stay one jump ahead of him.

Our mother knew everything. I could tell her anything. She would be frightened for us. She had a terrible time, stuck in the middle. Mother stayed with our father because she loved him. She did leave him once but not for long. I feel there is nothing lovable about him. In some ways I'm angry with my mother for staying while knowing what he did to us.

I was sexually abused by my father when I was 21 years old. I had married but my husband was violent and sexually abusive so I went back to live with my parents. It was then that my father attempted to have sex with me although he did not manage to penetrate. I could hardly believe what was happening. I had escaped during childhood then all of a sudden my nightmare came true. (Early adulthood account continues on page 209.)

Point for reflection

You have 'listened' to the voice of Marie. Now think about what you have heard from Marie's account about the perspective of the abused child. Try to identify at least two messages.

Comment: There is no right or wrong 'answer' as long as you were hearing the voice of the child not for example ignoring it, preferring to make judgements about the parents' behaviour. For me, one thing I heard was the voice of a child who had too much responsibility too early. 'I always used to calm the others and tried to look after them'; this should be the role of the parent when the children are worried or upset. These words coming from a mother or father in relation to their family would be appropriate but not when articulated by a child of the family.

A second thing I heard was a child burdened with too much responsibility in another respect. Recognising her sister had attempted an overdose, Marie said 'When I did realise I felt it was my fault. I should have stopped her'. Children so often think it is they who are to blame for the consequences of abuse, when they are not, and this can be a millstone of guilt they carry well into adult life.

Lloyd's account

My father was away a lot and when I was conceived he was elsewhere so in fact I was illegitimate and my father was not my biological one. I think I am a constant reminder for both parents of mum's infidelity and I guess this is why I was mistreated. My brothers who were my father's own children were not ill treated in the same way.

I was given no love by either parent. I was an outcast. A typical scene when the family was watching TV was for my oldest brother and mother to sit close together and my youngest brother and father to sit together, with me isolated on the floor. When it came to birthdays and Christmas the other two had presents and parties; I was lucky if I had a card. If I fell over I was hit and told to get up. I was given no sympathy and shown no kindness. My older brother copied my parents and was abusive and bullying towards me. My younger brother would try to be kind but only in secret.

My mother's cousin died in a house fire so my parents fostered the children. One of them was a boy aged sixteen and from the age of nine years I was being sexually abused by him. He gave me cigarettes and drink in exchange for sex. My parents knew but did nothing. There were no other family members to help me.

In primary school I settled quite well especially as one teacher found out I was really good at maths and spent time with me. This made me feel special so in some ways it made me think that I was treated differently at home because I was special and clever not because I was unwanted.

But then we emigrated. In my next school my appearance and accent meant I was immediately subjected to negative stereotypes. I was seen as a 'trouble' and because book learning came so easily I was labelled lazy. At that point I gave up and picked fights with teachers and other pupils – they expected me to be a troublemaker – so I was. The sexual abuse also made me worry about being a boy. I had to prove I was not a girl so became very tough. My brothers fared better because they were good at sports so were more accepted.

In my teens I more or less left home. I was lifted by police when I was eleven for smashing up an American's camper van. I was having to sleep rough and they were staying overnight in a field, my field. I became angry and thrashed out. I felt jealous of all they had.

My misery was so great that when I was about fourteen or fifteen years old I tried to hang myself but the rope was not long enough and I twisted my ankle. My family never knew. I also tried to overdose a couple of times but I vomited and slept it off. I was escaping through drink and drugs much of the time.

I did not have many friends although Bevis, a local yob turned good, taught me martial arts and showed interest in me. I also had one good friend of my own age, Gilroy. I had a fight with him and because neither of us could win, we decided to be pals. From about the age of twelve we beat up all the other children together. When I was about fifteen I had a row with him on the Friday. I told him to 'Fuck off and die'. I didn't see him again. Gilroy drowned (by accident) on the Sunday. I felt responsible and very guilty but I could not talk to anyone about this. (Early adulthood account continues on page 211.)

Point for reflection

You have listened to Lloyd but what have you heard? Are there any similarities between the messages conveyed in Marie's account and Lloyd's? Are there any additional ones?

Comment: Like Marie, Lloyd felt responsible for many adverse events including the drowning of Gilroy.

Also in Lloyd's story I heard the voice of a young person whose experience of abuse had made him question his identity, including his sexual identity. Unable to share these doubts with anyone he simply had to work out his own solution which was to adopt an aggressive male stereotype.

Above all I heard a child who was very, very forlorn and isolated; whether in the family, school or outside he had absolutely no one in whom he had real trust. A primary school teacher, Bevis and, with some ambivalence, Gilroy gave him some sense of value but Lloyd's was the voice of a very lonely child.

Sarah's account

I actually decided fairly early on that I didn't like my father, which is a big decision for a child. It was because I was frightened of his strict discipline and use of corporal punishment but I also hated the way he treated my mother. My younger sister, Barbara, and I used to compete not to sit behind him in the car because we could not bear to be that close to him.

I used to get spanked a lot. He was a headmaster and I went to his school. The role of father and headmaster became muddled but I didn't realise anything was wrong I just thought that what he did was what all teachers did. I was isolated and had no comparison of my family life with any other.

My father used to tell me not to put my hands in my pockets because it was, in his opinion, slovenly. Once I was at my grandparent's when my father arrived. He caught me with my hands in my pockets. He saw this as an act of defiance although in fact I had been playing happily and hadn't realised what I was doing. He grabbed me, bundled me into the car, took me home and beat me. My grandmother had cried and pleaded with him not to hurt me but he brushed her out of the way. After he had beaten me, I was heart-warmed to find my other grandmother sitting on the stairs weeping because of the way I had been treated.

He bullied everyone either in a straightforward way or by using a judicious combination of good looks, charm and manipulation. He was used to having his own way. I accepted the fact he had a right to hit me. The beatings hurt and I wanted them to stop. The pain didn't leave a lot of space in my mind for any other thoughts. I was very miserable afterwards feeling rejected, cast out, punished, not worthy. The effect of this situation was to make life such that, because punishment might happen at any time, no day was a safe day, a good day, until it was over. I resented not owning my life.

Besides the beatings my father used other strange ways of punishing us, for example he would put us in the car then drive very fast to teach us a lesson. I can remember the liberation that came when I was eighteen and was so unhappy that I didn't care whether I lived or died. This meant that when he drove fast he could no longer frighten me. I found that experience almost exhilarating.

One New Year there was a party next door. Both my parents drank heavily. I came back with my father and sister but the following morning my mother still hadn't returned. There was thick snow on the ground. My father told me that my mother was probably dead and sent me out to look everywhere, under all the hedges, for her body. I still carry the horror of that episode. She had in fact stayed overnight with the people next door but I didn't realise that and believed my father.

I always felt that if anything happened to my mother I wouldn't know what to do. Whatever kindness came from our home was from her. I always thought of her as my father's first victim and myself as second. I was distressed by the way I had to witness his treatment of my mother. He would constantly undermine her – for example, she was once enjoying music on the car radio when my father decided to stop the car and get out. He switched off the radio saying that he had to save the batteries. Even as a young child I realised it had nothing to do with batteries. Another time, on holiday, my mother sat on a wall and standing up had some tar on her skirt. My father shouted 'God, woman, you've sh … d yourself as usual.' Yet he constantly told us how beautiful she was and how lucky we were to have her as a mother. This, however, struck me as false.

I felt protective towards my mother. She was fascinated by my father and even when they finally separated she never became a whole person again. She needed to be fighting disasters and crises. She couldn't accept herself and turned more and more to drink. She was so unhappy that a lot of me parented her; I tried to cheer her up. It was only as a parent myself that I became angry that she never protected us. I have never told her how angry I felt.

I remember truly hating my sister. My father used to say to me 'Why can't you be like your sister, she's gregarious, has lots of friends and is cheerful? You are just a sour puss.' I was jealous of her. I did not realise he said the same to her about me, making her jealous as well. I could not afford to protect her. When I eventually decided to leave home, my father threatened me with the fact that Barbara would be made to suffer because I was not there. But I had to close my mind to that. I used however to draw his fire because, when I dared, I stood up to him. I now only have a superficial relationship with my sister. He made me have my hair cut very short like a boy so I wore headscarves. He said by doing this I was trying to look like 'a duchess', trying to show that I was better than the rest of the family. Once, when we were having a picnic, he made me sit some distance from the family in a field by myself to eat. I cringed up inside. He always made us feel he was in the right. In order to escape I used to daydream. One place that could be mine was inside my head, but he even resented this. We were in the car when I was imagining the dog I would give my grandmother for a present. I was hauled out of my reverie by father shouting, 'Look at that bloody, snotty cow in the back, too hoity-toity to talk to the rest of us.' His verbal attack was vitriolic. Another time when I wore a new bathing costume and felt quite proud of it he shouted across a quiet beach, 'Hold your belly in woman, you look like a pregnant cow.'

I was eleven years old and the only girl in my father's school. As the headmaster's daughter I was not popular. I felt very isolated but in a desperate attempt to gain popularity I became involved in some sex play with the boys. When I heard that my father had found out I fainted with fear. I was also frightened of one of the boys and so I withheld his name from my father who, when he discovered this, made me change into some of his thin rugby shorts. Then he caned me really hard. Half way through he showed my mother my bottom and she was sick, then he carried on caning me. A fortnight later when my mother jokingly patted my bottom I cried out because the pain was still so intense.

I asked my mother if I would have to go away after this incident. She said 'Yes, perhaps'. I thought I would just be thrown out of the house into the proverbial darkness. I wondered if I could live in a cave that I knew about in the mountain and hoped someone would put out food for me. In fact I was sent to boarding school although it was the summer term. I was very unhappy. I cried so much at bedtime that the staff had to intervene. They thought I was home-sick, missing a loving family but I was crying because I felt rejected and did not seem to belong to anyone. Because I started in the summer term, friendships were already made in that year and yet by the next term I did not belong in the new intake. I made no real friends. My father kept telling me that if I didn't achieve high academic results I would be sent to a state school implying that I would be virtually 'chucked in the bin'. I spent my time on the fringes wishing I had the confidence and the time to socialise. My father kept me short of money so I could not join in any school activities that cost money. I tried to tell some of my schoolmates about my home life but generally they did not believe me. My father was handsome and charming and when he came to school the pupils would all try to catch a glimpse of him and say how lucky I was. I was so grateful to one friend who stayed with us for a while and, realising what I had been saying was true, told me she believed me. I used to look forward to going home for the holidays because I always hoped that this time the nightmare would end and we would be an ordinary family.

As a teenager I was subjected to sexual bullying. He used to take me out making comments such as, 'People will think you are my girl friend'. He would have a lot to drink. On the way back he would stop the car and fondle me. I could smell the drink on his breath. I did not believe I could say 'no' to him so I just used to freeze. When I tried to refuse to masturbate him he said that I shouldn't get married because I was frigid and any man who took me on would be getting a poor deal. I wished he wouldn't do it and I felt guilty because I thought that I was letting my mother down and committing an infidelity. He would describe to me the merits of various women with whom he had affairs.

When I was seventeen I met a man many years older than myself and fell deeply in love with him. Perhaps in an attempt to escape from home I became engaged to him. He was a man very like my father. He found another girl friend. The engagement was broken. I was devastated. But other people didn't let me down. Aged eight-een I decided to leave home for good. My father threatened me in order to keep me from leaving. My mother rang my uncle and aunt. I took a bus to their home and my uncle met me at the bus stop.

They took me into their home and made me feel valued and cared for. When I was ready to move on they let me go. (Early adulthood account continues on page 212.)

Point for reflection

Having listened to Sarah's account what did you hear about the child's perspective? What aspects did you find remarkable?

Comment: Sarah's statement 'no day was a safe day, a good day, until it was over' indicated a truly frightened child. Such a comment might be have been understandable in the context of a child in parts of Belfast in the height of the Irish 'Troubles' in the late twentieth century or in Baghdad in the worst of the post-2003 invasion chaos. War and social upheaval might understandably result in a child feeling that every day might bring new dangers. But Sarah's story demonstrates the profound effect of abuse when a child can feel so insecure in the calm of a peacetime democracy when the danger comes from within the family.

I also heard the agony of a child whose family was so 'respectable' and the abusing parent so apparently attractive that she knew that she would not be believed.

Another message was from a child who is removed from home and sees this as abandonment. She wants to return home despite all the abusive experiences because she has the constant hope that 'this time the nightmare would end and we would be an ordinary family'.

Roy's account

I did not have any brothers or sisters. Mum was pregnant with another baby after me but she carried cement around the garden and lost the baby. My father constantly told me I was useless and worthless. I would not make anything of my life. I was a waste of space, a 'fat slob'. He would stand over me forcing me to eat food I did not like. I would have to sit in front of it for ages until I managed to eat it. It used to make me sick. But I began to over-eat things I did like for comfort, and I became very fat. Dad would also make me sit and write until I managed it perfectly. He kept screwing up the paper and put it in the bin. This could go on for two or three hours. If I wanted to watch television I was only allowed to do so if I could name the programme correctly. Mum was too frightened to stop Dad treating me in this way.

I witnessed a lot of marital violence. Dad used to beat Mum up although he did not hit me. But I used to feel very angry. I desperately wanted to hit out at Dad but knew I did not stand a chance. Once he put a stiletto heel through my mother's skull. Another time I was upstairs, Mum was downstairs and Dad was carving the chicken. Suddenly he started, and she went at him with a fork. She stormed out taking me too and went to the police. But she had him back on a six-month trial, which made me feel very bad. Both Mum and I were nervous wrecks. On one occasion, Dad told Mum to 'write your will out' just as she was going into hospital for an operation, this made me see red and I threw a hot cup of tea at Dad who looked completely stunned. After this my father stopped hitting Mum for a while.

Dad also had interest in very young girls; he was into gymslips. When Mum went in hospital for a hysterectomy he was in bed with a girl. At first he had an affair with her mother who had an abortion because he made her pregnant. Then he started knocking off her daughter, she was about twelve years old at the time.

After years of abuse, Mum left home for good taking me with her. I had to grow up so quickly when my mother left Dad that I pushed things to the back of my mind.

I tried to understand my father. His mother, my grandmother, walked out when his father had an affair. My grandfather remarried and Dad's stepmother was really cruel. She would beat Dad until her hands were blue and my grandfather did nothing protect him. My mother was born illegitimately and brought up in a children's home. Neither parent had many relatives and Mum none, but those that there were supported Dad. They felt it was normal for a man to beat his wife and children. My mother had a best friend I called 'Aunty' and she would always say nice things about me and was always ready to listen. I also had a pet cat, Tallulah, who was always a good companion.

In school I was quiet and very withdrawn. I did not have many friends. In fact, I was so fat that I was bullied a lot. I was off sick much of the time but this was a problem when Dad was at home. There was one teacher who encouraged me and I was able to talk to him a bit about things at home. But at the next school I started to play up and was threatened with expulsion. I never told the teachers there about home.

I left school when sixteen and started an apprenticeship. I was still fat, over nineteen stone. Then one day I was really upset by a cutting remark and I stopped eating. I lost weight, went down to six stone and had less than a year to live. Hospital did not help much but then I went to a day centre where there was counselling and other people with problems. It was really the other patients who gave me support. I was nearly twenty however before I managed to gain a reasonable weight and eat normally. Mum was not able to help much as she had so many problems of her own. (Early adulthood account continues on page 213.)

Point for reflection

In Roy's account, what did you hear? Again try to identify two messages that the voice of Roy as a child and young person conveyed to you.

Comment: I heard a child for whom food became a substitute parent. 'I began to over-eat things I did like for comfort.' But food brought with it as many problems as it solved so ultimately he virtually rejected it.

Another comment I heard was 'I tried to understand my father.' Normally, it is the parent who tries to comprehend their developing child. As in several of the accounts we have an abused child taking on parental responsibilities

Josie and Jake's story

Josie and Jake are brother and sister; Josie is the elder by four years. They provide an account of abuse in the same family from two different perspectives.

Josie

We seemed a poor but happy, respectable family living in a village with two decent loving parents. Our dad had been a soldier, serving in Northern Ireland and then the first Gulf War. When dad left for the Gulf, I was four years old and Jake was only a few months old. I have some quite happy memories of those early years. We lived near our nan and grandad, my father's parents. I never knew my mother's family; apparently there had been a falling out and she did not speak to them.

Things started to change. I'm not quite sure of the timing but not too long after dad came back from the Gulf. I know that he became very tired and developed some sort of chest complaint, I think bronchitis. He left the army but had difficulty holding down a job. He'd been in the catering corps and according to granddad had always loved cooking but after he came back from the Gulf, he used to get so tired that the long hours working in restaurants and hotels was too much for him.

Mum started to get more and more impatient with him. She always had a quick temper and would whack me and Jake with anything she had to hand; not enough to cause many bruises but it still hurt. Now she would push dad around, sometimes thumping him. 'Get out you useless lump!' she'd scream at him. He'd go off to the pub or out into a little shed in the garden. We had a small house but because it was a village all the houses had quite big gardens. Dad spent a lot of time out in the garden; it was an escape for him. The pub was his other escape but he rarely became violent with the drink, more like sad. I saw him weeping sometimes when he'd had a lot to drink.

Dad's health seemed to get worse. This led to a downward spiral. He found working more and more difficult. This meant mum had to go out to work, poorly paid cleaning jobs which she hated but was the only work she could get. Living in a village and unable to drive, she didn't have much choice. She became more and more stressed and angry. She went to the doctor and was put on pills but she also started drinking. She also took over-the-counter tablets like codeine and started to have to have them. Every Saturday she caught the bus into town. I went with her a couple of times and was puzzled because she went from chemist to chemist buying tablets. She told me to say nothing to anyone about the chemists.

All this meant mum's behaviour became really erratic and while she cleaned other people's houses, ours became a mess. The housework became my job. I was only aged about eight but before and after school I had to clean everything. I'd do the polishing and sweeping especially the floors; I remember mopping the kitchen floor. It was always smeary however hard I tried to clean it. It made me really tired, it's the one job I really hated. I had to wash the clothes. When I was younger, mum hung the washing out because she did not want the neighbours to see me doing it but once I was older she didn't mind. I did all the ironing and after a day at school it was really tiring. Apart from a bit of washing up Jake was not expected to help because mum claimed 'boys don't do pansy domestic things'. Mum had clear ideas that 'men should be men' and she showed her disgust that dad was no longer a soldier, that he couldn't earn a decent living for his family, that he liked what mum saw as the 'feminine' activity of cooking and that he would not stand up to her. She would hit him with a broom handle or soup ladle and mock him but he would not retaliate. His view was that men did not hit women and I knew deep down he wasn't weak because he was strong enough to keep to his principles despite huge provocation.

When we were young, Jake and me would spend time at nan's and grandad's house. They were kind and good fun; granddad could wiggle his ears and cracked really daft jokes. But they weren't young; they had had dad late in life and so by the time I was in my teens they had both became frail. Nan had some form of dementia and had to go into a home and shortly after granddad, who had lung cancer, became very ill, was admitted to hospital and never came out. Dad never let on to them how violent mum was especially to him and somehow Jake and me knew not to say anything,

Once I was in my teens, mum's drinking and dependence on drugs became worse. We had very little money because she spent it on alcohol and tablets. All the drugs were legal from chemists but she was still addicted to them. She would sometimes be incontinent, being sick and weeing all over the house. I tried my best to keep everything clean but I was really tired so found excuses to stay off school to give myself time to catch up on the cleaning. The worst thing was that I had no friends. I was not in school a lot and also I know that sometimes when I was there I smelt because I had not had time and energy to wash all my clothes. I could not bring any friends back to my home I was terrified that mum would be drunk and start to puke on them or say really rude things. I was too busy trying to help dad, look after mum, protect Jake and keep the home okay. All this meant that I was bullied inside and outside home. We went to school on the school bus which was dreadful. There were no teachers or prefects to control the bullies who would taunt me.

I suppose nowadays I would be seen as a 'young carer' as I was looking after everyone. But it did not feel as if I was doing anything valuable. I didn't manage to help mum with whatever her problems were. I couldn't make dad better. I didn't always manage to keep the house clean. I didn't manage to protect Jake. Once mum gave him a really bad beating but he will tell you about that himself. The other thing mum did to us children was to lock us in our bedrooms. We didn't realise how she was locking the doors. I didn't find out 'til I was adult. There was just a little hole and a straight round key. The hole was covered by a little plaque with our names on.

In school the teachers more or less ignored me. I was quiet, didn't want to draw attention to myself. There was one male teacher who took an interest in me. He taught English and gave me an interest in reading. I do not know if he suspected something but he lent me a book about a boy abused by his aunt and uncle, *Harry Potter*. The book was probably a first edition and worth a fortune now. Despite all my absences I managed to get six good GCSEs but I didn't stay on at school. I had too much to do looking after the family. (Early adulthood account continues on page 214.)

Jake

I remember even when very young I was very confused and quite frightened about what was happening to my parents. I hated the way mum pushed dad around, shouted and sometimes hit him. It didn't seem right and I spent a lot of time at my grandparents. Nan was always nice to granddad, who always seemed to be laughing and joking. I have memories of helping him in the garden where he grew lots of fruit and vegetables. I remember picking huge sweet strawberries and blackberries with granddad, always in sunshine.

Home was different. Mum was always shouting, losing her temper, she'd hit me often with a wooden spoon. She'd bully dad so badly. As I grew older I became really angry. I didn't see so much of nan and granddad because they were becoming ill. Dad also always seemed to be ill so he couldn't do things like play football or cricket with me. Josie was so busy cleaning everything and looking after dad. She also had to mop up after mum when she was puking or worse. I began to understand that she was often drunk and also had a lot of pills. I didn't dare show my anger but it was burning away inside.

I was nine years old when the burning angry feeling burst out to became a reality. I had always been fascinated by fire and mum smoked so it was easy to find a lighter and matches. There was a rubbish bin just outside the village shop. It was full of papers and stuff. One evening when the shop was closed I started a fire in the bin which caught alight. But we lived in a village, it was summer so still light and someone spotted me and knew who I was. The villager phoned the fire service and the police. I was too young to be prosecuted so the police told me off, took me home and told my mum what I had done. Mum ordered me up to my bedroom. After a while she came up. She had already measured out and cut some strips of gaffer tape which she was holding. I didn't understand what she was intending but I felt really frightened. She told me to take off my jumper and shirt. As I was doing so, she put the tape round my ankles, then round my wrists and over my mouth. I had been too frightened to yell out or try to escape and by the time I wanted to yell I couldn't scream or move very much because of the tape. Mum then put a length of thin rope around my ankles and wrists. I was really frightened I thought she was going to hang me. She pushed me over my bed and tied the rope to the bed legs so that I could not move. She then started to thrash me with a belt over my back, bottom and legs. It felt like she was hitting me for ever; I thought she wouldn't stop. Then she left me like that, still tied and locked the door. It was even worse because I could not rub the pain away. I just had to lie there in agony and I couldn't breathe properly; I felt I couldn't get enough air in through my nose. I was desperate to gasp for air, to scream but it hurt to stretch my mouth underneath the tape. After ages she returned. She told me she'd take the tape off my mouth if I didn't scream out. If I did, the tape would go back on and I would get another leathering even worse than the one I'd had. I didn't dare scream and she took off the tape and ropes. I'd wet myself. She kept me locked in my room for days. It was the summer holidays so I wasn't missed at school and I didn't have any real friends so no one asked where I was. I don't know what dad, Josie or my grandparents made of my disappearance but nothing was said. I wasn't allowed out of the house for a long while.

The beating made me even angrier but even more afraid. It did not stop me from starting fires. I lived in a village near countryside so I walked out into copses where I couldn't be seen and started fires. Fortunately we did not have any really long heat waves. I can see how forest fires are started deliberately. At the time I would have loved to have started a really, really huge fire. Mine just fizzled out or were dampened down by rain. I suppose I was lucky because I lived in a village and although my dad had been a soldier he had not been interested in guns once he had left the army, so I couldn't nick one from him. If I'd been in a city I would have joined a gang, smashed the place up, shot someone or, with mates, started really big fires. As it was I was a loner, only had one friend at school, Billy. He was partially deaf and I learnt a sort of sign language so we could communicate easily. He was over-protected by his mum and he lived in a different village miles away, so we did not see each other outside school.

Basically I was lonely, frightened yet really angry as a child. I think eventually I turned the anger against myself because I became more and more depressed. It got so much worse when nan went into a home and granddad died. Dad also seemed to be really ill and depressed. Sometimes things got better. During my teens mum was often tearful and regretful. She would apologise, not to Dad, but to Josie and me and say that she was not going to drink and be the best ever mother. But it didn't last long and it almost made things worse because I didn't know what to expect, I wouldn't know what mood she would be in. It also made me feel guilty about sometimes hating her. When she was all regretful it made me feel really sorry for her. So it was all like being on an emotional roller coaster. (Early adulthood account continues on page 215.)

Point for reflection

So having listened to Josie and Jake what did you hear? Were there some feelings they had in common? What did they experience and perceive differently?

Comment: I heard two children who felt they had to keep the family secret. Although largely isolated, there were people they could have talked to at school, there were neighbours in the small village and grandparents nearby. As Josie said 'Jake and me knew not to say anything.'

You might perhaps have heard two children who were suffering from loss; mourning their lost childhoods, lost parents, lost grandparents, lost education, lost friendships. They both expressed feelings of either tiredness or depression and self-blame.

In Josie's account I heard the message of a child who, despite virtually running the household felt useless because she could not put things right, she commented 'it did not feel as if I was doing anything valuable'.

Emerging from Jake's story was a child pitched this way and that by strong emotions of anger, depression, sorrow and guilt 'it was all like being on an emotional roller coaster'.

Comment on the accounts

One of the key features of the six accounts is that although the children were all clearly suffering at the hands of family members, on the whole, they were 'suffering in silence'. The accounts show how assiduously children will hide the abusive situation at home and how difficult it is for them to disclose any maltreatment. Josie and Jake felt so ashamed of their mother's behaviour that they diligently guarded the family secrets. Sarah, on the other hand, tried to tell her schoolmates what was happening but was not believed. Even when there was overwhelming evidence of something amiss, the extent of the family problems was not recognised, as shown by the cases of Roy and Marie whose family members were hospitalised and the cases of Marie's sister and Lloyd who both made suicide attempts.

The accounts also show how very damaging the experience of abuse is. The depth of the children's suffering is clear. As well as the suicide attempts, there was evidence of eating disorders, behavioural problems, drug taking, criminal offending on the part of Lloyd and Jake, educational underachievement and massive damage to the children's sense of self-esteem and self-worth. It is, however, important to note that, despite the harm, maltreatment does not always lead to permanent damage. The six survivors will be revisited in Chapter 10, where it will be shown that, with help, abused children can achieve fulfilled adult lives.

Point for reflection

Chose one or two of the stories of abuse outlined in this chapter. Identify who the main players in the case are including professional agencies such as schools or the police. Who held what sort of power? How might shifts and alterations in power have alleviated the situation? Could the victim have been helped by empowering either the children or other people in their lives? Might it have been useful to 'disempower' or limit the power of any of the significant people?

Comment: This activity is an extension of the second exercise in the previous chapter (p. 12), where you were asked to analyse the power in a family known to you, Here, instead, you are applying the analysis to a clear case of abuse by examining one of the above accounts. This activity is designed to help you identify the importance of power dynamics in relation to working with cases of abuse. It is also designed to help you consider the issue of 'empowerment' which often results in the limitation of the power of other people.

Putting it into practice

Look at the accounts above and examine how the children might be communicating distress. This might not be simply by what they say but there may be indications through their appearance or behaviour. Think of your own cases, whether in work or on placement. Have there been any similar indications, if not of abuse then of distress, either in the past or present?

Comment: It is important not to leap to conclusions. Children may show distress but this might not be rooted in abuse. For example, a much loved pet might have died and for a child, whose experiences are immediate and all encompassing, grief for a pet might be profound. This is where additional information from the family and other professionals can help build up a picture of what is happening to the child.

By chance, several of the accounts included domestic violence and abuse. This is not to say that intimate partner violence is always related to child protection. However, distorted relationships and the misuse of power in a family can often lead to both child and partner maltreatment. The significance of domestic violence in relation to child protection is explored further in Mullender *et al.* (2002), Humphreys and Stanley (2006) and Sterne and Poole (2010), with excellent advice on communicating with children and relevant legislation given by Hester *et al.* (2007).

Although there are many signs of abuse, as numerous public enquiries into child deaths have shown, recognising that maltreatment is occurring and being aware of the extent and severity of abuse, is by no means easy. As we have seen, there are many obstacles to recognition. One of the key ways of overcoming these obstacles is by increasing your understanding of theories and ideas that explain why and how children relate to others and cope with adversity. This understanding is the focus of the next chapter.

Further resources

Accounts by former victims of child abuse abound and give valuable perspectives, for example physical and emotional abuse accounts are given by Ben (1991) and Yen Mah (2002).

Algate, J., Jones, D., Rose, W. and Jeffrey, C. (eds) (2006) *The Developing World of the Child*. London: Jessica Kingsley.
Although not designed as a work on child protection, it is very informative about the developing child and there are some highly relevant chapters such as that by Dr Jones on communication with children about diverse experiences.

Humphries, C., Thiara, R. K., Skamballis, A. and Mullender, A. (2006a) *Talking to My Mum: A Picture Workbook for Workers, Mothers and Children Affected by Domestic Abuse*. London: Jessica Kingsley.

Humphries, C., Thiara, R. K., Skamballis, A. and Mullender, A. (2006b) *Talking about Domestic Abuse: A Photo Activity Workbook to Develop Communication between Mothers and Young People*, London: Jessica Kingsley.
These are two companion books, the first for younger children and the second for older ones. Colchester and Tendring Women's Refuge helped in the development of the books and they are informed by those directly affected by domestic abuse. There is information and clarification for adults but also photocopiable worksheets which can be used by children.

For practitioners and students wishing to undertake research with children, two books devoted to the ethics of research with children that could usefully be consulted before undertaking research are:

Alderson, P. and Morrow, V. (2011) *The Ethics of Research with Children and Young People: A Practical Handbook*. London: Sage.

Farrell, A. (ed.) (2005) *Ethical Research with Children*. Maidenhead: Open University Press/McGraw-Hill.

CHAPTER 3

Understanding and assessing abused children

CHAPTER OVERVIEW

This chapter has three main sections and deals with the following subjects:

- communication with children;
- attachments and the Stockholm syndrome – abuse, counter-intuitively, can increase attachments
- additional emotions evoked by abuse – may either obscure children's communications or lead to physiological and psychological harm

---

In keeping with the theme of this book, this chapter focuses on the child. It throws some light on abused children's reactions, actions, emotions and cognitions which might help or hinder recognition and assessment. It does not give a full account of assessing potential abuse in families; the complexities of a full safeguarding assessment cannot be dealt with sufficiently in one chapter. Other authors have comprehensively examined this topic, including Calder and Hackett (2002), Calder (2008), Bentovim *et al.* (2009), Helm (2010), Holland (2010), Parker and Bradley (2010) and Turney *et al.* (2012).

Practitioners will encounter abused children who are able to explain what has happened to them and be only too happy to be rescued from their homes. However, they are far more likely to meet those who cannot articulate their experiences. Child victims often defend their abusers and hide their injuries. As we heard from Josie and Jake, they guard the family secret and, as illustrated by Sarah's story, try to avoid removal from home. This chapter continues the examination of abuse from the child's perspective and examines how children might, often indirectly, cry out for help. It will also throw some light on one of the greatest barriers to the recognition of abuse, that is, the manifestation of the Stockholm syndrome, the often apparently paradoxical behaviour of defending abusers and resisting assistance.

Working with diversity

Most of the reactions and emotions described in the chapter will be common to all children whatever their culture, creed, colour, class, gender and abilities. There are, however, issues for some groups of children, which need to be borne in mind and are touched on in this section.

Children from minorities might find disclosing abuse even more difficult than those in majority groups. This is particularly true if they are aware that the group to which they belong is stigmatised by mainstream society. For example, a child from a minority cultural, religious or ethnic group might feel that disclosure will not only be a betrayal of their family but also of their group. Already, they may believe, too much discrimination is shown against their community without giving its detractors more ammunition.

Many children with disabilities might also be more reluctant to disclose abuse if they have received messages that they are a 'problem' or 'less worthy': they might believe that the added label 'abused' will simply heighten the perceived problems they cause or inflate their 'less worthy' status.

Cries for help

The six accounts in the previous chapter were all given by adults. It is generally harder for children to talk so directly and clearly about their experiences. However, children indicate their distress in a variety of ways and many of these are outlined below.

Verbal communication

Small children who have learned to talk, but who cannot fully appreciate the consequences of what they say, may describe their abuse spontaneously. This can, however, go unrecognised. 'Daddy tickles me with his hammer' or 'Mummy saggled me' (*strangled*) may be dismissed as childish nonsense. Sometimes children do not have the words to describe their experiences so they make words up. One little boy kept repeating 'Uncle Harry gooed on me'. It was only with careful questioning that he was able to indicate that he had been sexually abused and had been trying to describe the way the perpetrator ejaculated on him. A small child often has difficulty indicating the degree of the abuse so may say, 'Mummy smacked me and made me sad', which could equally mean that the mother administered a mild slap or that she lashed out harshly and recklessly for no good reason. Small children may also lack clarity in their enunciation leaving adults unsure whether the child is saying something like 'Daddy showed me his willie' or 'Danny showed me his wellie'.

Older children may be able to articulate what has happened to them but are more aware of possible consequences. They sometimes start to tell somebody in a manner that gives them a way out if they change their mind and also tests the reactions of the person in whom they confide. They may therefore start with a question such as 'What is meant by intercourse?' or by a statement such as 'I don't really want to go home this afternoon.'

Certain disabilities may make verbal communication, or its signing equivalent, particularly difficult. Speech may be impaired, so that what the child is saying is indistinct and misinterpreted. Complex concepts, embarrassing incidents, confusing experiences are difficult enough for children well able to manipulate the language of the majority. Seeking help becomes all the more difficult for those with a restricted or minority language. Furthermore, as Kennedy (2002) explains, children who use alternative communication such as word boards may only be understood by a couple of key people who may in fact be their abusers.

Children, with or without disabilities, may find that they are not believed as happened in the case of Sarah who had a superficially charming father. They rarely totally lie about abusive experiences within the family. However, like adults in emotionally difficult situations, they may not be absolutely truthful either. For example, one girl accused her stepfather of sexually abusing her. Investigations eventually revealed that the abuser was not her stepfather but her grandfather. She had been desperate for help but had wanted to protect her much-loved grandparent. Young children will sometimes make up stories about their home background. Primary school teachers wisely view some tales of fantastic events and magical relatives with circumspection. However, if these stories are negative ones they may well indicate some form of abuse, albeit not the mistreatment described.

It is not unusual for children to retract their allegations. This does not necessarily mean that they were originally lying. A common reason is that they cannot cope with the consequences of disclosure, especially if the family is disrupted and its members reject the child. He or she may feel that a retraction will result in the family being reunited and everything 'being alright'.

Non-verbal communication

Not all communication is verbal. When children's gestures, facial expression or demeanour do not accord with their words there is cause for concern especially if, for example, they say are fine but look nervous or despondent. Nonetheless, some children are very good at compartmentalising their emotions so they may maintain the fiction that everything is alright and look perfectly happy when, in reality, they are facing distress and abuse.

An important factor to bear in mind is that there are social and cultural conventions about some types of non-verbal communication. For example, in Western cultures eye contact tends to convey interest and sincerity. But in other cultures it may signal status; subordinates, including children, are expected to lower the eyes and those who maintain eye contact are seen as rude and insufficiently deferential.

Physical appearance

There are non-verbal, physical indicators of abuse. Sometimes abused children will draw attention to a physical injury in a straightforward way. They may have had enough and want the abuse to stop whatever the consequences. Sometimes they may indicate an injury indirectly in the hope that someone will notice their discomfort, for example, refusing to do PE because their leg hurts. More usually, children will try to cover up bruising or wheals and, if they are asked about them, will give an explanation, but one inconsistent with the injuries.

Although the cause of many injuries can be only identified by skilled paediatricians, there are some patterns of injury which should alert an observant lay person. Bruises and lesions on different parts of the body especially of different ages will not have occurred during one incident such as falling off a bike. Generally, concerns are legitimate when common sense suggests the injury does not fit the explanation. Finally, patterns of absence from nursery or school should be noted if there is any suspicion of abuse because, as we heard in the accounts of Marie and Jake, children may be kept at home until injuries heal.

It is thought that it is difficult to detect bruising on children with disabilities because they are more likely to fall. However, research by Goldberg *et al.* (2009, p. 608) showed that the problems of detecting physical abuse in children with disabilities is not so challenging. They found that while children with disabilities tend to have more bruises, importantly:

> the body surfaces that are uncommonly bruised in typical children and likely associated with physical abuse (neck, ears, chin, anterior chest, and buttocks) are also uncommonly bruised in disabled children.

Neglected children may have evident physical signs. A poorly clad, dirty, emaciated child will be readily identified, although neglect has to be distinguished from the effects of poverty. A neglected child might not be easy to recognise because clothing can mask serious underweight, while babies often have naturally rounded faces, which can belie an emaciated body.

The child's facial expression and body movements can be indicators of abuse. Distressed babies will usually cry but some infants who have been persistently attacked will show 'frozen watchfulness'. The baby will have a fixed smile and her eyes will follow adults around in a wary manner. She will not laugh, cry and gurgle in a spontaneous way. Older children may look apprehensive and again lack spontaneity in the presence of adults while a marked 'startle' response can indicate a child who has been significantly traumatised.

Behavioural signs

The reactions of children to abuse can vary greatly. It is therefore difficult to list the full range of behavioural symptoms of abuse. For disabled children, behaviour difficulties may be attributed to their impairment rather than the emotional impact of abuse (Kennedy, 2002). However, in all children a sudden change of behaviour can be significant, for example, the normally outgoing child who becomes withdrawn. Extremes of good or bad behaviour may also be an indication of mistreatment at home. Had Jake's arson attempts been discovered this would not have been an indication of a 'bad' child but rather one who was angered, disempowered and distressed by the abuse he experienced. Many abused children, like Marie, truant from school because they feel so different from other children. They are ashamed of what is happening and want to hide away from the world. As illustrated by Josie's account, sometimes they are forced to stay away to look after other family members.

Small children who have been sexually abused may act out their experiences with other children or toys. Nursery staff, who have a profound expertise in how young children behave, often recognise when children are going beyond the normal games of 'mummies and daddies'. Older children may become promiscuous or show extreme naivety and lack of interest in sexual matters. Children who are subjected to physical or verbal violence in the home may well show aggressive behaviour and bully other children. Conversely, they may be very passive and seem to invite the attentions of the school bully. Lloyd who became, for a while, pugnacious and criminally aggressive, and Roy and Josie, who were bullied, exemplify these two alternatives.

Eating disorders may be a sign of abuse as exemplified by Roy. Self-harming often has its roots in maltreatment and for some children life may become so intolerable that suicide is attempted, as illustrated by Marie's sister and Lloyd.

Finally, children may show no extremes or oddities of behaviour because they compartmentalise their lives. They metaphorically put the abuse into a separate box and forget about it during the times when it is not occurring. Nevertheless, there will be faint clues as most abused children feel isolated, unworthy and afraid. Perhaps the child will daydream a lot, be forgetful – the memory blanks out bad experiences – or be tired as night-time abuse and nightmares take their toll.

Ways of listening to children

When working with abused children, as Laming (2009, p. 22) advised, we need to put ourselves 'in the place of the child or young person and consider first and foremost how the situation must feel for them'. This means that we have to hear what children are trying to communicate to us.

Among the experts in communication, especially with children who have limited oral language, are early years workers. Daily, they communicate to and relate effortlessly with babies, toddlers and young children who have limited speech. Most take in their stride those children whose first developing language is not English or who have disabilities that impair language development. The communication repertoire of these professionals is outstanding.

The Mosaic approach (Clark and Moss, 2011) is a framework for listening to young children's perspectives on their daily lives and focused mainly on their experiences in day-care settings. However, with a little imagination the approach can be adapted for work with maltreated children.

'Mosaic' refers to the use of a range of inventive strategies for listening to children. Although primarily for three- to four-year olds, the strategy has, as Clark and Moss (2011, p.1) pointed out, been adapted for 'work with children under two, children for whom English is an additional language, keyworkers and parents'.

The authors remind us that children's 'voices' begin at birth. There is value in talking with children but there are other tools and symbolic ways that children communicate their feelings and experiences. Among the techniques suggested are careful observations of children, letting children take pictures of what they like or dislike, role-playing situations and encouraging children to talk, often 'on the move' because they do not always want to sit and talk.

Part of the Mosaic method includes views of parents and carers. However, this is focused on the child. There is the danger that, in working with parents and carers, the professionals become adult-centric and forget the child's perspective but the views of parents and carers can be important and telling. Parents' reports of being puzzled and concerned about their child might, when added to what the child has indicated, point towards abuse by others. This was illustrated by the inquiry into sexual abuse at Little Teds Nursery (Plymouth Safeguarding Children's Board, 2010, p. 14) where in 'March 2009 a parent made a telephone complaint to Ofsted regarding a member of staff shouting at a child and causing that child and other children to be frightened' and another parent observed that their child's experiences at Little Teds 'had resulted in the child fearing any contact with the nursery environment' (p. 17).

Grief and mourning

Abused children may have underlying symptoms of grief because, often, they are suffering multiple losses. There may be tangible losses such as the Christmas presents that Marie's father destroyed. But more often, they are psychological losses such as the negation of the sense of security that can be seen in the cases of Sarah and

Jake when they were savagely beaten. A further example is the denial of pride and self-worth apparent as a consequence of the emotional abuse of Roy and Lloyd.

In babies and very young children, the sense of loss might lead initially to increased distress, crying and anxiety but then if they are not comforted and reassured sensitively, they may withdraw and become quiet, functioning almost automatically. Repeated experiences of loss may well lead to an underlying detachment and limitation of emotional repertoire. Older children tend to demonstrate a grief process similar to that of adults but may have a more limited understanding.

It is important to note that with the 'process' of mourning, there is not a neat movement from one stage to the next but rather a complex development with children regressing to an earlier set of feelings, or becoming stuck in one phase or showing no apparent grief.

- There is often an initial phase of shock, disbelief and denial. This can be expressed through behaviours such as sleeping problems, regression or an apparent indifference to what is happening.
- There may then anger and frustration; this was illustrated in the account of Jake when much of his sense of security and of self-worth was destroyed particularly by the severe beating he experienced. His anger led him to fire-raise but he also turned much of the anger against himself leading to isolation and withdrawal. In contrast, Roy on one occasion, when facing the loss of his mother, exploded with anger and threw tea over his father.
- There is sometimes a stage of bargaining, 'if I am really good everything will be alright'. Marie and Josie always hoped if they worked hard and helped perhaps the family would heal.
- There can be a later stage of despair, seen in children who just accept what is happening or attempt to destroy themselves. Roy eventually just comforted himself with food. A more extreme example was Lloyd's attempt to hang himself and Marie's sister's attempted overdose.
- Finally, there can be a type of acceptance. In terms of bereavement, grief commentators talk about 'reorganisation' (Daniel *et al.*, 2010) where the child gains some control and looks to the future. But for many abused children this is more an 'accommodation', where they learn to live with abuse and

sometimes begin to identify with the abuser, emerging as the next generation of abuse perpetrators.

When working with maltreated children it can be difficult to disentangle grief processes from those of traumatic stress and the abnormal attachments recognised as part of the Stockholm syndrome. These are examined in the next two sections.

Post-traumatic stress

The signs of post-traumatic stress may be apparent, particularly in children who have been subjected to, or witnessed, abuse, terror and violence (Dwivedi, 2000; Cohen *et al.*, 2003; Margolin and Vickerman, 2007; Wechsler-Zimring and Kearney, 2011). There tend to be three broad areas of response: *intrusion, avoidance* and *physiological reactions.*

• *Intrusion:* memories of the trauma keep intruding. Children may consequently show signs of repetitive play associated with the trauma. However, the events might be transposed into apparent fantasies. So for example one five-year-old child repeatedly played a game where he waved a wand and his 'good' mother became a 'bad witch'. Disconcertingly the child clearly felt he was responsible for his mother's sudden change from caring parent to abuser.

Flashbacks can re-occur at any time; these are not just memories but a reliving of the traumatic events. Children may recall visual and oral images as well as odours, tastes and sensations, including pain, associated with the trauma. Flashbacks are experienced when children are awake but when they are asleep the memories may again intrude as nightmares.

Traumatised children may become very fearful and have an exaggerated judgement of danger. But equally they might have a foreshortened sense of the future. Because of this some may take substantial risks and disregard any consequences. While it is always worth warning a young person about the dangers of stealing a performance car and driving it at high speeds, there should be no surprise if a traumatised teenager ignores such advice. Margolin and Vickerman (2007, p. 616) observe:

> Youth may engage in risky behaviors such as substance abuse, risky sexual practices, or delinquent acts as ways to cope with PTSD, that is, to self-medicate, reduce their sense of isolation, or improve their esteem.

- *Avoidance:* children may avoid thoughts and feelings about trauma and situations which remind them of the trauma. If interviewed and expected to give details, they may experience a genuine inability to recall aspects of trauma. They can sometimes 'switch off' in order to protect themselves from intrusion. This may result in a more general loss of interest in activities and regression, for example very young children may lose newly acquired language or toileting skills. In slightly older children, the withdrawal can lead to heavy sleep, although the opposite can be evident, as intrusion can conversely result in insomnia. Another worrying outcome is increased feelings of detachment and estrangement from others with a restricted range of feelings. This can be difficult, especially for family members and foster carers because the child may have very limited ability to show affection.

- *Physiological reactions*: traumatised children may also demonstrate increased arousal including sleeping difficulties, irritability and outbursts of anger, difficulty concentrating, over-vigilance (being alert all the time especially to the mood and behaviour of adults) and an exaggerated startle response. They might suddenly react to a situation which reminds them of the trauma, for example the sight of a football boot if they were hit with one. If no one is aware of the abuse, the child's reaction will be apparently irrational, 'making a fuss about nothing!'

More worryingly, children's brains are still developing and there is evidence of potentially more permanent neurological damage, for example, problems in memory because of functional abnormalities in the hippocampi (Carrión *et al.*, 2010, De Bellis *et al.*, 2010). There may also be substantial changes in the biochemistry of the body and brain due to prolonged exposure to stress hormones and mechanisms (Margolin and Vickerman, 2007). There is growing awareness that chronic post-traumatic stress can be an underlying psychiatric disorder for some children constantly exposed to violence and abuse.

It is possible for intrusion, avoidance and physiological reactions to be manifest more or less at the same time. Therefore a child might have flashbacks but refuse to talk about his experiences and have an exaggerated startle response. Other children may have a predominant response, for example showing a general withdrawal and avoiding anything to do with their traumatic experiences. This can help explain why when a family of children are interviewed, the various members may give very different accounts of the abuse they all experienced with some denying anything untoward took place.

Attachments, entrapment and the Stockholm syndrome

All too often, child protection workers are urged to apply 'basic common sense' to their assessments. However, the expected outcome of maltreatment, namely loathing and a wish to be free of their oppressors, is not always present. Bowlby (1969, p. 80) spotted this when developing his attachment theory. He wrote:

> The attachment of children to parents, who by all ordinary standards, are very bad is a never-ceasing source of wonder to those who seek to help them. Even when they are with kindly foster-parents these children feel their roots to be in the homes where, perhaps, they have been neglected and ill-treated and keenly resent criticisms directed against their parents.

This section therefore explores the reasons for this apparent affectionate bond and the defence of their abuser by maltreated children. The first part looks at the natural attachment to parents in particular and families in general. However, this attachment and defence behaviour is not just directed towards abusive parents or family members. It can sometimes occur when the offender is someone on the margins or outside the family. In Victoria Climbié's history (Laming, 2003) it was Carl Manning, a man loosely associated with her great-aunt, who admitted to most of the physical abuse. Victoria had little chance to speak out, no one was listening. But even when workers listen to children there is no guarantee they will disclose what is happening, whether or not the abuser is a close relative. Even adult hostages, kidnap victims and concentration camp prisoners can, despite their suffering, demonstrate loyalty and affection towards their persecutors. An examination of the circumstances in which this may arise will provide some understanding of the child/abuser attachment.

Family matters

Bowlby (1951, 1969) contended that the primary caregiver for babies is their mother and this was largely supported by research indicating that infants of only a few days old prefer their mother's face to other faces (Carpenter, 1974), their mother's voice to other voices (Mills and Melhuish, 1974) and can distinguish their own mother's milk from that of other women (MacFarlane, 1977). Waters *et al.* (1995), using a more ethical determination of attachment styles, the qualitative Q-sort method, found across a diversity of cultures that babies tend to rely on their mother as a secure base. Rutter (1981), however, argued that a group of consistent carers provides this attachment and subsequent studies confirmed that babies are likely to have a similar attachment to their fathers (Lamb, 1987; Geiger, 1996; Goodsell and Meldrum, 2010). It is therefore probable that children develop strong attachments to parents and other caregivers even where the adults may feel ambivalence towards the child.

Despite criticisms on ethical, practical and cultural grounds (Washington, 2008; Woodhead and Faulkner, 2008) of Ainsworth's 'Strange Situation Procedure' (SSP) (Bowlby, 1969) and her classification of attachments, her great contribution was to identify that, while nearly all children have an attachment to at least one primary carer, not all such attachments are beneficial. Some abused children live in such physically, socially or emotionally isolated families that there seems to be no alternative to the mistreating parent. They cannot redirect their attachment behaviour because a substitute is not available. They have little option but to continue to focus all their energies on trying to attract the abusive parent. For others, their maltreatment does not start until after they have developed an attachment to their parents.

Children can become attached to alternative caregivers. This ability to redirect attachment behaviour is the basis of successful adoptions and step-parenting. However, it again means that the child may attach to a foster, step or adoptive parent who has little affection for the girl or boy in question. Children, whose attempts to be cared for by their natural parent have been thwarted, will be all the more desperate to cling to substitute caregivers, once they have given up hope of being nurtured by their natural parents.

Meanwhile, in terms of the wider family, it is an important unit in most societies. It has played a significant role in politics and in the exchange of property, and therefore children from a variety of cultures are brought up to have a healthy respect for their families. The focal importance of family is encapsulated in the United Nations Declaration of Human Rights, Article 16 (3), which states:

> The family is the natural and fundamental group unit of society and is entitled to protection by society and the State.

In many countries, demographic and economic conditions mean that ageing parents depend on their offspring for material support. The older generation therefore has a vested interest in emphasising the importance of loyalty to family members or obligations to the older generation. This is reinforced by religious texts: 'Honour your father and mother' (The Old Testament, Orchard and Fuller, 1966, p. 63); 'Honour the mothers who bore you' (The Koran, Dawood, 1990, p. 60); 'Shall I kill my own masters, who though greedy of my kingdom are yet my sacred teachers?' (Sanskrit poem, *The Bhagavad Gita,* Mascaro, 1962, p. 48).

Associated with the concept of family is a strong belief in the blood-tie. 'Blood is thicker than water' is a familiar saying. This is inculcated in early childhood through fairy-stories and nursery rhymes. A study of folk tales worldwide shows that where a child is mistreated, this is generally at the hands of a non-family member or a step-parent. From their infancy, children learn that they may be mistreated by people who are not really part of their family, but if they suffer at the hands of their parents it is either because they deserve punishment or because the parent is acting in their best interests. For the adopted, fostered or step-child there is still the spectre of the blood-tie because in its absence they may feel unable to take the care of substitute parents for granted.

Point for reflection

Think of folk tales that might have been told to you in your childhood, whatever your cultural heritage. Were birth parents ever the perpetrators of misfortune to any of the child characters? If they were what was the motivation of the parents? Was any ill-treatment for the child's ultimate benefit?

Comment: Even in some modern 'fairy-like' tales, any abuse is perpetrated by carers other than birth parents, one of the most prominent being Harry Potter by J.K. Rowling whose wonderful birth parents were killed and Harry is emotionally abused and neglected by his aunt and uncle.

Familiar phrases such as 'like father, like son' and 'a chip off the old block' reflect the belief that aspects of personality are inherited. Children are reluctant to think of their parents as weak or cruel because these characteristics reflect on the children themselves. They have a vested interest in, for example, interpreting their parent's violent behaviour as a display of strength. Sarah, whose account was given in Chapter 2, came to dislike her father early in childhood. She recognised that this was, in her own words, 'a big decision for a child'. Sarah's disapproval of her father led, inevitably, to self-disapproval. This resulted in a loss of self-esteem, which meant that she submitted to physical, emotional and sexual abuse because she felt she had no right to resist.

Anatomy of the Stockholm syndrome

In kidnap, hijack and hostage situations, negotiators recognise that captives frequently develop positive feelings towards their captors and show hostility towards any rescuers.

> Even in the face of an armed officer of the law, the victim would offer himself as a human shield for his abductor. As absurd as this may seem, such behaviour had been observed by law enforcement officers throughout the world (Strenz, 1980, p. 147)

This paradoxical phenomenon has been termed the 'Stockholm syndrome'. Its name derives from the events in Sweden in August 1973 when four employees of the Svergis Kredit Bank were held hostage for 131 hours by two bank robbers. It became clear that during the siege, the hostages, despite being law-abiding citizens, were more afraid of the police than they were of their captors and subsequently defended the robbers.

There are a number of similarities between the victims of hostage situations, concentration camp prisoners and abused children (Doyle, 1985, 1997a). All are innocent, unsuspecting victims imprisoned and mistreated emotionally and/or physically by aggressors who feel that they have to hold the balance of power and have to be in total control of the victims.

There appear to be a number of psychological factors which enable a victim, whether adult or child, to cope with the stress of the situation and which may explain the Stockholm syndrome. The phases involved in the syndrome bear some similarities to grief processes with an initial shock and denial to final assimilation and acceptance.

Frozen fright, denial and isolation

At a time of disaster and terror in which there is some possibility of escape, individuals may panic, scream and run. However, in most hostage situations the captors ensure that the victims are trapped with no means of exit. This results in what Martin Symonds (1980, pp. 131–2) has termed 'frozen fright':

This superficially appears to be a cooperative and friendly behaviour that confuses even the victim, the criminal, the family and friends of the victim ... the victims narrowly focus all their energy on survival, exclusively concentrating on the [abuser] ... The victim then feels isolated from others, powerless and helpless.

All this is reminiscent of the frozen watchfulness of the battered infant and the feelings of helplessness and isolation recounted by many victims of child abuse.

Another early emotion is denial. It is more reassuring to believe that the captors intend no harm, than to recognise that they may well be prepared to maim and kill. One hostage of the hijack of TWA flight 355 in 1976 expressed the belief that the bombs held by the hijackers were fakes even after one of the bombs had killed or injured four bomb disposal officers. Chodoff (1981, p. 4), who studied concentration camp survivors, noted:

It appears that the most important personality defenses among concentration camp inmates were denial and isolation of affect. Some form of companionship with others was indispensable, since a completely isolated individual could not have survived in the camps, but the depth of such companionship was usually limited by the overpowering egotistical demands of self-preservation.

This is an echo of the isolation felt by child abuse victims. The relationship problems caused by the need for self-preservation was illustrated in the last chapter by Sarah, in relation to her sister, Barbara.

Fear and anger

Fear and anger may be repressed or turned, *not* against the subjugator because in the victims' impotent state that would be too uncomfortable, but against the rescuing authorities. There is a sense in which both abused and abusers feel united against the outside world. The threat 'within' is transferred to an external menace. This does not disappear as soon as rescue is achieved. Victims may:

remain hostile toward the police after the siege has ended. The 'original' victims in Stockholm still visit their abductors, and one former hostage is engaged to Olofsson. South American victims visit their former captors in jail. Others have begun defense funds for them. A hostile hostage is the price that law enforcement must pay for a living hostage. (Strenz, 1980, p. 149)

This fear and anger of 'outsiders' is sometimes seen in abused children. It is not uncommon for practitioners to find that the children they are attempting to help view them with hostility, mistrust and resentment.

Hope and gratitude

Having externalised much of their fear and anger, victims will search for evidence to confirm their hope that those maltreating them are really acting in their interests. There is more hope of survival if those in whose power victims reside are basically benevolent. For example, in the case of acts by hijackers, such as allowing food on board, these are seen by the captives as proof of the hostage-takers' kindness and concern for their welfare. Hostages and abused children have in common the fact that, although they are in the power of someone who may threaten their safety, they cling to him or her because they are dependent on their abuser to provide life's necessities.

There is also a sense in which victims feel that they owe their lives to their captors. Bahn (1980) explains that in the case of hostage situations when a threat to life is not carried out there is a build up of intense gratitude. A concentration camp prisoner will therefore attach great importance to any slight gesture of kindness from the guards. Solzhenitsyn (1974) recalling his time as a Russian Gulag prisoner describes the deep indebtedness felt towards a jailer who greeted the prisoners with a friendly 'good morning' (pp. 541–2).

When adult hostages and prisoners can react with such gratitude and lack of resentment, it is hardly surprising that children should feel grateful and forgiving towards parents who, although seeming to threaten their lives, do not (in most cases) actually kill them. All children, but particularly abused ones, can believe that their parents could kill them. Bloch (1979, p. 3) after years of working with children and studying their fears and fantasies concluded:

> Children are universally disposed to the fear of infanticide by both their physical and their physiological stage of development and the intensity of that fear depends on the incidence of traumatic events and on the degree of violence and of love they have experienced.

Despair and acceptance

Once victims have convinced themselves that their abuser is good and worthy of gratitude, they reach the inevitable conclusion that they are suffering because they are bad and therefore deserve to suffer. This can lead to anger being turned against the self and overwhelming feelings of depression and despair.

The child psychiatrist Bruno Bettleheim (1979) was himself a concentration camp victim and he observed prisoners' stages of adaptation. They became increasingly compliant as they realised how dependent they were on the goodwill of the guards. Eventually many went beyond compliance and began to accept the values of the guards.

Another study of adaptive behaviour in the camps noted that after the initial response of shock and terror, apathy set in. This 'was often psychologically protective and may be thought of as providing a kind of transitional emotional hibernation' (Chodoff, 1981, p. 4). A concentration camp survivor, Sherry Weiss-Rosenfeld recalled: 'The feeling was something indescribable; it was a feeling of total despair ... And I said to myself, even if I were to sprout wings all of a sudden I could not fly out of here' (Dwork, 1991 p. 225). A similar apathy can engulf some abused children so that they no longer look for any escape and simply accept their mistreatment.

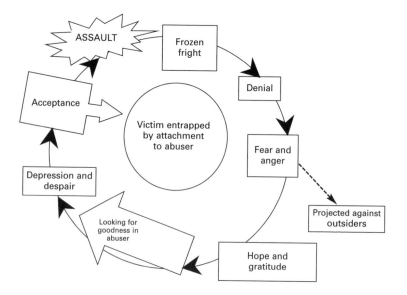

Figure 3.1 The Stockholm syndrome: psychological processes of entrapment

The final stage of acceptance can mean that victims adopt the self-concept of themselves as 'damaged' goods and become prey for other predators. Radford *et al.* (2010) and Finkelhor *et al.* (2009) confirm this; their research indicated that children who experience abuse from one carer were increasingly likely to be victimised by others. Figure 3.1 summarises the stages of the Stockholm syndrome leading to final acceptance. However, not all children will experience all the stages in an orderly progression.

Psychological contrast and weakening resistance

'Psychological contrast' was the term used by Solzhenitsyn (1974, p. 104) to describe the 'good guy, bad guy' tactics used in many interrogation situations and by hostage-takers.

> For a whole or part of the interrogation period, the interrogator would be extremely friendly ... Suddenly he would brandish a paperweight and shout 'Foo, you rat! I'll put nine grams of lead in your skull! ...' or as a variation on this: two interrogators would take turns. One would shout and bully, the others would be friendly, almost gentle.

This is reminiscent of the experiences of abused children. Their abuser may be violent, threatening or coldly callous one moment and then, perhaps feeling remorseful, be loving and tender the next; alternatively one parent may be persistently cruel whereas the other parent is kind and caring. This has the effect of making the victim even less secure and more compliant. When Jake's mother alternated between trying to care and failing to do so Jake found this so difficult to deal with, 'I didn't know what to expect, I wouldn't know what mood she would be in. It also made me feel guilty'.

In *The Gulag Archipelago*, Solzhenitsyn (1974) also lists the various tortures used to weaken the resistance of prisoners. Many of these are reminiscent of the behaviour of abusing carers.

- Psychological methods include the use of night-time when the victim lacks his day-time equanimity; Marie, it will be recalled, described being pulled out of bed at one o'clock in the morning to be interrogated by her father about his uncleaned shoes.
- Foul language and humiliation are often used in torture situations; these were very much part of Sarah, Roy, Josie and Jake's account of their parents' behaviour.

- Inducing confusion, intimidation accompanied by enticement, promises and 'playing on one's affection for those one loved' were other psychological methods of torture cited by Solzhenitsyn and illustrated by Marie's account.
- Physical torture methods include: burning with cigarettes, tickling, beating, locking in a bed-bug infested room, not allowing victims to sleep and forcing them to stand or kneel for long periods. All such methods are familiar in the field of child abuse. We remember that Victoria Climbié was left, at night, naked, beaten, in a bin bag in the bath.

It is therefore hardly surprising that mistreated children, like prisoners subjected to torture, will become compliant and offer little resistance to the demands of their abusers.

The roots of resistance

Many, but not all, victims of hostage situations, concentration camps or child abuse show compliant behaviour or respond positively to their aggressors. Those that show some resistance often have a strong value system or an alternative model of behaviour to which they cling tenaciously. Solzhenitsyn himself condemned the treatment to which he was subjected. Similarly, children who are subjected to mistreatment at the hands of a newly arrived step-parent or who have other positive influences may resist and complain because they know there are alternative forms of parental behaviour.

Strenz (1980, p. 143) noted that the Stockholm syndrome is likely to be absent when abusers showed no kindness towards their victims:

> Those victims who had negative contacts with the subjects did not evidence concern for them … They obviously did not like their abuse and advocated the maximum penalty be imposed.

It seems that if children live with two constantly abusing parents, they will not have the same sense of loyalty and concern for the parents. The same is true if one parent is actively abusive and the other indifferent to the children's plight.

Putting it into practice

Roy, Sarah, Marie, Josie and Jake (see Chapter 2) witnessed emotional and physical abuse by one parent against the other. Terminology describing this form of oppression is evolving but 'domestic violence' and 'intimate partner abuse' are commonly used terms at the time of writing. Consider what you know about these cases and what you have learnt in this chapter about the Stockholm syndrome. How far do you think that the Stockholm syndrome might be at least a partial explanation of why victimised parents, such as, the mothers of Marie, Sarah or Roy and father of Josie and Jake, have difficulty leaving their partners? If in your work or placement you are working with, or have good knowledge of, similar cases, consider whether the Stockholm syndrome might apply to either the parents or children in your cases.

Comment: The purpose of this activity is to help you think about how the Stockholm syndrome can entrap anyone, adults or children, in an oppressive situation. It is a positive psychological and often adaptive response to dangerous, threatening situations but unfortunately there can be negative outcomes, which further entrap victims of abuse. The other purpose of this activity is to help you think about the links between child abuse and domestic violence (including emotional aggression, such as that suffered by Sarah's mother or Josie and Jake's father). This double-faceted oppression can substantially increase the complexity of working with abused children.

The victim as a child

Many hostage, kidnap and concentration camp victims are adults who have experiences of life from which they can draw strength plus a fully developed intellect, which they can use to rationalise their experiences. Abused children do not have these advantages. They are imprisoned by overwhelming emotions and, in cases of long-standing abuse, possibly by cognitive distortions and alterations in brain architecture.

There are many emotions leading abused children to believe that they are in the wrong, and the abusing adults in the right. Many of the emotions appear to mirror those identified by Erikson's (1965) life-span theory, namely mistrust, shame/doubt, guilt, inferiority, role confusion, isolation and despair.

Fear and mistrust

Feelings of fear and mistrust are closely related. Abused children are unable to trust those who are meant to be protecting and caring for them. In their state of mistrust and uncertainty they are beset by a number of worries. In some cases, the fear is quite straightforward and is due to apprehension about future harm or that abusers will carry out threats (e.g. Angelou, 1984). Often children are not so much afraid for themselves as for their loved ones. Marie kept quiet about her father's behaviour because she was worried about what would happen to her mother and siblings if she was removed from the family.

Practice focus

Dino

Dino had a moderate level of learning disability. He was brought up in a semi-detached house with both his parents. However, when he was aged 11 his father developed a cancer which proved terminal within six months of diagnosis. Dino's mother found and married a new partner within a year of her husband's death. However, the new partner was emotionally and physically violent to Dino. To protect him, his mother took Dino and moved out of the family home into a flat. However, Dino kept returning to the home maintaining he wanted to live with his step-father.

This behaviour seemed so extraordinary that the practitioners vaguely assumed that it must be 'something to do with his learning disability'. However, one social worker took the time to talk with Dino and listen to him. He explained with palpable logic that he was devoted to his aviary full of birds, which he and his father had built up. Not only was he attached to the birds but the aviary was a link to his dead father. The aviary was too large to move to his mother's new flat and he was so worried about it and the birds that he preferred to risk his own well-being in order to return to his step-father to protect them.

Fear of alternatives is another common and understandable anxiety. Many young children assume that if their parents mistreat them, it is because every parent behaves in that way. Sarah believed that all headmasters and fathers beat the children in their care. She would have resisted any attempt to place her with foster parents because in her inexperienced eyes they would probably have been as bad if not worse than her father. Many abusive families and abused children are isolated with little opportunity of observing alternative family models. Mistreated children, lacking basic trust, may well take a long time before they can accept that other adults are well-intentioned.

Children have a realistic albeit subconscious fear of being killed. Freud dwelt at length on Oedipus murdering his father to marry his mother but there is little mention of the first part of the story which tells of the attempts of the parents to kill the baby Oedipus. The fear of infanticide held by children has its roots in reality and will be all the more intense for children who have been abused, attacked and threatened. Their hope of survival lies in parental love overcoming parental aggression, so they have to make themselves lovable and valuable to the parent. This may be achieved by accepting abuse without resistance and without causing problems.

Some abused children instinctively recognise that they will survive if they can find a useful role for themselves in the family system. This may explain why some children accept being made the scapegoat or take over the parental, caring role.

The sibling of an abused child or a child abused by siblings may well harbour the same fear of being killed and will therefore develop the same mistrust, sense of unworthiness and need to win parental love whatever the cost. Dorothy Bloch (1979, pp. 6–7) noted that:

> It did not need to be necessary for the child himself to be the target ... It was sufficient if the parents committed violent acts of any kind ... towards each other, or towards another child or even towards an animal.

Neglected children, similarly, have a realistic fear of death. Children who are ignored are in danger: consequently, they may behave badly in order to attract attention. If they can feel a beating or hear a rebuking they know that they are alive and that someone is taking notice of them.

Finally, as the previous section on the Stockholm syndrome indicated, victims can become paralysed by fear. A baby's 'frozen watchfulness' is one example. This paralysis will result in the child's inability to resist the abuser or seek assistance. Some will grow so quiet that they are literally unable to cry for help. Laming (2003, p. 1) in his report on the death of Victoria Climbié noted that, at his trial, Carl Manning admitted 'that at times he would hit Victoria with a bicycle chain. Chillingly, he said, "You could beat her and she wouldn't cry ... she could take the beatings and the pain like anything." '

Messages from research

Masten *et al.* (2008)

Despite reservations about using experiments to explore aspects of child protection, this one by Masten and colleagues produced some thought-provoking findings. The team selected 29 children, from ethnically diverse backgrounds, who had been removed from home due to severe abuse and/or neglect. These were matched with 17 'controls' from the same neighbourhoods who had not knowingly been abused. In both groups there were roughly equal numbers of boys and girls and the age range was from eight to fifteen years. Proper consideration appears to have been given to ethical considerations. The assent and informed consent of both the children and their carers was obtained.

The children were presented with standardised photos of four male and four female morphed faces showing a continuum of emotions from happy, through neutral, to fearful. The children were also tested to see if they were suffering symptoms of post-traumatic stress disorder (PTSD). The researchers were hoping to find if there was a difference in reaction to the emotions shown between those with PTSD and those without.

What the researchers found was that children who had been maltreated, with or without PTSD, recognised emotions, and especially fear, significantly faster than those who had not been maltreated.

Comment: The findings were in line with other research (e.g., Pollack and Tolley-Schell, 2003), which has shown that maltreated children have increased sensitivity to negative facial expressions. It is possible that constant exposure to menacing behaviour leads to increased cognitive investment in identifying negative expressions so that abuse victims can rapidly guard against threats. An interesting speculation is whether practitioners who were abused in childhood are better at detecting a frightened child than those who were not.

Doubt, shame and guilt

Abused children, riddled with fears, not only mistrust others but also question their own capabilities. They are trying to win their parents' love but as long as the abuse continues they seem to be failing. Consequently, they doubt themselves, the safety of their environment, the ability of other people to rescue them, the ability of substitute parents to love them and the ability of the rest of the family to survive without them.

Shame is another enduring emotion besetting abused children. First, there is the shame associated with being bad and deserving punishment. Smacking, scolding and sending to bed without supper are all common ways of punishing misbehaviour. In the straightforward logic of children, if they are severely beaten, continually shouted at or locked away without food it must be because they are very wicked. The consequent disgrace and sense of shame overshadows the lives of abuse victims.

Children who are intimidated or distressed can find it difficult to control their bowels and bladder and, once old enough to be toilet-trained, will be ashamed of wetting or soiling themselves. To compound matters they are often told they are lazy, dirty and disgusting for doing so.

Sexually abused children often feel that they are to blame for the abuse. Sometimes they enjoy the sexual activities or willingly accept the advances of the perpetrator because they are lonely or succumb to bribes. Even some material designed to prevent sexual abuse may have the effect of compounding the guilt. 'Danger–stranger' protection strategies can have an adverse effect because children are told to say 'no' to a sexual advance. If they fail to do so they may feel they have disobeyed instructions.

Infants cry and, unless grossly neglected, are fed and tended to. They seem to have magical powers to control their environment. Consequently, small children begin to feel responsible for whatever happens. Older children may have to contend with the feeling that they were old enough to have done something about events.

Children can also feel responsible for others. If they tell someone about the abuse their parents may be prosecuted or the family split up. The reason for so many retractions lies in the guilty feelings weighing on a child whose disclosure has led to such distressing events. Those removed into care may be unable to enjoy their freedom from abuse because they believe that it was achieved at the expense of other family members. Guilt may also be induced in the child if, as happened with Jake, a parent is abusive one moment and caring the next.

Finally, children may be blamed for having provoked the abuser. There is still a belief in sexually abused children seducing 'innocent', unsuspecting adults. In relation to physical abuse there is the concept of over-chastisement; the child has deserved punishment and provoked the parents so much that they have lost control. A constantly crying baby is regarded as provocative. In all these cases the child is seen as the agent of abuse, the person to blame, while sympathy is reserved for the adult who claims to have been pushed beyond the limits of endurance.

- *Inferiority.* Abused children develop a sense of unworthiness because of the feelings of shame and guilt evoked by mistreatment. The outcome is a sense of inferiority, reinforced by the child's seeming inability to win parental approval and love. It follows that abused children may be reticent about seeking or accepting help; they conclude that if their parents do not think that they are worth protecting and loving there is no reason why any other adult would do so.
- *Role confusion.* Inappropriate role adoption is a recognised aspect of child abuse. Children may accept the role of family scapegoat or victim in order to be of some value to the parents. They may cling tenaciously to their role, fearing rejection, even annihilation if they lose it. This explains why abused children sometimes resist change and rescue. They know no other role and if removed from the family attempt to establish themselves as scapegoat and victim in their substitute families. Role confusion also occurs when the child becomes responsible for family members and takes on a parental function as happened with Josie and Marie.
- *Isolation and despair.* A sense of isolation is apparent in the accounts given by many abused children. They often feel different from their peers. They may be ashamed of their families or their condition. Furthermore abusive parents tend to discourage friendships. Abused children cannot be intimate with anyone outside the family owing to their feelings of guilt and shame and may keep people at arm's length, carrying the burden of their secret alone.

Children who feel mistrustful and isolated will be heading towards despair rather than being full of ideas for change and hope for the future. They will resist disclosure and removal from home because they may, in their despair, doubt that the situation will ever improve for them. Even when settled in a loving foster home they may expect things to deteriorate and will try to provoke the foster parents into abusing and rejecting them rather than wait for the inevitable (they believe) abuse and rejection to occur.

Putting it into practice

If you are involved in working with children or in a child care placement, listen for the way adults around you, whether professionals or lay, talk about children, especially when they are behaving badly. If this is not possible, listen to the discourse about children who have behaved badly and also those who have been abused in the media, newspapers, television, radio or the internet. Hopefully, you will not hear indiscriminate condemnation of children or young people, but you might.

Comment: Children will test boundaries and in this sense their behaviour might justifiably be seen as challenging. However, the idea that children deserve violence and abuse requires questioning. Children hold little power and therefore loss of control or abuse of power is the perpetrators' and not the children's responsibility.

Abnormal cognitive development and learning

Prior to the current knowledge gained through brain imaging and advances in biomedical sciences, Sigmund Freud (see Jacob, 2003), Erikson (1965) and Bowlby (1951) all hypothesised that maltreatment in the earliest years could cause problems for the developing child. This idea is now supported by modern biomedical scientists who are demonstrating the damage that early abuse and neglect can cause to brain development. As Perry (2009, p. 241) explains 'These adverse experiences interfere with normal patterns of experience-guided neurodevelopment by creating extreme and abnormal patterns of neural and neurohormonal activity'.

There is, for example, evidence that verbal abuse and parental criticism results in changes in neural pathways in the brain (Choi *et al.*, 2009) and in the parts of the brain involved in processing language and speech (Tomoda *et al.*, 2011). This may have implications for any verbal therapies because of possible alterations in language comprehension abilities.

Neglected children can fail to develop because their environment lacks stimulation (Iwaniec, 2006) and emotionally or physically abused children may be prevented from exploring their world and satisfying their curiosity because if they go beyond very tight limits or cause any disruption they will be punished. Eventually it becomes more expedient not to reach out, not to try anything different, not to seek a change in their circumstances.

Another theory of interest related to the way children learn is that of 'learned helplessness', which is associated with despair. It is a term coined by psychologist, Martin Seligman (1975). His experiments showed that if animals, and possibly people, attempt to escape but are unable to do so, they will eventually give up even when given the opportunity. Some victims of abuse seek help indirectly. If time and again adults fail to understand the children's messages, they will give up hope of any help being forthcoming. Alternatively, some children are able to ask for assistance directly but often they are not believed or nothing happens because the parents are unable to change and the legal grounds to force a change or protect them are absent. Children could then be in a worse situation as now they will despair of receiving help. Subsequently, they may resist offers of help even when, eventually, someone with the power to intervene tries to assist.

Behaviourist theories relate to learning and teach us that training children is a simple matter of conditioning. Children are taught how to behave by being given rewards for good behaviour and punished for bad. They will seek pleasure and avoid pain. But this can be deceptive as life is rarely so straightforward. Abuse victims may accept pain and suffering rather than lose something less tangible. Those outside the family may not understand why victims choose to remain at home even though they are likely to be beaten, molested or go hungry. But for the abused child some things such as security in what is familiar or the chance to win parental love are more important than simple avoidance of pain and discomfort.

Point for reflection

Think back to Chapter 2 and the case stories of Marie, Lloyd, Sarah, Roy, Josie and Jake, then review the ideas presented in this chapter. List, in each of the cases, any obstacles to recognising the severity of the abuse that professional workers are likely to have encountered

Comment: The purpose of this activity is to help you identify the factors that might prevent even skilled, committed and well-trained professionals from recognising that a child is being abused.

The next three chapters examine ways of working with children in order to overcome or alleviate some of the more negative emotions and perceptions that result in children becoming imprisoned in abusive situations. They explore individual, family and group work, which can be undertaken by professionals, especially those with only modest training or experience and constrained by limits on time, space or facilities. These chapters are designed to offer practical guidance and encouragement to a wide variety of workers and are not confined to 'experts' in specialised settings. The suggestions have all been tried, tested and found to be helpful by myself and by colleagues, including those in local authority settings.

Further resources

Davis, L. and Duckett, N. (2008) *Proactive Child Protection and Social Work*. Exeter: Learning Matters.
This highly informative book is organised to look in detail at each of the key forms of maltreatment and includes examples from inquires. It also specifically addresses issues for children with disabilities.

Howarth, J. (ed.) (2009) *The Child's World: The Comprehensive Guide to Assessing Child in Need*. London: Jessica Kingsley.
This is a highly informative book of chapters written by different authors which provides a comprehensive guide to assessing children. The chapter by Norma Howes 'Here to Listen!' is about communication, stressing that children cannot always 'just tell' about what has happened to them.

Triangle: http://www.triangle.org.uk
Triangle is an independent organisation helping children and families especially in relation to communication issues. Among other tasks, they can provide BSL interpreters, speech and language therapists, communication support workers plus spoken language interpreters especially in relation to ascertaining children's wishes and feelings.

CHAPTER 4

Working with individual children

CHAPTER OVERVIEW

This chapter is about direct work that front-line staff can use to help children understand what has happened to them. The chapter addresses:

- requirements of the practitioner
- planning individual work then starting work and establishing boundaries
- the helping process including trust, exploring feelings, countering misconceptions and protective strategies
- the sometimes difficult issue of ending individual work

The preceding chapter helped to demonstrate how abused children are so often imprisoned in a world of fear, mistrust, self-denigration and isolation even after the abuse itself has stopped. They will therefore benefit from work aimed as releasing them from the misconceptions and negative emotions illustrated in the accounts by Sarah, Roy, Marie, Lloyd, Josie and Jake in Chapter 2 and further explored in Chapter 3.

Victims of abuse who present as severely disturbed will require skilled therapy. It is not the purpose of this book to teach general child-care workers about psychotherapy or similar interventions requiring specific training. Children needing this form of treatment are usefully referred to specialist agencies. However, the majority of abused children and their siblings can be helped through various forms of direct assistance, well within the capabilities of child-care workers.

The word 'therapist' is used here to indicate the person who is offering structured, direct help to enable the child to come to terms with what has happened. This help can embrace a variety of methods based on a wide range of theoretical perspectives. The term should not be confused with the word 'psychotherapist', which usually indicates a purely psychoanalytic approach.

The focus of this chapter is not on the investigative process, procedures, parental perspectives or policy. There are a number of publications looking at these issues (for example, Masson *et al.*, 2007; Munro, 2008; Cleaver *et al.*, 2009). Instead it concentrates on the therapeutic needs of children once an investigation has elucidated the situation. However, investigative and therapeutic work are closely allied, so much so that a well-conducted investigation will begin the helping process. Conversely, therapeutic interviews can become the start of an investigation if during therapy a child discloses that the severity or extent of the abuse was greater than first thought. Many of the suggestions therefore will apply as much to investigative work as to therapy.

Working with diversity

Children from all sectors of society can be abused. There is no one type of child who is exempt from maltreatment. Therefore, inevitably, helping professionals will work with a diverse range of people including those from minority ethnic groups, asylum seekers, traveller children and children with a range of disabilities.

Kennedy (2002) outlines key issues in relation to children with disabilities. There may be communication problems, not all of which are readily anticipated, such as the difficulties she encountered when her own sign language was different from that used by a deaf child she was helping. She recommends a communication assessment at the outset as well as the use of facilitators, and the co-working of disability and child protection workers. She also highlights the emotional impact of having a disability and the experience of abuse.

Other issues relating to working with diversity are integrated throughout this chapter.

Requirements of the therapist

There are two opposing views of the type of people able to help abused children. At one extreme it is held that only 'experts' should be allowed to work with them, at the other extreme it is maintained that anyone can do so. Certainly some expertise is required but this can be acquired by practitioners with skills in other areas, notably early years practice, which are transferable to child abuse cases. Some professionals cannot relate easily to children and these should bow out of direct work gracefully. Children can readily sense an uneasy adult and will believe that they are the source of that unease, compounding their feelings of guilt and unworthiness. Conversely, as illustrated by Frank Beck (see Kirkwood, 1993) and Vanessa George (see Plymouth Safeguarding Children Board, 2010), there are people who are extremely good at relating to children but who readily capitalise on these abilities to exploit them.

Therapists should be comfortable with children and adolescents, and should be able to tolerate:

- sitting, kneeling, even lying on the floor;
- biscuit crumbs and paint falling on their clothes;
- displays of violent behaviour and strings of swear words.

A lively imagination, inventiveness and a willingness to learn from the child are additional requirements. Above all, the therapist must respect children and acknowledge that they should be given the same dignity, value and right to know what is happening to them as is given to adults.

An ability to communicate with children is obviously required. Simply talking may be adequate when counselling adults but is insufficient with children. As Piaget's theories (see Muller *et al.*, 2009) indicate, younger people need to relate abstract concepts to concrete reality. They communicate through play, spontaneous body language and actions. On the other hand, even young children appreciate the opportunity to talk, ask questions, and listen to explanations. One eight-year-old began a therapy session by asking me if he could 'talk first and play later'.

Some children will require the therapist to have specific skills in communication, including those who have physical impairments, which restrict speech and hearing. A number of children may not be familiar with the English language. In such instances advice may need to be taken from specialist practitioners or people who know the child well, and toys and materials adapted to individual needs. Therapists also need to be aware of possible undiscovered disabilities such as dyslexia, which may mean children are unable to read or write as proficiently as their age would suggest.

Despite the recognition that some children will not behave in a way expected of their chronological age, knowledge of normal child development will help in the choice of age-appropriate toys and activities. Abusive parents sometimes have over-high expectations of their children and workers will only add to the child's self-doubt if they also demand too much. A therapist with a good knowledge of child development will also be able to assess how far development has been impaired.

Working with abused children requires emotional resilience. Some adults may find the child's pain unbearable, resulting in an avoidance of any discussion of the abuse itself and a superficial interview. But this can give children the impression that they have been involved in something so dreadful that it cannot be discussed. Moreover, practitioners unable to bear the pain shown by victims may blame them because the children's suffering seems more bearable if they have 'deserved it'.

Inevitably, there will be a number of therapists who were themselves abused in childhood and, for some, the distress of the child becomes their own distress. But if they have been able to come to terms with their experiences, they may have valuable insights to offer. Therapists who were not abused do not have this advantage and may have difficulty understanding the victims' perspectives. Nevertheless, their relative detachment can be of value, as long as they are able to use their imagination, powers of observation and natural sensitivity to respond appropriately.

Therapists who are themselves parents may find the mistreatment suffered by children who look like their own offspring hard to cope with. Alternatively, they may over-identify with the abused child's parents, particularly if they come from the same social group, or the child behaves in a way that any adult would find difficult to tolerate. However, practitioners who are parents might be more comfortable in the company of children and more readily recognise unreasonable parental behaviour.

Consideration also needs to be given to the cultural heritage of the child and therapist. Kadj Rouf (1991a) who has a white mother and Asian father, reflected, 'I wish some one who understood my culture and abuse could have come and talked to me and my family … how being abused affected me in terms of my Asian culture'. The ideal is to give children a choice of whether or not they wish for a therapist of the same culture. But where this ideal is not possible there are two important principles. The first is that children should not be denied individual work because there is no therapist from the same background. Second, practitioners should be sensitive to issues of cultural heritage, and should endeavour to find ways of addressing these where they are important to the child.

The gender of the therapist requires careful consideration. A child abused by a woman may be unable to tolerate a female worker whereas one who has only experienced female company may be uneasy with a male worker. It is ideal if, in the initial stages, the child's wishes and fears can be met by a choice of a therapist of the appropriate gender. Later the child can be introduced to one of the opposite sex, thereby learning that not all people of the feared gender are abusive and uncaring. But when considering the gender of the therapist, cultural issues need to be addressed. For example, in some cultures it is uncommon or even unacceptable for adolescents to spend time alone with a member of the opposite sex.

One fear, especially for male practitioners, is that they will be accused of molesting the children during therapy. Young people who have learnt that all relationships with adults lead to sexual activities, may misinterpret actions by the therapist. To overcome unwarranted accusations, sessions can be witnessed by a supervisor, using a video monitor or a one-way screen. A video camera, or even an audio recorder similar to those used for police interviews, could be used to tape the sessions. Another option is for a familiar adult to stay in the room with the therapist and child.

Whether the therapists are male or female, young or old, parents or non-parents, new to the work or experienced they all require a competent, supportive supervisor. This is particularly important because some therapists, who have forgotten their own childhood mistreatment, will start to recall it because a client's distress can be a powerful reminder of their own. Doyle (1986) outlines the problems faced by professionals in this situation and suicidal feelings cannot be discounted. The supervisor should be prepared to listen and discuss with the therapist the impact of her or his experiences but rather than offering direct therapy could usefully help identify an acceptable counsellor. A supervisor trying to act as counsellor may create considerable role confusion while the needs of the client may be neglected in the face of the overwhelming emotional demands of the practitioner being supervised.

Planning individual work

Invariably abused children and their siblings will benefit from individual work. This may take place before, or in conjunction with, other forms of therapy such as family or group work. One-to-one work is directed towards:

- listening, showing respect for and understanding the child's views;
- allowing expression of feelings in a safer context than in a family or group session;
- communicating positive messages to the child;
- enabling the child to adopt new roles;
- 'protective behaviours', that is, teaching them that they have a right not to be abused in future.

Individual work can vary in depth, content and setting. For example, severely neglected children may require many sessions, simply learning to respond to stimuli, play with toys and relate to one person, before they can cope with any other help. Some older teenagers may welcome counselling and the opportunity to talk with no play element whereas others may welcome the opportunity to play freely and recapture some of their lost childhood. Individual therapy will therefore have to be tailored to the individual. The suggestions in the rest of this chapter should only be followed after the specific needs of each child have been considered.

Before individual work can start there is the planning stage which includes such matters as duration, frequency, choice of personnel and location.

Duration and frequency

Duration applies both to the number of sessions and to their length. A single session may well be worse than none. Children who share aspects of themselves about which they feel ashamed may, if no follow-up is offered, conclude that they are so awful that the therapist does not want to see them again. Usually a minimum of four sessions is required but however many are planned there should be provision for an extra meeting in case the child reveals something unpleasant in the final planned session. The therapist can use the additional meeting to show the child that he or she is still liked and accepted.

When the sessions have lasted beyond a few months it is worth assessing whether the child would benefit from the deeper experience of psychotherapy or the wider experience of a therapeutic group.

At least two hours will have to be allocated for each session although much of this is for preparation and evaluation. An initial period should be set aside for the therapist's mental and emotional preparation. Even if there is access to a proper playroom, time will be needed to ensure that materials appropriate for the particular child are to hand. After the session it will take at least half-an-hour for the therapist to assess, evaluate and record what has happened. He or she should also be allowed some time to relax and unwind before starting on the next task. This leaves approximately one hour for direct contact with the child. This may be shorter, especially in the early stages if the child is uneasy in the one-to-one situation, or longer for children who need time to settle.

Sessions may also be longer if the therapist chooses an activity such as taking the child out for a meal. These excursions can provide new stimuli for neglected children who have not had experience of them or a relaxing environment for children for whom such activities are familiar. However therapists need to reflect on whether over-reliance on excursions is an avoidance of deeper communication.

Sessions are usually held once a week, preferably on the same day at the same time. Some children benefit, particularly in the early stages, from more frequent contact, especially younger ones for whom time passes slowly and who need to build up a comfortable relationship as quickly as possible. Towards the end of therapy, sessions may be reduced, particularly if family or group work is planned to take the place of individual interviews.

Allocating tasks

If transport is needed to ferry the child to the session it is preferable that the therapist is not expected to drive. It can seem economical for one person to undertake both tasks but practitioners need all their energy for the therapeutic session. Some therapists report that service users talk to them more readily in the car. This is valuable in some instances especially with adults or when undertaking informal work (see Ferguson, 2011). But when it comes to planned direct work, if a child will talk in the car rather than in the session, it usually indicates that there is something wrong with the interview. This could be that the child does not like a lot of eye contact when talking – in which case communication can be through a pretend telephone or sitting side-by-side. Children might feel more secure that conversations will not be overheard in the car – in which case they can be encouraged to test the soundproofing of the interview room or play background music to counter the fear of being overheard. Apart from evident safety aspects on busy roads, another reason why a therapist should not double as a driver is that the session then lacks a proper start and finish. Beginnings and endings are important in all forms of therapy.

A careful decision has to be taken over whether or not the therapist is also to be involved with other members of the family or with a group to which the children or their relatives belong. There might be conflicts of loyalty if the therapist helps other family members, on the other hand there may be conflicts with colleagues if he or she does not.

Location, materials and environment

Sometimes there are good reasons for undertaking individual work in the child's own home. But often it is more appropriate to use an alternative location because, in the family home, children may feel the ties of loyalty binding them more tightly, preventing them from disclosing further abuse or from expressing anger against family members. In a foster home or residential setting the children may wish to distance themselves from their former unhappy experiences and will not want them introduced into their new environment. If work has to be undertaken in the home then, unless children make a specific request to do so, their own bedroom should not be used. They should be allowed to preserve a 'safe-space' where they can relax without the intrusion of painful reminders. Therapists also have to consider whether or not interviewing a child in the bedroom could be adversely interpreted, leaving themselves open to accusations of sexual impropriety.

The interview room should be comfortable, soundproof and not a thoroughfare for other people. The floor should have a clean, soft covering. Easy chairs, a coffee table and cushions are all useful. If play work is to be undertaken then too few toys are better than too many. It is important that the child is not overwhelmed and distracted by an abundance of play equipment. Spare toys and equipment such as computers or televisions, not destined for use, are best kept out of sight in bags, a cupboard or in boxes well out of reach.

Play materials and play space need to be safe. Protections such as fireguards or electric socket covers may be needed while small parts, which may choke, will have to be removed when planning for the very young. Children, of any age, in distress may well start to suck or chew play materials so lead paint and anything that is dangerous, if swallowed, should not be used. Children may become very angry or excited so sharp implements, very hot radiators and fires and similar hazards have to be avoided in case the children fall or bump onto these.

Jennings (1999) also advises having some aprons, old shirts and smocks available in order to protect children's own clothing. In addition, dressing up clothes are welcomed by children and need not be unduly elaborate.

Equipment and toys need to be appropriate for each child. It is essential to have a mix of black and white dolls and play figures, as well as toy animals, which do not represent any particular colour. Books should be chosen to reflect the multi-cultural nature of our society. If a black child selects a white doll or a white child chooses a black one to represent themselves, that is their choice and should be accepted without comment. One white, blonde, blue-eyed six-year old chose a black, brown-eyed action-man figure as himself. This was explained when a casual inquiry revealed the star player of his favourite football team was black. Similarly, a range of toys traditionally associated with specific genders should be available and if girls wish to play with cars or boys with dolls then that is their prerogative.

It is important that people with disabilities are not invisible in reading and play materials. There are some specialist dolls available but there are also popular brands of play figures with wheel-chairs and other visible disabilities. Such toys all need to be available to all children because they may well have in their family or circle of acquaintances people of a different culture or colour or with a disability and may wish to play out scenes to include them.

Older children may seek the comfort of playing with toys associated with an earlier stage. It is therefore useful to have a range of materials, including ones associated with babies and toddlers so that they can choose them, free of the fear of being ridiculed.

There should be easy access to a sink and toilet as well as to a room where a familiar adult accompanying the child can wait. Consideration needs to be given to wheelchair access and provision for people unable to walk far or climb stairs. It must be remembered that mobility can be an issue for the children or for their carers. Finally, it is also preferable that the same room, looking more or less the same, is used for each session.

Starting the session

When children first arrive they should be introduced to anyone they do not already know and then be given time to familiarise themselves with the geography of the building, unless sessions are held in their school or other places familiar to them. It is important to check that the children know the whereabouts of a hand basin and toilet.

The next step is to ensure that the child does not feel isolated and trapped with the worker. This is particularly important in sexual abuse cases where he or she might have been closeted in a room with an adult, engaging in sexual matters. The similarities between the abusive and therapeutic scenarios might lead the child to fear abuse, this time by the worker. The child can be reassured by people monitoring the situation through a video or screen although equally effective is the availability of a trusted adult in a nearby room. The child is given permission to go to that adult whenever he or she wants to. If there is no adult available the next best alternative is to show the child the way to reception and again give him or her permission to leave the room and go to reception at any time.

It is useful to start the work of the first session by asking the child to write labels for the doors of the therapy room and of the room where the familiar adult is waiting or labels showing the way out to reception. This has a number of benefits. Firstly it empha-sises to children that they can leave the room and will not get lost. A label such as 'Jane's room, please keep out' demonstrates that the therapy room is the child's territory for the duration of the session which increases feelings of security and of being special. While the children are writing the labels their ability to use pen and paper can be assessed. Those unable to write can draw a picture of themselves and their familiar adult. One four-year-old said she could write and proceeded to put obscure symbols on the labels. These were pinned to the doors because the child knew what was meant and was happy with them. Another option is to use stickers or stencils for the labels.

Care has to be taken to place the labels on the doors at the appropriate height. Usually this is at the child's eye level. However, one thirteen-year-old who had been neglected and had conse-quently failed to grow properly was indignant when I unthinkingly began to place her label at her eye level. 'What are you putting it there for? I'm not a child you know.'

An important preliminary is the establishment of boundaries. Geldard and Geldard (2007, p. 11) emphasise that the counsellor or therapist 'must create a permissive environment in which the child feels free to act out and to gain mastery over their feelings in safety'. They advocate three rules for children; they are not permitted to hurt themselves, the therapist or property. It is perhaps advisable to have joint rules. Neither child nor therapist will hurt themselves, each other or property. Another important agreement is no touching that makes either participant uncomfortable such as the touching of private parts. Whether referred for sexual abuse or not, in the safety of the playroom children may start to act out sexually abusive experiences or test out what is appropriate sexual behaviour. If the 'no uncomfortable touching' rule is established at the outset, children can be gently reminded of the rule if they attempt to touch the therapist inappropriately rather than meeting a sudden unexpected rebuff.

It is important to ensure early in the first session that the children understand why they are attending and what they can expect from the therapist. It is worth asking them why they think they are coming. A frequent response is 'don't know', even when they have already been well prepared for the session. This is often because they are rather confused about what is happening and are afraid of giving the 'wrong answer'. It is worth clarifying the reasons by asking questions. 'Have you been feeling sad?' The child nods. 'Do you think that coming here is something to do with feeling sad?' Children who show no desire to offer an explanation can be told in a direct way but any implication of fault is to be avoided, for example, not 'Because you told your teacher mummy and daddy were hitting you and making you sad' but rather 'Because we heard that your mummy and daddy were hitting you and making you sad'.

At the beginning of the first session children need time to play freely and explore any toys. This helps them to relax and feel comfortable. Allowing children free play will also show the worker which toys they like best. In the case of those teenagers who do not want to use toys, a general talk about their hobbies and interests serves a similar purpose, helping them to relax and become familiar with both therapist and setting.

Provision of a drink and biscuits is another useful preliminary. Making a drink and finding the biscuits can be used in subsequent sessions as an opening ritual which children often find reassuring. Experience shows that sometimes they consume neither drink nor biscuits until the end of the session but it is worth having them available during the interview.

It is important to ensure that the same toys are available for a particular child from session to session. One child, Zarina, played the same game with a small plastic duck repeatedly for weeks. She would have been devastated if the duck had been lost and searched anxiously for it at the beginning of each session, so care had to be taken to keep it safe.

The preliminaries having been completed, it is time to start the core work. It is often helpful to begin by asking the children to draw their families. Such drawings reveal a considerable amount of information about their view of themselves and their family relationships. The names given to various father figures can be demonstrated in those families where a mother has a number of cohabitees and vice versa. Interpretations must, however, be made with extreme care; a nine-year-old who was not very adept at using pencils drew her mother as much larger than her father. This was not because the mother was more important than her father but simply because she had difficulty drawing her mother's shape and kept redrawing the lines until the figure became very large.

Older children may prefer to draw up a family-tree. This usually involves going back as far as possible in the family history. This exercise can reveal hidden worries, for example one teenage boy commented, 'Uncle John was no good, he was sent away from home because he stole money. I've had to leave home so I guess I'm as bad as he was.'

BASIC Ph

Workers are often perplexed when activities that work supremely well with one child fail to engage another. The work of Mooli Lahad (1992) offers some explanation of why this happens and how failure to engage can be avoided. He has developed a theory and approach to work called BASIC Ph. This has its complexities and practitioners would be well advised to attend several days of a training course before using the approach. However, in essence it has a straightforward logic.

From his extensive experience of working with traumatised adults and children, he observed that people have a range of coping mechanisms and these are based on beliefs (B), affect (emotions) (A), social relationships and support (S), the use of imagination (I), cognition (C) and physical activity (Ph). While ideally people will marshal all these mechanisms, for most people one or two will be prominent. The practical application of this theory is that in the initial stages children will be more successfully engaged if the therapist utilises the children's own survival mechanisms. A child using imagination and physical activity for coping will quickly engage with a therapist offering therapy through imaginative, active games. Another child who copes using social relationships and cognitive processes will be happy to talk issues through with the therapist but will feel uncomfortable and possibly alienated by exhortations to engage in imaginative games.

Individual children's prominent coping mechanisms are assessed by helping them devise a 'six-part story'. This story is usually drawn or painted but other media such as clay, fuzzy felt or drama can be used. The child is then asked to describe the story and their words faithfully recorded. The nature of the story and the types of words used indicate the child's preferred way of coping. A decision about appropriate activities and materials for individual sessions is then made on the basis of initially harnessing the child's most prominent coping mechanism.

The difficult aspect of this method is the scoring of the words because care has to be taken not to make judgements through the use of interpretation, and some words may be difficult to categorise, hence the need for therapists wanting to use this method to attend a training course or refer directly to publications by Lahad (e.g., Lahad, 1992; Lahad, 2002; Berger and Lahad, 2010).

The helping process

There are a number of components of the helping process in relation to abused children and their siblings. These include:

- establishing trust;
- the exploration of feelings;
- messages to counter misconceptions;
- the acquisition of new roles and protective strategies.

Establishing trust

The most important task of the therapist is to watch and listen to the children, allowing them to express, both verbally and non-verbally, their fears and feelings. At first sight, this seems a relatively simple task but there are many factors which inhibit abused children and which will have to be overcome before they can express any strong feelings.

They may not be able to trust anyone, and here again an understanding of Erikson's Stage theory is useful. The therapist has to prove that he or she is trustworthy. Being open about what is happening will help. As the Cleveland Inquiry report (Butler-Sloss, 1988) recommends 'Children are entitled to a proper explanation appropriate to their age ... and given some idea of what is going to happen to them' (p. 245).

The therapist should be introduced by his or her name and job title not as 'aunty Y' or 'a friend'. The comments of Fraiberg (1952, pp. 59–60) despite the passage of decades are still valid:

> Sometimes, with the uneasy acknowledgement of the differences in the relationship of adult and child clients, we feel that it is necessary to go under an assumed name for the benefit of the child. In this way a social worker may refer to himself not as a 'caseworker' but as a 'friend'. Unfortunately this avowal of friendship may be received cynically by the child.

It is worth reiterating that when recording equipment or one-way screens are being used they should be shown to the children. They have as much right as adults to raise objections and have the equipment switched off or the curtains drawn across the screen. If a child is very interested in, or upset by, the camera or screen then the time spent allowing him or her to play with them may help to satisfy curiosity and allay fears.

The therapist also needs to be honest in relation to the issue of confidentiality. The children can be assured that only people who are in a position to help either them or others at risk will be allowed to know what the child does or says in a session. Complete confidentiality cannot be guaranteed because during therapy children may indicate that they or another child was more seriously injured or mistreated than first thought; this will require the involvement of investigating agencies in response to the new allegations. The Cleveland Report again recommends, 'Professionals should not make promises which cannot be kept to the child, and in the light of possible court proceedings should not promise a child that what is said in confidence can be kept in confidence' (Butler-Sloss, 1988, p. 245).

Another aspect of confidentiality is that some of the work will inevitably be very emotive and bring distressing memories and emotions to the fore. The child may seem calm and unaffected during the session, only to react with substantial distress afterwards. Carers need to be able to understand the reason for and nature of the children's reactions. Therapists therefore should give some thought to what information those responsible for the day-to-day care of the child require in order to cope with any subsequent problems.

Exploring emotions

Children need to be helped to describe at least some aspects of their abuse if their emotions are to be understood and their experiences accepted. Assuming the matter has been properly investigated, there will be no need for the therapist to extract precise details from the child but some aspects have to be shared. Children might be encouraged to begin by using a doll's house or a drawing of the home to say which rooms they disliked and where they felt safe. Dolls or modelling clay figures representing the family may help them re-enact events or they may prefer to describe what happened through a puppet or cuddly toy. Children can also be persuaded to talk down a 'no-secrets' telephone, which is simply a disused or toy telephone decorated to look special.

'Anatomical dolls' which have representations of genitals help sexually abused children reveal their experiences. However, in legal proceedings they have been viewed as the equivalent of 'leading' questioning, so it is wise to clear their use with the appropriate local authority managers and legal department. If used they should he introduced, with clothes on, to the child as special dolls, which can help children who have had uncomfortable experiences.

Despite the need for openness, workers are wise to avoid 'pressing the bruise', recognising when a child does not want to pursue a particular line and noticing 'the triggers to withdrawal' (Compton, 2002, pp. 406–7). These may be moving to another activity, rushing around, becoming very still and silent, changing the conversation or leaving the room. There is a difficult balance to achieve because 'Pressing too hard for overt responses may lead to distortion, even lying' (Compton, 2002, p. 407). However, it may be fear, shame or guilt underlying a child's reluctance to share experiences and these feelings need to be sensitively and gently challenged.

Children may be inhibited by both imaginary and well-founded fears some of which can be anticipated and allayed. Victims whose abuse has involved their bottoms and other private parts may worry that they will be in trouble for using 'rude words'. Using books like *A Very Touching Book* (Hindmann, 1983, still available and still unsurpassed), which contains cartoon sketches of naked bodies can help.

Erikson's (1965) theory helps us understand the prominence of shame, doubt and guilt for many abused children. Therapists can demonstrate that they accept such matters without condemnation by playing with a whoopee cushion, sharing moderately rude jokes or by encouraging messy play. Sticky poster paints for hand and finger pictures or sand and water provide delightful sensations and can be used to show how the therapist is unperturbed by mess.

On the other hand, if given too much freedom children may fear that the situation will run out of control. The therapist has to demonstrate that some limits will be maintained by for example finishing on time, insisting that the mess is eventually cleared up and being gently firm if the child's behaviour becomes unmanageable. On the other hand, there will be occasions when control is difficult and objects get broken or spoilt. It is therefore advisable to avoid using anything valuable that cannot be easily replaced.

Guilt may also prevent children from expressing their feelings. A non-judgemental attitude on the part of the therapist is essential and this also needs to be maintained in relation to any activities of the perpetrators described by the child. It is fine to say, 'You have the right to be angry with her' if the child shows anger against an abusive mother but not, 'I'm really angry with your mum.' This is because the children's feelings towards their abusers may range from the intensely loyal (remember the Stockholm syndrome) to the ambivalent. Children may believe that any adult who expresses anger against their abuser will think them stupid for feeling affection for that same abuser.

Anger is often a powerful emotion experienced by abuse victims. This may not be directed towards the perpetrator. Often it is turned against themselves in the form of self-denigration and depression. There are games and exercises designed to help children express anger safely and direct it towards those with whom they have a right to be angry. For example, children choose a doll to represent the abuser and are then encouraged to express anger against the doll. Similarly, they can model or draw a representation of the abuser then screw it up, toss it away or throw objects at it. Some children do not find this direct expression of anger easy. One girl, for example, preferred to keep winding a toy turntable round and round, getting faster and rougher as she talked.

Marie, Lloyd, Sarah, Roy, Josie and Jake all emphasised how isolated they felt. Through stories, children can be helped to realise that they are not the only children who are abused. Storytelling is an important therapeutic tool. Compton (2002, p. 413) writes, 'The most influential books are usually those chosen by the individual child and it is useful to be aware of the children's favourite or least favourite texts'.

Additionally, there are some special texts, designed for children in distress, such as the truly wonderful *The Frog Who Longed for the Moon to Smile*, and similar stories by Margot Sunderland, illustrated by Nicky Armstrong (2001). Children can also benefit from acting out or role-playing the stories.

One reason for their isolation is that the victims have been so hurt that they have built up a protective barrier. Here a hedgehog puppet is useful. They can be shown how the hedgehog is so prickly on the outside that nobody can cuddle him when he feels in danger. But underneath he is soft and if he feels safe he can get close to people.

Another useful exercise helps children explore feelings. The therapist draws three blank heads. The children are then invited to fill in the faces, drawing expressions to demonstrate how the people are feeling. Often they choose sadness, happiness and anger. The therapist can join in by filling in additional sets of faces with other feelings such as embarrassment, fear and loneliness. When the child has finished the worker can ask 'What makes you angry?' 'What used to make you sad?' 'What would make you happy?' Where appropriate, the therapists can use their own drawings to explore additional emotions.

Practitioners familiar with bereavement counselling will recognise that expression of fear, guilt, anger, isolation and confusion is often associated with loss and the process of mourning (see Kubler-Ross, 1970). Abused children are 'bereaved' because they will have lost, at the very least, security, self-esteem and unconditional love. Many games and exercises that help bereaved young people express feelings will also be of benefit to abused ones.

Practice focus

Mandy

This case illustrates Vygotsky's (1978) idea that adults need to help children to move forward in terms of problem solving and progressing to the next step in development.

Mandy was a 6-year-old who had witnessed a considerable amount of family violence. When offered therapy she clearly wanted to explain what she had witnessed but did not have sufficient vocabulary. She made some attempt at drawing. But with little early experience of scribbling and limited school attendance, her ability to draw and manipulate crayons was not well advanced.

Had I been her teacher, my task would have been to help her to manipulate crayons. However, my job was more that of learner than teacher because to help her therapeutically I needed to understand her experiences from her perspective. Guided by Vygotsky's ideas of the adult's role in providing a means for a child to advance, I judged that I was justified in intervening to help her express herself. Therefore, we agreed that I would undertake the drawing under Mandy's instructions. The resulting scenes and figures were simple but showed a series of events of considerable domestic violence with Mandy featured trying variously to hide or to help. The drawings would not have been accepted as evidence in a court but they were valuable in giving us a shared understanding and providing me with insights into how the family situation must have felt for her.

Countering misconceptions

Children are often very confused about what has happened to them and a child who has experienced a lot of life changes can be helped through a 'life-story book'. Usually this is associated with looked-after or adopted children but those remaining at home can also make sense of changes in their lives through tracing their life story and it gives them opportunities to ask questions that they might have been afraid to ask before or to realise certain events were not their fault.

Life-story work involves recording important information about the child and events in the child's history illustrated by documents and photographs. Experience has shown that a loose-leaf book is preferable because additional information can be inserted at a later date. Other media can be used such as a video or audio tapes. This work is a task undertaken as a partnership between child and practitioner; therefore the child is given choices, such as, whether the accounts of events are written in the first or third person, for example, 'My first school' or 'Sean's first school'. There are a number of helpful publications on life-story work such as Rose and Philpot (2005), Shah and Argent (2006) and Ryan and Walker (2007).

Children's experiences of sexual abuse can be clarified through the use of simple 'facts of life' books. Twelve-year-old Emma, whose father had attempted to rape her older sister, could not understand why there were restrictions on her father's activities. Concepts such as exploitation and the denial of informed consent were difficult for her to grasp. However, she was told, with the help of diagrams and age-appropriate books, how her father's actions might have resulted in her sister having a baby by him. Emma and the therapist then tried to draw a family tree including the hypothetical baby. As she saw how difficult it would be for the baby to sort out parents from grandparents or aunts from sisters, Emma began to appreciate why her father's abuse of her sister had to stop and some of her confused feelings subsided.

One feature shared by most abuse victims is that they have a low opinion of themselves and low self-esteem is reinforced by the feelings of shame and guilt. There are a number of ways of assessing the extent of the damage to abused children's self-esteem. One way is by asking children whether or not they like their name. It can be useful to explore this theme further by asking if they know why they were given particular names and if they have a family nick name. Sarah's father, to show his contempt for his wife and daughters, gave the two girls nicknames usually given to boys.

Young people who do not like themselves are often reluctant to look in a mirror or draw or model themselves. Slow, gentle encouragement to look in a mirror or to create an image of themselves as attractive is one way of helping enhance their self-esteem. Older, imaginative children may like to draw themselves as trees then explain the drawing. One teenager drew herself as a stark tree with no roots or leaves but with big patches on the trunk. This provided an eloquent witness to her feelings of bleakness, loneliness and of being defiled by the abuse. In later sessions she was able to add leaves, draw in roots and erase the patches. This exercise reflected her progress towards a happier self-image.

Children, including non-abused siblings who witness abuse, often blame themselves for the mistreatment and need to hear they were not to blame. If they are old enough to understand analogies then these can be used to illustrate the concept of adult responsibility. They could be asked who would be to blame if an adult stole some money then bought sweets for them with the stolen cash. This demonstrates that even if the child appears to enjoy or benefit from the activity he or she is not to blame. However, they need to understand that they bear a degree of responsibility if they bully or sexually exploit other children. Ryan (1989) warns of the dangers of taking the messages of not being to blame too far and generalising it to all situations.

When children have managed to draw attention to the abuse, they need to hear that:

- they have done the right thing;
- that by their disclosure they have helped to protect themselves and other children;
- they may have enabled their parent to receive help;
- it is not their fault if disclosure has led to their removal into care or the disintegration of the family.

Some therapists do not believe children should be touched in therapy. However, Ferguson (2011) states 'every worker should be prepared to touch children as a routine part of their practice'. My experience has led me to the view that social workers and therapists should be willing, appropriately and with sensitivity, to touch service users particularly young children. There are a number of reasons.

The first is illustrated by Ferguson (2011) who explores the whole nature of touch in child-protection work. He gives the example of a neglected two-year-old wearing loose clothing; a team leader did not realise how neglected she was until she picked her up. A similar situation occurred in the case of Maria Colwell (Field-Fisher, 1974) when, of all the professionals who saw her, only a teacher who lifted her up realised how emaciated she was.

Another reason for touch is that some children believe that they are so defiled by the abuse that they are 'untouchable'. While particularly true of those sexually abused, Josie's account illustrated how this can also apply to children suffering physical and emotional abuse and neglect. She was not surprised that teachers and peers appeared to shun her. People in distress can benefit from physical comfort and it can demonstrate to abused children that they are not untouchable.

Nevertheless, for some victims gentle touching and cuddling is either unknown and alien, or interpreted as a preliminary to sexual activities. To create a sense of safety and security and to avoid alarming children, therapists can begin to give physical comfort through the use of puppets. Their hand touches the child's hand, both safely enclosed by the puppet. Sometimes puppets are not needed as the child is able to accept a reassuring squeeze of the hand or shoulder. However, children should always be in a position to move away from any embrace and therapists need to ensure any physical contact is not intrusive and cannot be misinterpreted.

Messages from research

Lynch and Garrett (2010)

Lynch and Garrett interviewed six female and two male child welfare social workers in the Republic of Ireland to explore their views on physical touch in relation to the people with whom they worked. From the interviews they identified six themes.

The first was the need to differentiate between appropriate and inappropriate touching. The workers felt that touch initiated by the worker, in intimate places and for long were inappropriate.

The second was that all felt that touch was important in showing empathy, in enhancing relationships and communication and in showing support for children.

In contrast the third theme was that touch was associated with risk. For one interviewee who worked with children with disabilities the association of touch with abuse was marked. There was also the fear that touch would be misinterpreted.

The fourth theme was that in their own personal relationships they were tactile and used touch but at least one would never do so professionally. Two had fond memories of being cuddled and hugged as children.

The interviewees were asked to read an extract appearing to criticise the social workers in the Peter Connelly case for not having touched and examined him. Most felt touching and examining Peter was a medical role not a social work one.

The sixth point made was that generally the interviewees felt that the topic of touch should be discussed more among social workers.

New roles and protective strategies

In any family or group, members will take different roles – parent, leader, facilitator, clown. When the family or group has problems, individual members become scapegoats, victims or 'invalids'. Abused children usually have a negative role and, like Lloyd, begin to behave in a way which fulfils this. Others, like Marie or Josie take on a parenting role comforting their mother or father and protecting siblings. If, during therapy, children do not learn new roles they will remain as parent or scapegoat when they join their original or new family. For example, if their role was a parental one they need to learn that responsibility lies with adults and not with children.

Practice focus

Lisa

Eight-year-old, Lisa, had tried to protect her two younger brothers and sister from abuse and domestic violence. All the children were taken into care and remarkably all four children went to the same foster carer. Lisa was seen as a particularly burdened child and offered therapy. During the first session she devised a game for herself. Using a farm set, she put all the baby animals into an enclosure lying them down so they could sleep. For several sessions she placed one lamb standing in the middle to 'look after the babies'.

After a few sessions she lay the lamb down with the other baby animals and chose two strong carthorses which she placed in the middle of the sleeping baby animals. She said that it was for the adult animals to look after the babies and glanced up at me for reassurance. I smiled, nodded and said 'yes'. After this, for several sessions, she played the game over and over again until she was convinced that both she and her siblings had a right to be looked after by adults and she did not have to wear herself out protecting the other children.

Children can also be encouraged to role-play possible situations in which they might be exploited or bullied, learning through these how to defend themselves.

Although children may not be able to resist someone more powerful, they nevertheless have a right to try to protect themselves and to seek help. One game emphasises this right and encourages them to think about the people they can turn to for assistance. The child

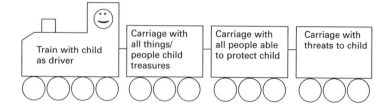

This is a variation on the game which can be used with a toy train, cardboard shapes or a drawing. The child chooses what will be put in each carriage, although he or she might need helpful suggestions especially with the second carriage.

Figure 4.1 The 'Who can help me?' game

chooses something, such as a box, to signify a castle of which they are sovereign. The child then selects little figures to represent themselves and also all the people and things they like – their parents, ice cream, going to the cinema, their brothers and sisters, grandma, birthdays. This is put in the box/castle. Outside the castle threatening the child's happiness and security is an army of figures representing all the people and things they do not like – spiders, a certain teacher, ghosts, crocodiles, being hit, 'mummy/daddy drinking and being angry'. Between the threatening army and the castle is another army of all the people who can protect them – their parent or grandparent, a favourite teacher, a social worker, the police. This theme can be adapted to concur with the child's interests such as a farm threatened by wild animals, a planet under attack from aliens, a train with three carriages or a boat under fire from pirates (see Figure 4.1).

Putting it into practice

This activity revolves around the 'castle' game. The basic principle of the game is that children explore whom and what they can draw upon to protect themselves from the people, things and situations that may threaten their well-being.

Think of any child with whose interests and enthusiasms you are familiar. Then try to devise a version of the 'castle' game that reflects these. For example, the castle could become Hogwarts for children who love *Harry Potter* or a boat threatened by pirates for the fans of *Pirates of the Caribbean*. If you do not have figures then you can make some from modelling clay 'Playdo' or 'plasticine' or use paper either to draw out the game or cut out figures.

Comment: The purpose of this exercise is to show that when working with children it is important to tailor games and activities to the child and not expect the child to fit in with set ideas. Most play activities can be adapted to reflect individual children's interests and enthusiasms.

Point for reflection

Reflect on the same game. How might the game be adapted to include children in diverse situations? For example, how could you adapt it for a sight-impaired child? How could you ensure that it is relevant to a child from a minority ethnic group? If you have specialist skills, for example working with children with an autistic spectrum condition, could you adapt the game to make it meaningful for them?

Comment: The aim of this activity is to illustrate that play work can be offered to nearly all children without huge quantities of specialist materials. Although there are some very valuable, specially designed play items for specific groups, it is often feasible, given understanding and imagination, to adjust general activities so that they are suitable for specific needs and for children from a variety of backgrounds and heritages.

Children can be made aware of their rights to be looked after and not harmed. Returning to the theme of touch, in the case of children who have been sexually abused, it is worth ensuring that they understand the difference between benign and inappropriate touch. There is good touching like stroking a cuddly toy, bad touching such as being pinched and 'not good' touching which makes them feel uncomfortable and embarrassed especially when it involves their private parts.

Finally, children need to learn that there are different types of secrets and some should be kept and others should not. If by keeping a secret they, or someone else, is hurt or made to feel uncomfortable then the secret should be told to someone who can help. If they fear that there will be terrible consequences from telling someone then they can be encouraged to use a trick like crossing their fingers behind their back to ward off any evil while telling. Unfortunately, this may not help those abused children who have a realistic fear of being taken away from home or upsetting their parents but it will help in cases where the threat is unrealistic, for example where a child is told he will be turned into a frog if he discloses.

Harnessing modern technology

Anyone who spends time with children and young people will be aware of how effortlessly they use media such as mobile phones with their texting and apps, Skype, social networking with pokes, walls and comments, and on-line forums, not to mention a wide range of electronic and computer games.

Increasingly, there is development of technology-based ways of working with distressed children. 'Walk in My Shoes', for example, is a computer program enabling children and adults to communicate potentially difficult situations. Use of the program requires a short training course. Subsequently, the trained interviewer can work through the program with vulnerable children and adults helping them communicate their experiences including distressing events or relationships. A program similar to this can be adapted for therapeutic work. Programs could also be customised for children with disabilities. For example, the very visual nature of the program means that it could be used with hearing-impaired and deaf children, while a computer version which uses sound and speech could be provided for sign impaired and blind children.

There are other possibilities to reach children for whom currently there is no provision. Although direct one-to-one work is the ideal, March *et al.* (2009) found that for children suffering from anxiety those participating in an internet-based therapy programme did better than those on a waiting list so receiving no help. Rothbaum (2009), meanwhile, explores and points to the benefits of using virtual reality as a therapeutic resource especially for children in the future.

Ending individual work

The end of individual work may signify that the child is unlikely to see the therapist again. Therefore care has to be taken to end on a positive note. Sometimes on the last planned session children divulge potentially damaging information. In these cases the therapist needs to arrange a follow-up meeting to demonstrate to the child that she or he has not been rejected nor has the therapist been harmed by anything that the child has said. For practitioners short of time, a brief, informal follow-up, a phone call or even nowadays a Skype link is better than nothing at all.

If there are only to be a few planned sessions then the child can be told at the outset that they will see the therapist for, perhaps, six meetings. After each meeting there is a reminder of how many sessions are left. If the number of sessions has been left open, then, as the worker feels termination is drawing near, the child should be prepared for the fact that he or she will be moving on to a new stage.

Most children enjoy individual work despite the fact that sessions can be painful for them. Sometimes they become attached to a certain toy, but it is rarely possible for them to keep it. Generally children accept the fact that play equipment has to stay where it belongs. However, they can be given a photograph of their favourite toy or a memento. Compton (2002) suggested a personal set of coloured pencils for the child, which can be kept by the child when sessions end. Children can also become fond of their therapist. Again they can be given a photograph or some other memento such as a badge, button or a drawing. Therapists may wish to draw a picture of a trophy and give it to the child as a prize for being courageous or some other positive attribute. This exchange is particularly useful if the therapist has asked to keep some of the child's drawings.

Practice focus

Emil

Emil, aged six, had been physically and emotionally abused by his mother and her boyfriend and removed to foster carers. His behaviour at the foster home fluctuated between withdrawal and temper tantrums. He was given individual play work during which he was able to express a range of emotions. He had become attached to a toy rabbit through which he talked to the therapist. He would not directly answer the therapist's questions but instead would tell the rabbit but talking out loud the therapist was able to listen and understand his issues. During the period of therapy the boyfriend left and Emil returned to his mother's care. He seemed delighted to be home and all appeared well. As the therapy came to an end the therapist felt that Emil was so attached to the rabbit that at the very end of the therapy he was allowed to keep the rabbit as a memento of the sessions.

Less than a year later, Emil came back into care after a catalogue of concerns. His absences from school had been frequent. When he was in school, he had been involved in bullying younger children and stealing, especially other children's packed lunches. There had been concerns about his appearance because he had put on a lot of weight and his clothes were old, worn and too small. There had been complaints of anti-social behaviour against neighbours. Finally, he had been admitted to hospital with an alcohol overdose. While in care for this second time, his key social worker found out that his mother had used his beloved toy rabbit as a weapon with which to taunt him, constantly threatening to destroy it. Eventually she had burnt it slowly in front of him.

Comment: The case of Emil demonstrates the care which needs to be taken in the choice of memento. One that has too much meaning attached can become the source of great distress if lost or damaged. This is why a small one which a child can hide easily or which can be readily replaced is preferable.

Finally, individual therapy may help victims cope for a while but sometimes they need assistance later in life when they reach another significant point such as the birth of their own baby. Such events can awaken long-buried memories and emotions. Children can be prepared for this by being told that occasionally people's problems re-occur and when that happens they have the right to seek support again.

Individual work is unquestionably of considerable value. However, it is not the only way of intervening therapeutically. The next chapter explores working with children in the family context which can provide a useful supplement or alternative to individual work.

Further resources

Rymaszewska, J. and Philpot, T. (2006) *Reaching the Vulnerable Child.* London: Jessica Kingsley.
  This is one in a series of books about promoting recovery for abused and traumatised children. It is absorbing and provides insights into ways of helping children.

Sunderland, M. and Armstrong, N. (2008) *Draw on Your Emotions.* Bicester: Speechmark Publishing.
  Margot Sunderland's books for children are always fun to use and can help them express their emotions. Sunderland has also produced other books to be read with or by children who are

coping with distress; who can resist titles like *A Wibble called Bipley* or *A Nifflenoo called Nevermind*?

Thomas, B. (2009) *Creative Coping Skills for Children*. London: Jessica Kingsley.
A rich source of suggestions for activities to cope with different needs or feelings. There are for example ideas for helping children relax or for those who are grieving.

More information about Walk in my Shoes can be obtained from:
http://www.inmyshoes.org.uk/ In_My_ Shoes/ Introduction. html.

CHAPTER 5

Working with children in the family context

CHAPTER OVERVIEW
The following topics are addressed:

- the diversity of family life
- the advantages and pitfalls of family work, assessing families, using family trees and SLOT analyses
- ways of working with families including co-working, live supervision, case-team manager models, family group conferences and family centres
- facilitating family communication and harnessing modern technologies

Child maltreatment occurs primarily within the family and, therefore, it is appropriate to help children in the family context. This chapter is not designed as an in-depth study of family therapy. Instead it looks at the type of family-based assistance that a social or other welfare worker, with some understanding of family dynamics, can undertake. Dogra *et al.* (2009, p. 234) point out that in mental health work with young people:

> Although most workers do not have formal family therapy training, they draw on some of the key concepts to inform their work which is one distinction between family-based work and family therapy undertaken by professionals with specialist training.

All the suggestions in this chapter are rooted in the practical experience of 'family-based work' by front-line practitioners. Those who used the methods described were all busy practitioners with many other demands on their time and with few facilities. They did not regard themselves as 'experts' but they acquired an expertise by careful planning, accepting guidance from colleagues, understanding underpinning theories, practising techniques and by always being sensitive to the feelings and needs of the families.

Working with diversity

As Morris (2011, p. 2) explains, families can be diverse with 'geographical location, blood ties and proximity not necessarily being key determinants of the membership of a child's family network'. In a multi-cultural society, abused children will come from a range of ethnic backgrounds. Problems are encountered when workers and the family are from different cultural groups and Lau (2002) highlights the value of families having therapists from the same ethno-cultural backgrounds. But that is not always possible. Often it is a simple matter of statistics. In one area there may be a dozen cultural groups but only a couple of workers able to engage in family work. Moreover, in small towns the family may not want a professional who is a member of the same small community 'knowing their business'. Furthermore, families, particularly in the UK, may comprise different cultures. But those from minority ethnic groups should not be denied family work simply because they cannot be matched to a worker from the same group. Instead, the differences in race, symbolic and belief systems, family structure, language and communication can be acknowledged.

Maitra and Miller (2002) also explore many of the dilemmas of working with non-Western cultures in Western society. A worker may seek a consultation with a professional from the same cultural background as the family. However, care is needed because as the authors acknowledge, culture is an evolving process, rather than a static one. People from minority cultures and religions are sometimes dismayed by the pronouncements, in the name of their culture, of others from their group. Those who interpret beliefs more liberally may be deeply irked by the assertions of the more orthodox or fundamentalist members and vice versa.

There is cultural diversity not just between non-white families or white non-British ones but also within apparently cohesive groups. There are micro-cultural differences between different socio-economic classes and even different geographical areas. For example, working in one traditional coal-mining area we found that we excluded the grandmother (the mother's mother) at our peril. Invariably these women exerted a powerful influence, whether by undermining any intervention or by offering valuable support. Morris (2011) underlines the importance of not using 'family' to mean 'parents' or immediate carers and there may be important figures in the extended family.

There are other aspects of diversity. Families in which parents, children, or both, have a significant disability will have their own unique ways of functioning in order to manage the disability. A paper looking at the impact, on siblings, of having a brother or sister with disabilities was written by Burke (2010). Such siblings tend to experience disability by association and less ability to participate in the community but equally they gain knowledge and understanding that their peers do not have. It is therefore particularly important that they, and their siblings with disabilities, do not miss out on receiving therapeutic family work just because therapeutic tasks become more complex when a member has a disability. There may be communication issues, therefore a co-worker who can use the same communication system may be necessary (see Kennedy, 1990, 2002). Consideration has to be given to adapting materials so that they can be used by all family members and, in some families, wheelchair access will be needed.

Finally, there is a huge diversity of family structures with not just male/female parents but also two same-sex parent figures or single parents of either sex. The reasons for single-parenthood can be equally diverse and the reason will have an influence on family functioning. The absence of a much-loved parent who has died will have a different impact on the remaining family compared to one who has left in the wake of anger and bitterness to find happiness with a new family. There are reconstituted families with numbers of step-parents and siblings. Sometimes children are adopted and others fostered into the family. Some children will have two or more equally important families. Extended family members may be significant with several generations living in the same home. In contrast, others will be living in relative isolation as the only child of one available parent and very distant, uninvolved extended relatives. Account has to be taken of the role and impact of all potential and absent family members before undertaking family-based work.

Benefits and problems

Benefits

Attachment theory teaches us that children can become devoted to abusing parents. They often want the abuse to stop but crave the abuser's love. In many cases, abusive parents have a degree of affection for their offspring despite maltreating them, and family work can develop this into a more protective affection. It can transform an 'ineffective' family into one that can provide a 'good-enough' environment. This is in the child's best interests because children have a strong need to belong to a family; a need reinforced by the emphasis on the 'family' in advertising, in school, on television, in magazines and comics.

A further advantage of family work is that, according to systems theory, if there is change in one member, the system as a whole will be changed. For example, during family work a parent who has accepted responsibility for the abuse can be helped to express this to the children. This results in the children being relieved of guilt and shame, marking the beginning of new, honest, open forms of family communication.

Treating children without treating family members can lead to problems because abused children learn to adapt to the maltreatment and while their behaviour may seem to be 'abnormal', when seen in the family context it is a normal adjustment to an abnormal situation. Jessica Cameronchild (1987) was physically and emotionally abused from her earliest years. As a teenager she attempted suicide. She was hospitalised and given intensive therapy. She wrote:

> The psychiatrist and hospital staff were, in fact, setting up a very futile and destructive double bind by putting me on a program that required me to give up defenses which were vital to my survival at home ... the course of my treatment exacerbated the violence for my brothers at home, condoned our parents' past mistreatment of us, reinforced their denial, and augmented my futile view of the world in general. (p. 148)

Treating the parents without involving the children can be equally unsatisfactory. The aim of treatment for abusive parents is likely to be directed at a change in their behaviour towards their children. This is usually a long, slow process. But the children themselves will have adapted to the parents' abusive behaviour. Marie talked about learning to stay one step ahead of her father. When the parents alone are given therapy, *they* might change but their children can, as a consequence, become more confused and frightened. They were secure with the 'devil' they knew. Now they are insecure as they can no longer anticipate parental behaviour. Children who had a role as family scapegoat or surrogate parent may no longer feel of value to the parents. Consequently, they might react by trying to provoke the parent into abusing them again in order to restore the former, familiar situation.

Patterns and forms of communication are important in families. Parents given help will learn to communicate more openly and directly with the children. But if not included in the therapy, the children will again become confused. For example, an eldest daughter had protected her younger siblings. She had always acted as their spokesperson, bearing the brunt of her father's anger and violence. Intervention resulted in the parents trying to relate more directly to the younger children, who did not understand what was happening and became frightened and unresponsive, whereas the eldest girl felt ignored and rejected. The parents experienced frustration as their new behaviour seemed to make the situation worse. Family-work, which teaches all members to learn new patterns of communication together, would have avoided these difficulties.

Practice focus

Sinead

While family work is valuable, Sinead, an adult survivor, cautions against too rigid an adherence to it:

> My parents were utter tyrants. By the time I was about five-years-old and my brother was nine, we were completely withdrawn. We would not move or talk without permission. We could not play and were very quiet. My parents were having problems so we went to stay with an aunt. She was so worried about us that she referred us to a psychiatrist. Because my parents would not be included in any therapy, the psychiatrist said that nothing could be done. He would not treat children without their parents. So we were offered no help and just left to get on with life.

Sinead reflected on how valuable play therapy or individual work would have been and how much she had needed the opportunity to play spontaneously, express her terrors and frustration in safety, and have the attention of an understanding adult without fearing punishment. The ideal is to intervene in the whole family, but if this is not possible the child should not be abandoned; individual or group work have their benefits too (see Chapters 4 and 6).

Problems and pitfalls

Bentovim (2002, p. 464) offers useful guidance about situations where family work is contra-indicated. These include families in which there is:

- a complete rejection of the child;
- a parental failure to take any responsibility or acknowledge there are any problems;
- the needs of the parent taking primacy over those of the children;
- a combative oppositional stance to the professionals;
- severe personality or related problems in the parents.

Even in families without the above features, problems will still be encountered. For the majority of people the familiar is comfortable, the unknown is feared. Change often means moving from the familiar to the unknown. A sudden crisis may cause a sudden change but without any other intervention the family system will re-create the situation which existed before the crisis. Disclosure or professional intervention in an abusing family constitutes a crisis. The family may change temporarily but, once the crisis has passed, the family will try to revert to the former situation. In cases of sexual abuse, the non-abusing parent may bar the abusing partner from the home at first, only to have him or her back once the case conference or legal proceedings have been completed.

A lone child-care worker is unlikely to be able to resist the powerful processes, inherent in all systems, of returning to the status quo – called 'homeostasis'. The main problem encountered by a therapist attempting to intervene single-handed is the possibility of being absorbed into the family system. Families are adept at finding roles for people who could be a threat. Roles include 'rich uncle/aunt' – the constant provider of material goods, 'family friend' – the confidant who can be trusted to keep family secrets or 'fairy god-parent' – the person who will solve all problems instantly by magic. In some cases the worker may become clearly allied with the abusing parent, condemning the children's behaviour as 'provocative' or 'seductive'. Because the needs and demands of its members often conflict, a single professional trying to meet the requirements of the whole family is faced with an impossible task. He or she is likely to become emotionally exhausted or will only find sufficient energy to spare for just one or two members.

A major criticism of family-work based on systems theories was voiced by MacLeod and Saraga (1988) because, particularly in cases of sexual abuse, the perpetrator avoids responsibility as blame for the abuse is located in the family 'system' and therefore other members of the system – the non-abusing parent and victim – are given equal responsibility. Anyone working with families has to be clear about who has responsibility for what is going wrong; power imbalances have to be acknowledged. Parents are given considerable power over their children and they are required to use this power for the welfare of the children. In a patriarchal society, there is a strong likelihood that the father will hold most power. If he has exploited this then he has to take responsibility for his behaviour.

Assessing families

There are various official guidelines and some excellent texts about assessing families (Bentovim *et al.*, 2009; Helm, 2010; Holland, 2010; Sperry, 2012; Turney *et al.*, 2012; Wiffin, 2012) and this section is not designed to provide comprehensive assessment guidelines. However, there are a couple of techniques used with families which can be particularly effective in helping workers understand their dynamics.

Working on the family tree

Family history can have a huge impact on family dynamics and it is surprising how often history has a propensity to repeat itself. Drawing up the family tree going back if possible three or four generations can be a truly enlightening journey.

Practically speaking, it is not always easy to draw out the tree and it can require considerable use of initiative. When faced with a father who was one of 22 surviving children, I had to hastily decide how much time to devote to all of his siblings. I was however mostly guided by the father's opinion of which parts of his family history were most important.

Practice focus

Hayley

Hayley was referred by a hospital because her two-year-old son, Jamie, had cystic fibrosis. Despite previously being a conscientious mother, she had recently failed to keep essential hospital appointments for her son and was refusing visits from her GP, health visitor and specialist nurse. There were concerns that without appropriate physical therapy Jamie might not survive.

When visited, Hayley seemed a devoted mother and Jamie an outgoing, relaxed toddler, therefore it seemed surprising that she was putting her son's life at risk. The family consisted of Jamie, Hayley and Louise, her sister. Jamie's father was unknown and Hayley had little contact with the rest of the family.

With Jamie joining in, we started to draw the family tree. On the second visit Hayley asked Louise if she would run an errand. When Louise left, Hayley, cuddling Jamie, asked to continue with the family tree. She explained all her other babies were miscarriages. She did not know the babies' genders so I drew triangles. As I was drawing one, Hayley became agitated and stopped me, saying one of the triangles was wrong; it should be a circle because the baby was a girl, called Lily. She explained that Lily was not a miscarriage but a child that had lived for two years. Five years ago, Hayley explained, when living elsewhere, she had been holding Lily when her partner had attacked her. He stabbed Lily instead, killing her. As Jamie's second birthday had approached she had become more and more haunted by the memories of Lily's murder and had felt overwhelming guilt making her avoid medical professionals who, she thought, might condemn her.

With that information it was possible to verify the original incident with the police who confirmed that Hayley was not held responsible for Lily's death. Hayley was reassured and grief counselling was arranged. She allowed a specialist nurse to visit regularly and was gradually persuaded to return to the hospital for Jamie's checks.

Comment: Obviously in a short case example, I have had to skip the trust and relationship building techniques with Jamie, Hayley and Louise that preceded and followed the family- tree work. However, ultimately Hayley's worries were revealed because she felt unable to see Lily drawn as a triangle, a miscarriage. She was incapable of denying her daughter's existence when drawn in front of her. In this way, assembling a family tree can reveal some secrets that are impeding family functioning. There might, however, need to be opportunities for individual members to approach the worker on their own. Hayley asked for her sister to leave the session. Part of the work with Hayley was helping her explain events to her sister who had been a teenager in care five years earlier and had not known about Lily.

Point for reflection

Consider Hayley's story. Was it appropriate that she should be referred to me, a specialist child-protection worker? Was Hayley abusing Jamie in any way?

To address these questions try to work out:

- What power Hayley had and how she was using her parental power?
- What judgements should professionals make about Hayley?
- What is meant by non-judgemental attitudes in this case?

Comment: it could be argued that, as a parent, Hayley had considerable powers and she was failing to use them to maximise Jamie's chances of survival. Therefore it is appropriate for professionals to make the judgement that Hayley's behaviour had become 'abusive' and needed to change. Her parenting, which had been good, appeared to be less so and placed Jamie at risk as he celebrated his second birthday.

Non-judgemental attitudes could include that no judgements should be made about Hayley's motivation without evidence. For example, to simply assume she had stopped caring would have been judgemental.

Similarly, in relation to Lily's death, the only legitimate judgement was that confirmed by the police and original court evidence that her partner was solely responsible for Lily's death. To speculate that Hayley might be to blame for 'provoking' a violent partner or using Lily as a shield would be to make unwarranted judgements. However, if there had been evidence to support these possibilities they would need to be taken into account in any assessment of the risks to Jamie.

SLOT analysis

One of the problems when assessing a family is that it can be 'pathologised' when viewed from the perspective of professionals from different, and usually more powerful, social sectors. This has been highlighted in relation to class (Gittins, 1993) and cultural heritage, especially black families in a predominantly white society (Howitt and Owusu-Bempah, 1994; Phillips, 2002). On the other hand, some public inquiries suggest child-protection workers sometimes operate a 'rule of optimism', thereby failing to address family weaknesses (Dingwall *et al.*, 1983; Derby Safeguarding Board, 2009). Another risk is that practitioners ignore environmental factors and focus on deficiencies in the family rather than adverse external circumstances.

A SLOT analysis can counter these oversights. It is adapted from SWOT analyses of service and commercial organisations. It explores the family's potential on the basis of its internal strengths (S) and weaknesses (W), while taking account of external opportunities (O) and threats (T). When working the family it might be more appropriate to think of a SLOT analysis, with weaknesses being conceptualised as 'limitations'. In ideal circumstances, the family members undertake the exercise themselves, identifying the strengths and limitations within their own family and the opportunities and threats of their environment. They are the people most familiar with their family and how the environment affects them.

Undertaking a SLOT analysis does not call for elaborate preparation, all that is needed is a sheet of paper divided into four boxes or four separate sheets. Each box or sheet is given one of the four headings: strengths, limitations, opportunities, threats. Under each heading a list is made of the family attributes in terms of strengths, and so on. Sentences, key words or agreed symbols can be used. The diagrams can become more complex as some limitations might be redefined as strengths or threats redefined as opportunities and vice versa.

Practitioners can assist the family in several ways. First, there may be strengths or limitations that an outside observer can identify but which the family cannot see or do not want to acknowledge. Second, the practitioner may have had early warning of law and policy changes or other environmental factors of which the family are unaware. Third, the practitioner can work with the family on how to build on identified strengths, how to diminish the effect of limitations or how to turn a limitation into a strength. Finally, the practitioner can help the family to devise strategies to take advantage of environmental opportunities and protect themselves from external threats.

There are some families that, for whatever reason, are unable to undertake this evaluation themselves. In these instances, the SLOT analysis can be used as an assessment tool by the practitioners and fed back to the family. However, even in these cases where the family has been unable to participate fully, the opportunity for family members to add their own perspective can be given.

The great advantage of a SLOT analysis is that account is taken of the family's strengths whether drawn from their traditional culture, extended family members, their past experiences or the combination of the strengths of individual members. Families differing from the mainstream are less likely to be pathologised because members are given the opportunity to identify strengths. But it also provides an opportunity to be honest and clear about family limitations. Finally, the impact of the environment is acknowledged, so realistic proposals can be explored.

Putting it into practice

Try to undertake a SLOT analysis of a family with which you are familiar. This need not be a family in which abuse has occurred. What are the strengths that the family could build on for the future? Are there any limitations or weaknesses in the family structure, and can these be reconstructed as strengths? What opportunities are available to the family? What environmental threats are they facing? What conclusions can you draw about the functioning of the family?

Comment: This activity will help you to practise developing a SLOT analysis. Sometimes it can be difficult to decide where to place certain factors, for example, is the imminent demise of an adored grandparent a weakness, limitation or a threat? The important principle is that the categorisation makes sense to both the family and worker. As long as everyone involved is in reasonable agreement then the technicalities of the classification of factors does not matter.

Point for reflection

Using the family in the activity above, imagine a change in the structure and context of the family. For example, if your chosen family has a male and female parental partnership, in your mind, change the parental partnership to two female carers or maybe a single, male carer. You could change the ethnic or socio-economic background of the family members. Now try the SLOT analysis again. What differences are there? How important are these to the future functioning of the family? You can repeat the exercise making other alterations such as the physical capabilities of the family members or environmental factors, maybe placing a rural family in an urban area or vice versa.

Comment: The purpose of this activity is to show how a SLOT analysis can be undertaken with a wide variety of families. It will also help you explore how far a change in just one aspect such as whether the parent figures are heterosexual or homosexual can substantially change the strengths, limitations, opportunities and threats facing the family.

Ways of working with families

While the advantages of family work appear to outweigh the disadvantages, a major drawback is that just one worker can become absorbed into the system. There are however a number of strategies which can prevent this. Most require some form of joint work, that is, professionals working closely together to achieve the same objective. This is not the same as interdisciplinary cooperation; a health visitor and a teacher can work in close cooperation but the primary aim of the health visitor is the good health of the family whereas that of teacher is the proper education of the children.

Various models for joint working will be suggested in this chapter but it is acknowledged that sometimes local resources are such that there is only one therapist available for the whole family. In these circumstances, other agencies such as the school and primary medical team have a duty to help the family worker by monitoring the situation as far as possible and passing on relevant information. Too often such agencies expect the worker to seek information from them instead of volunteering potentially important details.

Practitioners who are having to work on their own should also have a supervisor able to provide an objective view of the family and of their involvement, thereby helping to guard against over-identification with part of the family and emotional exhaustion. In instances where the supervisor has insufficient knowledge of both family work and child abuse the worker should be encouraged to seek the advice of a consultant. The supervisor and consultant will then liaise in order to ensure that their approaches are consistent and are not presenting the worker with further conflicts.

Co-working

Working with a co-therapist is a tried and tested approach to both group and family work and offers considerable advantages to workers and family alike. Two workers are more able to resist the pressure of the family system. It is more difficult for a family to find roles for two new members than it is to absorb just one.

The needs of all the different members of the family can rarely be met by just one worker. Even where there is a single parent with one infant it is often difficult to give attention to both. A mother who is abusing her baby is likely to be under great stress and make considerable emotional demands. She is unlikely to tolerate the worker spending a lot of time relating to the baby because she needs the attention for herself. Yet the baby will also be distressed by the abuse he or she has suffered and by the mother's tension. The therapist needs to build up a relationship with the infant, becoming a familiar figure for the baby who will then accept handling or examination by the worker should this become necessary.

A useful role-play exercise illustrates the problems inherent in the one-therapist-for-one-family approach. Participants represent a family consisting of a single distressed parent with two children who are being neglected plus a lone social worker visiting the home in order to alleviate the family problems. Invariably participants report that the visit made matters worse, especially for those playing the parts of the children. If the worker gives most of his or her attention to the parent, the children feel doubly neglected. However, if the worker spends time with the children, a vulnerable parent can feel his or her needs are being ignored and experiences increased frustration. This situation is avoided if two therapists are involved, one attending to the needs of certain family members while the other concentrates on the remaining members. Often the split is between the parents and children or between the males and females in the family. Sometimes the needs of one person are so overwhelming that one worker concentrates all efforts on that person leaving a colleague to attend to all other demands.

Co-working, especially where there is conflict between two parents, can provide a model of adult cooperation and open communication for the parents. The two workers can demonstrate to both parents and children that mutual respect and joint decision making is possible. A further incidental benefit is that, in potentially violent situations, being accompanied by a colleague offers some protection.

The drawbacks of this way of working are self-evident. Both therapists must be competent and confident. A defensive co-worker who becomes possessive of the clients and keeps trying to 'score points' over his or her colleague is a destructive force. Two workers can start to mirror the split in the family; identifying with different factions, thereby reinforcing family conflict. The abused children may not only be criticised and scapegoated by siblings and parents but also by two workers. One worker absorbed into the family system is bad, two workers thus absorbed is more than twice as bad.

In hard-pressed social work agencies there may not be sufficient staff to allow for co-working of staff within the agency. One solution is to link up with another agency such as probation, education or health departments. However, probation officers, community teachers and health visitors may well have different objectives, constraints and priorities, making any commitment to long-term co-work difficult.

A further problem is that of supervision. Co-workers even from the same agency may have different supervisors. There are a number of solutions. One supervisor may agree to have a prime role, while the second simply retains an overview in order to satisfy the demands of accountability. Alternatively there may be periodical four-way supervision sessions. A third alternative is the appointment of a totally independent supervisor just for a particular case.

Where the therapists have the same supervisor there are still problems about whether they are seen individually or together. The best solution seems to be to have individual sessions, with arrangements made for the co-worker to be available for part of the time. Another solution is to alternate individual and joint sessions.

Recording and case accountability also present problems. If the therapists are from different agencies they will keep individual records but if they are from the same agency then only one is needed. Alternate recording of sessions evens out the workload but can cause confusion. The most practical solution appears to be for one worker to have prime responsibility for recording, booking facilities, liaison with other agencies and all other aspects of case management.

Live supervision

As its name implies, in live supervision, supervisors are present during the family session. They are more than mere observers; their task requires active participation (Blakey *et al.*, 1986). Live supervision can take a variety of forms depending on the facilities available. In its simplest form, one supervisor sits quietly in a corner of the same room as the therapists. At the other extreme, a group of colleagues can view one or two workers through a one-way screen or video monitor link. Experience shows that both therapists and family members can put cameras, screens and additional people to the back of their minds and concentrate on the task in hand.

An important principle is that all family members should agree to the involvement of the live supervisors. They should understand what is happening and accept that there will be interventions. It is made clear that the live supervisors are there to assist the worker who, in consequence, will be able to help the family more effectively. The family is usually introduced to all the supervisors, although if there is a group watching through a screen or monitor it can be more appropriate to introduce a representative of the group while inviting the family members to meet the rest after the session.

There are planned breaks during the session, when supervisors and therapists can reflect on events so far and when changes in direction may be suggested. In addition there will be *ad hoc* interventions by the supervisors if the workers and family members seem to be stuck or unnecessarily avoiding important issues. These interventions can be conveyed by telephone or through ear-phones or perhaps by a knock on the door. Notes for the session and for case files are usually made by one of the supervisors, thereby leaving the therapists free to focus all their energy on the direct work with the family.

This model can prevent therapists from becoming part of the family system. For example in one case, a single male worker was helping a family of mother, father, Martin their teenage son, and three younger children. The supervisors were able to observe how the family dynamics were making the worker take over the role of forceful father in relation to Martin instead of enabling all family members to express themselves and adopt more appropriate roles.

Live supervisors can also ensure that the therapists do not focus on the needs of certain family members to the exclusion of others. In another case, the supervisors observed how the two workers were focusing attention on the parents and were failing to see their daughter's anger and distress, which was such that the supervisors entertained the possibility that she might attempt suicide.

There are problems inherent in live supervision, including the threat posed to therapists by the presence of colleagues who are observing and analysing their work. Related to this is the fear of therapists that they will lose credibility in the family's eyes because they seem to be frequently 'corrected' by other people. But experience shows that workers, who have supervisors in whom they trust, find live supervision reassuring. Once it becomes an established practice in a team, members can come to depend on it to the extent that an unsupervised session can be unnerving. A family can be helped to appreciate this method of working by the explanation that two or more heads are better than one.

Another problem is that of the time and commitment required of more than one worker. However it is better in the long run to have effective therapy which achieves real and positive change in family functioning rather than one worker intervening to stave off yet another crisis for a while. Live supervision has a further advantage as it is a little more flexible than co-working because the live supervisor does not have to be the same person each time. It is important to clarify that live supervision and co-working can be combined with co-therapists being live supervised.

It is perhaps worth highlighting the fact that live supervision is not used exclusively in family work. It can be used with groups, pairs and individuals. However, it is especially valuable, as has already been noted, as a protection against the therapists becoming absorbed into a very powerful but ultimately destructive family system.

Case-team manager model

It has been shown that different family members have differing therapeutic requirements, yet it is difficult for one or even two workers to give effective help to each family member. The danger is that the needs of the quietest, most withdrawn person will be overlooked, yet he or she may be the most distressed individual who could, in silent despair, attempt suicide. Alternatively, the needs of the youngest member, especially a child not yet able to verbalise feelings coherently will be ignored. A total team approach therefore has much to commend it. But there are problems when several workers are involved. Teams can mirror the conflicts between individuals and sub-groups in the family, creating more confusion than already existed. Intervention can become disorganised because there is no clear line of responsibility and the needs of some members can be ignored.

In order to avoid the obvious pitfalls, a case-team manager can be appointed. He or she has had no direct involvement in the family but has a vital role in coordinating the intervention of the individual workers. The case-team manager is responsible for organising meetings of the workers at acceptable intervals. During meetings, the therapists outline their involvement subsequent to the previous meeting and report on the situation of the family members to whom they were committed. The case-team manager then:

- helps the workers to reflect on what was happening and to plan for the next stage of the work;
- identifies conflicts between workers especially when they mirror conflicts within the family;
- is responsible for keeping a record of all meetings;
- arranges the date and venue of subsequent meetings.

When this model is used the family have to be kept informed of what is happening and are made aware of the involvement and function of the case-team manager, although he or she does not usually meet the family. If the family ask to meet the manager this can most usefully be arranged towards the end of the intervention.

The main objection to this model is that it appears to be costly. However, each worker can be involved in several of these cases concurrently because the emotional demands are spread between a number of different practitioners. One worker trying to achieve the same objective on his or her own would have found the task overwhelming and time consuming. Instead of spending several hours each week contacting fellow workers by telephone, efforts are coordinated by a fortnightly or monthly two-hour session with only brief practical telephone calls in between, when necessary.

Supervision is another problem especially if the supervisor of any therapist feels threatened by the case-team manager's influence. It is inappropriate for agency supervisors to attend case management meetings. Their presence would make the sessions too large and unwieldy. Nevertheless, occasional additional meetings can be arranged at which individual supervisors can give voice to their concerns.

A final problem which may affect team functioning is that of hidden agendas. For example, one of the team might have been abused in childhood and might not have resolved this background problem. When a case-team manager suspects that there may be a personal issue involved, he or she should arrange for an individual discussion with the worker to sort out a way of helping other team members appreciate what is happening.

Family group conferences

Although many recommendations and some decisions about vulnerable children are made during formal case conferences, some areas convene family group conferences, not in place of case conferences and core groups but to supplement them, or in instances where there are family tensions yet a full case conference is not required. These are relatively formal meetings usually coordinated by an independent professional. Unlike case conferences, only those professionals with relevant information attend and may withdraw after sharing the information. The wider family with interests in the child's welfare participate and any family member who cannot attend is invited to contribute perhaps through a letter or recorded message.

Messages from research: family group conferences

1. Bell and Wilson (2006)

The authors sought the views of the children, aged six to sixteen years, in the first 20 families, none of whom were involved in current child protection investigations, who participated in a family group conference (FGC) pilot project.

Information about the views on the FGCs were obtained through questionnaires filled in by 20 FGC conveners, 55 adult family members and 15 children. In addition, six weeks after a conference, in-depth interviews were held with 19 key professionals, 35 adult family members and 9 children.

From the views expressed in the children's questionnaires it seemed that, for most, the FGC was a positive experience although one girl disliked everything about it. The interviews produced similar results with most children finding attendance beneficial, three having more mixed views and one child experiencing the process as a negative one. In that instance, the social worker and convenor left the room and also the girl felt 'that the focus of the meeting should have been on her mother's behaviour and not hers' (p. 677).

The children also appeared to be prepared for the conference but they were unsure about the role or even attendance of any advocates. Most also found the outcomes beneficial although there were some mixed views especially the girl who found it a negative experience and commented, 'I [left] feeling just mixed up' (p. 678).

Comment: From the negative experience of one girl it appears that children need at least one advocate at FGC to ensure that the family does not excuse parental behaviour by scapegoating the child, which in my professional experience can so often happen in families in which there is conflict.

2. O'Shaughnessy *et al.* (2010)

This paper is a report of the implementation and evaluation of a Family Group Conference (FGC) project in Liverpool focusing on the psychological welfare needs of black and minority ethnic (BME) children and families.

Seventy-two BME families took part in the project and an internal evaluation indicated improvements for many of the families. To delve into the processes in more detail the experiences of two families were explored in depth.

The authors concluded FGCs could be successful with BME families because they were 'respectful of family culture and prioritises the voice of the family over the voice of the professional' (p. 2043). The authors noted however that considerable preparation was needed and the culture of the families appreciated. For example, in the second family it was important to include the extended family from the start rather than the more traditional process of seeing the parents and children first then embracing the extended family. Another key point is that the FGC coordinators were not matched with the families, not least because the considerable diversity that the term 'BME' encompassed precluded matching. However, the authors highlight, the coordinators needed supervision and space for reflection to fulfil their roles adequately.

Comment: Clearly there are considerable benefits in using FGCs but indiscriminate use of FGCs may result in risks to children where there is multiple generational abuse and where maltreatment has become the family norm. When strengths outweigh limitations, FGCs will work well but where the opposite is true they might further disempower the children. Therefore careful preparation and supervision of the coordinators is required.

Family centres

Joint working is a characteristic of family centres. There are many different projects which are called family centres. In one model, parents and children attend a centre on several days a week. The objective is to help family relationships, provide play and structure for the children and training in parent craft for the parents. At family centres the parents may be taught practical skills such as how to cook, budget family finances, maintain hygiene and establish a routine. In relationship to their children they learn about normal development in order that they do not have unrealistic expectations of the youngsters and are helped to appreciate their children's needs for stimulation and security.

Some centres are not directed specifically towards vulnerable families. Rather they are a community provision. One notable example is the Pen Green Centre in Corby. Such centres are designed maximise the potential of families in general but by doing so prevent the abuse of children. This type of centre will be discussed more in Chapter 9, which explores prevention.

Facilitating communications

In family work it is important that all family members take part. This means that people beyond the nuclear family may have to be included if they are an important part of the family system. A common example is that of the grandparent who frequently looks after the children and has tried to protect them. It also means that all members who are present at a session need to participate actively. It is easy for the more assertive family members to dominate the session, while the youngest or quietest are virtually ignored. There are a number of techniques, which ensure that everyone present is included.

Verbal techniques

One way of including all family members in the verbal component of the session is by using circular questioning. One member is asked how another member reacts or would react in a given situation. The accuracy of the answer is checked with the second member. For example instead of asking the father what he does when the children arrive home late after school, the youngest child could be asked, 'What does dad do when you come home late?' The child may say, 'He gets angry.' The father is then asked, 'Do you get angry?' The father might explain, 'Yes, because I'm worried about them when they are late.' When one family member is very quiet, another can be asked on that member's behalf.

> ### Practice focus
>
> **Mandy**
>
> A subdued teenage girl, Mandy, who had been physically and sexually abused by her step-father understandably refused to say anything during the first few family sessions. The workers, having in vain already asked Mandy directly, asked another family member 'What would Mandy reply to that question if she was able to do so?' She was then asked if the response was accurate. She only had to nod or shake her head. Although she could not talk she was able to voice her opinions through other family members.

Care has to be taken in this form of questioning. Asking about the feelings of others poses difficulties for family members. The question, 'How does mum feel when you do that?' posed to a cynical adolescent may well be met with the response, 'Dunno, why don't you ask her yourself?' It is marginally better to ask, 'How do you think mum feels?' thereby inquiring about his opinion rather than directly about another's feelings. When the response, 'Dunno' is still forthcoming it is important not to make the young person feel condemned; so instead of irritably saying, 'But I'm asking you, not her' the most appropriate response might be a move to a new area of questioning.

Members can also be encouraged to ask each other questions. The therapist might say, 'Tommy can you ask mummy what she would like to happen?' Tommy may refuse. The mother is then invited to ask Tommy why he does not want to ask her. Yet again care has to be taken especially with children to guard against making them feel at fault if, because of shyness or anger, they cannot participate.

In some families, it is evident that the emphasis has been on condemnation and punishment. One useful exercise is to ask each family member in turn to say something they like about a chosen member. Then the spotlight moves on to the next person, so that each family member has heard something nice said about themselves by every other member. The therapist usually takes a turn in saying something positive about each family member but it is not necessary for the worker to be in the spotlight unless the family makes a specific request to that effect.

Non-verbal communication

One way in which the therapist can influence family dynamics is by changing the seating plan. This is obviously easier to do in a designated interview room rather than in the family's home. In one case where the daughter had taken over her mother's responsibility for her family, father and daughter used to sit together, while the mother and young son sat together leaving chairs in between each dyad for the workers. After a few sessions, the workers insisted on the mother and father sitting together, allowing the two children to sit next to each other. One aim of the work with the family was to distinguish between adults who were the parents and children who should be free of parental responsibility. The change in places provided a tangible demonstration of this. When a family member who should have been present at the session is absent, he or she can be included in the session by being designated an empty chair.

Family members can be asked to communicate non-verbally with other members. For example a child may start crying and the mother, if she does not do so spontaneously, can be invited to put her arm round her child. Again care has to be taken because if the mother refused point blank to do so the child might feel all the more rejected and distressed.

Exercises and role-play

One exercise helps to illustrate the different perspectives of the family. Members in turn are invited to draw either themselves or the family member they consider to be most important first. This can be on a blackboard or a large sheet of paper. Members are then invited to draw the rest of the family positioned on the paper near to or distant from each other depending on how the person creating the drawing sees the family relationships. With a large family it is probably less time consuming to represent its members as a large dot. If this exercise had been used with Sarah's family, the two sisters may have seen how they both believed that the other sister was closest to their father, thereby dissipating some of the jealousy and misconceptions that they had about each other. Furthermore, the father would no longer have been able to play the 'your sister is better than you' game. He would have had to have drawn each child at an equal distance from him or have specified a favourite (see Chapter 2, p. 37). Positioning coffee cups, buttons, coloured cardboard pieces or little play figures can be used instead of sketches.

Mandy, mentioned earlier in this section, refused to join in this exercise. The workers accepted her reluctance. They said that, although they would like her to take part because her opinion was as valid as that of the others, she was perhaps not ready to do so. Later when everyone else had had a chance to sketch the family, Mandy was again approached with the suggestion that she could tell another member or a worker where to put the family figures on her behalf. She agreed and chose her brother to act as scribe. Soon she was so involved that when her brother did not put the figures in exactly the right place she went over to the flip-chart and started drawing the family constellation herself.

Practice focus

Zoe

Role-play is useful in helping family members rehearse what they would like to do in a given situation. For example, a family was being helped through the case-team management model described earlier. The daughter, Zoe, had been sexually abused by her step-father. She was ambivalent about meeting him. She was frightened about being so angry that she would lose control when she met him and either attack him or dissolve into tears. Similarly Mr D was worried about his response when he met his step-daughter again for the first time since disclosure, yet he wanted to apologise to her and tell her that she was not to blame. There was a female worker supporting Zoe and a male probation officer supporting Mr D. Eventually the workers decided that Zoe could usefully rehearse what she would like to say to her step-father by meeting the probation officer who would represent Mr D. Conversely, Mr D met the female social worker to rehearse with her his apology to Zoe.

Finally, therapists can set tasks to be completed by the family between sessions. For example, a very isolated family may be encouraged to invite one of the children's friends to tea one evening before the next session. If the family does not manage this one week they can be encouraged to try again. If they still do not manage then the workers accept responsibility for setting a task which was too difficult, thereby avoiding giving the family any sense of failure. It is important, however, not to condone the family doing more than was asked, for example inviting three friends for tea when they were only asked to invite one. Sometimes doing too much reflects over-high expectations on the part of the family, when the therapists are trying to instil a sense of reality into the situation. Furthermore, some families are so sure that they will fail that they attempt more than they can manage in order to ensure their eventual failure.

One slightly paradoxical task, which is designed to succeed through failure but which usually brings some humour into the situation, is to ask the family to behave in a specific undesirable way but only under certain conditions. In a case of marital discord, for example the parents are told that they must have an argument but it must be at 9 p.m. precisely on Monday evening when all the children are in bed and it must take place in the kitchen. Usually couples find it difficult to argue to order but this exercise helps them to start thinking about the nature of their rows and how, when and why they occur.

Harnessing modern technologies

Film or Skype can be used to help family members communicate when direct contact might be impossible either because of physical or emotional distance. For example, in the case of Zoe above, after the completion of the various role-play meetings, Zoe still felt unable to meet her step-father, yet she needed to hear him accept responsibility if she was ever to appreciate that she was not in some way to blame. A video recording was made of Mr D assuring Zoe that the abuse was his fault and showing concern for her welfare. Zoe agreed to see the DVD and was supported by her therapist as she watched it. She was able to see her step-father's sincerity and was given further important evidence that she was not responsible for the abuse or the consequences of disclosure. It is important, however, that workers ensure in any sex offender–victim communication, such as showing a DVD or letter writing, that the perpetrator is not covertly threatening or blaming the child.

The next chapter looks at working with children, not so much in a family context, but in an unrelated group context.

Further resources

Hothersall, S. J. (2008) *Social work with children, young people and their families in Scotland*, 2nd edn. Exeter: Learning Matters.
  As the title suggest this book is directed towards those who work in Scotland. It would be useful not just for social workers but other

professionals working with children, and it has much to recommend it to all child care workers in the UK.

Lowenstein, L. (ed.) (2010) *Creative Family Therapy Techniques.* Toronto: Champion Press.
This is a delightfully eccentric book with wonderful ideas for family work. It describes a substantial range of creative activities and also outlines their purpose.

Further information about family group conferences can be obtained from the NSPCC: http://www.nspcc.org.uk/Inform/research/ questions/family_group_conferences_in_the_child_protection_ process_wda68725.html.

CHAPTER 6

Working with children in groups

CHAPTER OVERVIEW

This chapter looks at group work with children, examining:

- diversity and inclusion
- the benefits and problems of group work with abused children
- alternatives to standard group work including 'pairing', 'family groups' and the 'Bee Kind Garden' project
- group processes based on Tuckman's (1965) classic model
- planning and running groups for younger children and older children

Group work is a tried and tested method of enhancing the ability of people to function in a variety of settings. It has been used in recent years to help sexually abused children, and those who witness domestic violence or suffer a significant bereavement. Often these children are offered a place in a group *before* they show any symptoms of distress. An assumption is made that children who have been subjected to sexual abuse or witness domestic violence have had a potentially damaging experience warranting intervention. Group therapy is less readily used as a method of helping other abused children unless they have displayed developmental difficulties or behavioural signs of disturbance. Group work could usefully be used for all forms of abuse regardless of how far the children seem to be harmed by their experiences.

It is worth emphasising that children who have been subjected to different forms of abuse do not always benefit from being together in the same group. Members need to have enough in common to appreciate each other's experiences. In a mixed group the range of areas to be dealt with can become too broad for the group to be effective. Children who have been emotionally and physically neglected may have no problems over secrecy but may have to learn about playing with others, whereas those who were sexually abused will need to exchange ideas about appropriate touching, sexual behaviour, the keeping of secrets and ways they can be protected from sex offenders' advances. For many children who have suffered multiple abuses, therefore, it might be appropriate, for example, for individual work to help them with their experiences of sexual and physical abuse but be engaged in group work with other children who have witnessed domestic violence.

In selecting group members there are few hard and fast rules although it is necessary to avoid the inclusion of a very disruptive child or one who is not ready to cope in groups; a point made in the 1970s by McKnight (1972, p. 134) is still relevant today:

> One thing we have found as the result of hard experience is that it is unwise to include an extremely disturbed child in the group. The inclusion of such a child too early, and too quickly, leads to him becoming the immediate scapegoat, which can be harmful for the child and the group.

In their evaluation of two groups based in northern England schools, Parton and Manby (2009, p. 17) echo McKnight's words with their conclusion:

> that children with special needs and high anxiety levels could cause unmanageable disruption within the group. It was unrealistic to expect that involvement would resolve the problems of these children or of others, usually boys, whose behaviour was seriously disruptive.

Both sets of authors advise offering alternative, particularly individual, therapy for these troubled children.

Working with diversity

As with all other intervention, practitioners will be aware that children come from a range of different cultural and racial backgrounds and have different abilities and personalities. Therefore, anyone planning to run a group has to give consideration to group memberships and how far any group can meet the unique needs of each child.

Thought has to be given about including a child who seems very different from the rest of the group. One child using a wheelchair or with visual or hearing impairment will tend to be the focus of attention. Nevertheless children who are used to coping in other groups, as the only one with certain characteristics, will no doubt cope with the group; an example is that of a child with a visible disability who attends a mainstream school. A further point is that children with disabilities or other obvious 'differences' should not be denied services and therefore every attempt should be made to help them integrate into available groups.

Consideration has also to be given to the cultural mix of the group. Kadj Rouf (1991a) who was the only black child in her group recalls 'I would have felt happier if there had been more black girls in the Group'. Nevertheless, she appreciated the group and she has some suggestions for improving her experience, which could have been implemented even if no other black girls were included. Her first suggestion is that the group should address other cultures and religions and include representations of black people in materials used, such as books and films. Second, racist comments used by other group members need to be addressed. Third, the specific issues she had about her colour and culture needed to be acknowledged. This could have been done by asking all the members to share what particular personal problems they were encountering. For one child it might have been a mother's attempted suicide, for another it might be a court appearance as a witness and for Kadj (1991b) it would have been coping with the fact that her father was black leading to her desire to 'cut out the black part of me because it belonged to my dad'.

Mixing boys with girls is perfectly feasible but there will be some difficulties particularly with the seven-plus ages when boys begin to have a poor opinion of girls and vice versa. Consideration also has to be given to those cultural traditions that deem the mixing of sexes, particularly in adolescence, unacceptable. There may also be difficulties if there is only one girl in a group of several boys or vice versa.

Nevertheless, it is important that children are not denied a source of help simply because the ideal is not available. Research (Doyle, 1998) found that while black families received substantial material help, their children were less likely to receive help through individual counselling or group work. The concern is that they were not offered a service because there were no black counsellors or other black children in the groups. In Chapter 5, O'Shaughnessy et al. (2010) emphasised that in family group conferences they did not try to ensure the coordinator was an 'ethnic' match because in the UK ethnic diversity is extensive. In the real world the ideal is often not available; where this is the case, children should at least be given a choice of services and their cultural needs met through creative methods.

Benefits and problems

There are a number of benefits and pitfalls associated with group work.

The benefits

The six survivors in Chapter 2, Sarah, Lloyd, Marie, Roy, Josie and Jake, all recalled a pervading feeling of isolation. Mistreated children often feel they are the only ones to have experienced such treatment and there must be something wrong with them. By getting to know other children who have suffered similar experiences, they learn that others share their feelings. Participants sometimes admire a fellow group member such as the nine-year-old girl who felt that another girl in her group was very pretty. Through this she learnt that abuse does not necessarily make a child unattractive. So group work can assuage victims' feelings of isolation, of being abnormal, and unappealing.

Groups provide a means whereby positive messages are reinforced. This is particularly true for adolescents who are often influenced more by their peers than by adults. A teenage boy, told by a therapist that he is not to blame for the abuse, may take the attitude, 'You're paid to say that.' He might, however, be more easily convinced by a group of fellow adolescents all giving him the same message.

Glass (2010) also points out that for children who are living in neighbourhoods with gangs, or other problem community factions that have negative identities, a therapeutic group can give them an alternative, more positive, group identity.

Participants who have learnt new roles in individual therapy can practise these in the group. If, for example, they have always been a scapegoat they can try out new ways of ensuring that they do not unfairly take the blame for anything that goes wrong in the group. Generally, role-play between peers is more comfortable than between an adult and a child.

A further advantage of group work is that the children may feel that they are in a 'safer' environment than they are in individual therapy alone with an adult. This, especially for sexually abused children, avoids recreating the abusive scenario.

Humour is more likely to occur in a group setting than it is in individual or family work. Laughter is a good tonic and it can help children come to terms with negative experiences. Marie pointed to humour when asked what helped her survive her experiences. She explained that after incidents such as the destruction of the Christmas presents, her mother and siblings were able to laugh about their father's behaviour, reducing him to the status of a clown rather than an ogre.

Problems and pitfalls

The main problem for hard-pressed social workers hoping to establish a group is one of resources. Group work with children, as with adults, requires commitments of time, a suitable location, resources and transport. But, with children, there are additional considerations: how much should the carers know about their child's behaviour in the group, what to do with the people who bring them to the group, the need for a safe familiar adult nearby and the sheer mess and noise that is inevitable in most children's groups.

Ideally there is commitment by at least two therapists. They need to set aside time at regular intervals for the group sessions, as well as additional time for preparation and planning, review and recording. Parton and Manby (2009, p. 17) comment it 'is important not to underestimate the high level of skills required by group leaders'.

All participants have to be capable of handling the group situation. A young person must be able to relate to other children and share the leaders with others. Meanwhile the group leaders have to be capable of working with a number of children at once. They require skills in both direct work with abused children and in group therapy, and above all they need to be emotionally resilient. Commenting on her experiences of running groups for small children Eileen Vizard (1987, p. 19) writes:

> From the therapist's point of view, however, a lot of experience in doing this work does not protect one against a feeling of sickness when, for instance, as happened to myself and a new co-therapist recently, a 4-year-old girl turned to us in the middle of pinning on her name badge and said simply 'I was raped'.

The same room should be used on each occasion but, in many buildings, meeting rooms large enough for groups are at a premium. Unless other colleagues recognise the importance of the group, the workers may find that time and again their room is commandeered for a case conference or a training session.

Transport is sometimes a problem. In order to find enough children who have sufficient in common to make a viable group, members might have to be drawn from a fairly wide geographical area. Children cannot be expected to make their own way to meetings, yet sometimes their caretakers' ambivalence about the group means that they prove unreliable when it comes to bringing the children for sessions. It is however unsatisfactory if the group workers have to ferry the members themselves because they need to be free to devote all their time and energy to running the session itself.

When running children's groups, we find that caregivers are often very concerned about what is happening in the group and may put their child under pressure to give details. If they are overly suspicious of what is happening, they may attempt to persuade the child not to attend. Under such circumstances it is probably advisable to provide the carer with sketchy details, thereby satisfying curiosity without breaching the child's confidences. Bannister (2002) writing about group work with abused children noted, 'it cannot be emphasised too strongly that parents or carers should be carefully prepared for the group and also supported for its duration' (p. 494).

A major pitfall is the assumption that all problems can be helped through group work. This is not the case. A prime example is that of people suffering from eating disorders. Groups help people trying to lose weight, because the element of competition is a spur to greater efforts. Unfortunately, the same process can work in the same way with people suffering from anorexia nervosa. There is the danger that members will secretly compete to see who can lose the most weight. Anorexia nervosa can be linked to sexual abuse and the idea of a group for teenage girls, who have the experiences of sexual abuse and anorexia nervosa in common, is an inviting one. But, unless the group is run by someone with consummate skills it is more likely to compound the problem of weight loss rather than help it.

Messages from research

Wanlass et al. (2006)

This is a case study of one group for 8–12 girls who had been abused and were between the ages of 10 to14 years.

The authors give a vivid illustration of the issues facing group therapists especially because such therapists often have to cope with the dual challenges of being a group facilitator and child advocate. They explore how the therapists have to contain their own emotions and reactions while assisting the children to make sense of their experiences and work through their negative emotions. The group work can help to develop healthy and adaptive coping strategies.

However, the authors also point out that therapists can become the objects of transference and counter-transference. Although psychodynamic concepts tend to be dismissed by current social work trainers, anyone with experience of running groups for children who have been abused will know that being given meaningful roles by the members is a reality which needs to be understood and managed.

In the study, the authors identify several roles, the first being faced with children who take on the role of helpless victim and can make the therapist feel as helpless. They give the example of Becca who stated 'Oh, you can try to make me feel better, but I'm already ruined. Stains can't be washed out … get it?' (p. 319). Other transferences include the facilitator being viewed as an exploitive perpetrator exemplified by Cindy's' challenge to the therapist 'What's wrong with you? Do you get off on people's pain or something?' (p. 320). Then there is the silent partner, demonstrated by Lisa who refused to relate to the female therapist regarding her with the contempt she felt for her mother who she believed had stood by while she was victimised. Finally, there is the role of perfect parent encompassed by Mindy's comment 'I wish you were my mom. You would never let dad hurt me. I know you would take care of me. We kinda look alike, and sometimes I pretend that I am going to live with you' (p. 321).

As well as coping with these projections, group workers can also be advocates because as the authors explain 'therapists are the most likely party to hear about violations of court no-contact orders or retaliatory family events that threaten the child's safety' (p. 323). They may become aware of additional abuse to the group member or to other family members, which will require a review of the child protection plan. They add that therapists 'can facilitate communication between all parties trying to assist the abused child, including individual therapists, CPS caseworkers, and guardians *ad litem*'.

Comment: This paper serves as a very useful source of evidence and information about the benefits and pitfalls of working with children in groups.

Variations on the theme of group work

On occasions there are too few children with enough in common in one area to form a viable group. Furthermore, the problems outlined in the previous section may prove too daunting for professionals who might otherwise have used group therapy. There are two methods of intervention that provide many of the advantages of group work yet avoid some of the main problems. These are 'pairing' and 'family groups'.

Pairing

As its name implies 'pairing' refers to work with two children, who are not siblings but have much in common. Usually they will have already had some individual help. They reach a stage where they need to know for certain that other children are abused and consequently feel less isolated. They may also need to act out their experiences and practise strategies, both for avoiding the victim role and for asserting their right to be safe and properly cared for, which is more easily accomplished with a peer rather than an adult.

One abused child is invited to meet another one who has had similar experiences to him or herself. If one declines the invitation he or she is evidently not ready to cope with the situation and should not be pressurised into doing so. If both agree, the group can go ahead. Where the same person has provided individual work for both children he or she will probably continue as the group therapist. In cases where each child has had a different worker, a new therapist can be designated for the group work or, alternatively, the two original workers can become joint leaders.

Once the children are introduced and feel comfortable, they can be invited to draw up rules for the group. In individual work they may have each had different limits and expectations of themselves and the worker. For example, one child may have been used to entering and leaving the interview room at will whereas the other child may have felt it important to ask the worker's permission. In one group of two girls, aged seven and nine plus, one adult devised and wrote out a list which (with no apologies for the spelling) reads:

Rools of the group
no swaring
only leave the room if ask
no smoking
no breking toys
no hiting
no secrets

The last point about 'no secrets' required much discussion. The members had to draw a distinction between being honest with each other and yet having the right to some privacy. They also talked about not telling people outside the group what members had said. They agreed that if they really had to tell someone else about events in group sessions then they must discuss who they were telling and why with the other group members. This gave the worker the permission she needed to protect the children and their siblings in the event of their making further disclosures during group sessions. It also had the advantage of alerting the worker if at any stage either girl was placed under pressure by their caregivers to give an account of what was happening in the group.

In small groups, with only three or four members, the absence of a couple of participants will be keenly felt. However, in the case of pairing when one child cannot attend a session the leader can revert to giving the other an individual interview. As individual work should already be familiar, this is usually a relatively positive experience. There is, however, considerable difficulty if after a short while one child withdraws. The remaining member may feel that he or she has done something wrong, compounding the sense of rejection. It is therefore better to plan a limited number of meetings, perhaps two, to begin with. Assuming these are successful the leaders can suggest two further meetings, repeating this process until they sense that the members are so committed to the group that longer-term planning is feasible. Alternatively the leaders may feel that one child is reluctant to attend, in which case they can terminate the group in an ostensibly planned way.

Pairing is useful not only in alleviating the isolation of older children but also in helping younger children who have been physically or emotionally deprived and restricted. Some may have been so neglected or so inhibited by punitive parents that they have yet to learn to play, explore and experiment. Once they have learnt to play with toys and materials under the guidance of adults, the next big step is to play with other children. Pairing can bridge the gap between the comfortable but limited nature of individual play and the daunting prospect of being in a larger group.

Family groups

Work can be undertaken with a group of children from the same family where there are three or four children within an age range of about five years. Once these children feel fairly comfortable about their situation, they can be matched to a similar set of siblings. This results in a group of between six to eight children. It is difficult to assimilate three or four children from the same family into a group where all the other members are individuals rather than sibling groups. But in this way the two sets of children have a richer experience than they would otherwise have if they were only offered help in their own family group.

One advantage is that there is an almost ready-made group. There is little of the initial awkwardness associated with half-a-dozen strange children meeting one another for the first time. The time required for the usual preliminaries such as learning each other's names is cut by more than half. Another important advantage is that the children learn that theirs is not the only family with problems of abuse.

One possible drawback is that the two different families will remain separate and the group will not coalesce; however, in practice, this does not seem to happen. After a brief initial period new alliances are made which cut across the two families. Nevertheless, care has to be taken to ensure that the families are compatible and their structure suitable. It would probably not be appropriate, for example, to link a family with only one girl with another family with all boys, leaving the one girl without a female ally.

The Bee Kind Garden

The Bee Kind Garden based in Spokane in the USA is an example of a group project based in a natural and therapeutic environment. Children who have had experience of abuse attend in groups of about six to ten. They visit a natural garden space which has plants, flowers and a number of child-friendly animals. Trained volunteers support one or two children to relate to the animals, learning about and developing friendly, trusting relationships. The volunteers also help the children feel relaxed in a natural environment. In addition, once a week, children can have specific therapy from qualified therapists. There are also special sessions for parents who can learn about good-enough parenting.

The project was evaluated by Worsham and Goodvin (2007) although they were restricted to interviews with the adult volunteers and therapists rather than the children. Nevertheless, the project appeared to enhance the children's development of a sense of an autonomous self with an idea of some control over their lives, a capacity for exploration, and their formation of positive relationships with adults. In terms of Erikson's (1965) developmental theory, the Garden enhances the children's sense of trust, autonomy and initiative. The authors note that, according to Cowen's (1994) psychological wellness model, informants' descriptions indicated that time spent in the Garden enabled children to develop appropriate competencies and empowered them through encouraging control over their own activities.

The evaluators' two main concerns, which are ones shared by all proponents of group work, are first, that a simple time-limited scheme may not be able to undo all the damage to the child's relationships and functioning caused by the abuse and second, the possibility that children may experience loss at the conclusion of the relationship with their adult volunteer. However, the project does not claim to be the only type of therapy that is offered to the children and it also ensures that there are opportunities to cope with termination after each session and towards the end of each child's programme.

Group development

When working with any group, including those for children, the group will develop and progress through stages from the beginning 'getting to meet you' stage to the final parting. Despite my best efforts, I have been unable to find a better framework, and one which has greater resonance in reality, to describe group development than Tuckman's (1965) identification of four stages:

- 'forming', when the group first gathers together;
- 'storming', a testing of boundaries and sorting out of positions and roles;
- 'norming', when members explicitly or implicitly lay down basic ground rules;
- 'performing', the stage at which the group is able to work on then meet its aims and goals.

Each stage will be reached all the more smoothly, and the storming period minimised, if there is careful preliminary planning and preparation. Later, Tuckman and Jensen (1977) added 'adjourning' which is sometimes alternatively described in therapeutic groups as 'mourning' to refer to the ending phase. It is important to consider this stage as carefully as the other four in therapeutic group work if members are not to feel abandoned and rejected once the group ends or they have to leave the group.

Groups for younger children

There are many principles of groups that apply to all groups, whatever the age of the participants. These again are well documented in the standard works, such as Lindsay and Orton (2011), Benson (2010), Corey (2010) and Preston-Shoot (2007). This section will therefore examine areas specific to group work with young abused children.

Planning and preparation

When working with individual children, I tend to have about three bags of assorted toys, books and other play material then let the children choose from whatever is in the bags, because they have a remarkable ability to choose suitable media to work through their own problems with a little guidance and reassurance. However, with groups there needs to be rather more preparation and organisation because otherwise the result is simply a number of individuals in a room together rather than a group. While control needs to be by a light touch, it is useful to have planned materials and activities.

The main feature of group work with young children is that it will certainly be noisy and probably messy. Because of this, the room for meetings has to be chosen with care. It is likely that such a group will run during the day, rather than in the evening. This means that either the room has to be soundproof or well away from other people who are trying to work – unless you have remarkably tolerant colleagues. The room should be fairly easy to clean, while time has to be allowed for clearing up any mess. Access has to be considered, to both the group room and other facilities such as toilets, for people using wheelchairs or unable climb stairs.

While adult groups may need little more than a suitable room, chairs, maybe a table, pens and paper, children will require more materials. Toys, paints, modelling clay, a mirror and dressing-up clothes are all likely to be used. As with individual work, toys and materials that are not for use in a session should be kept out of sight, otherwise they can become an irresistible distraction.

The optimum size is probably about six children, although two adults may cope with as many as eight. Usually it is necessary to have two adults present especially if the children need accompanying to the toilet. One male and one female leader is preferable. Members who have been abused by, say, their mother will learn through the female worker that women can be kind and caring, while if they have been protected to some extent by their father they may be reassured by the presence in the group of a male helper. The two leaders represent a mother and a father figure and, for children with two opposite sex parents, this may be the first time that they experience this combination of adults communicating and showing respect for each other without either shouting or physical violence.

In groups with small children the leaders should be directive, ensuring that the sessions do not run out of control and taking the burden of decision making away from the children. McKnight (1972, p. 136) writes of her early experience of leading children's groups:

> My first lesson was in direct connection with my role. My experiences hitherto had been of discussion groups with a self-effacing sort of leader who was almost one of the group. The children, in fact, taught me that this was impossible in our setting and moreover it was not what they wanted.

Nevertheless, the children should be included in some decision making, for example they may express a preference for refreshments at the beginning of the session rather than halfway through, or they may be consulted about introducing a new member to the group.

Access to a group work consultant is advisable because young children's groups are fairly boisterous and it is easy for the adults to be distracted from the main issues by particularly demanding or difficult behaviour on the part of one or two members. The consultant needs to be knowledgeable about group dynamics, play work, child abuse and normal child development. The leaders should also be supervised, possibly by the consultant but preferably by a separate supervisor who will negotiate boundaries of responsibility with the consultant.

Other arrangements to be sorted out before sessions begin are transport, refreshments, recording, and timing. An additional issue is the decision over whether or not the group is a closed one or whether it will accept new members. Similarly leaders have to decide whether it will be an open-ended group or, if not, how many sessions will be held. For small children, a closed group with a fairly limited number of sessions is generally most appropriate.

Another important aspect of planning is liaison and confidentiality. Children attending the group should have their own individual worker who will help with practical arrangements and may be providing a child with individual therapy. Depending on the circumstances, the worker might be given full details of the child's progress or, on the other hand, may only be told that the child attended the session. Evidently if during a group session the child discloses something that indicates that he or any other person is in danger then the leaders must ensure that a protective agency is informed.

One feature of small children's groups is that there is likely to be an informal group of parents, caregivers or social workers waiting in a nearby room. This occurs because the children are too young to bring themselves to sessions and because they have a right to have a reassuring familiar adult to hand in the event of their becoming distressed. If the needs of this informal group of carers are overlooked they may well sabotage the efforts of the leaders by becoming noisy or demanding their attention before and after sessions. Vizard (1987, p. 18) solved this problem by evolving:

> the practice of having the little children's group and the caretakers group amalgamate for part of the last session, in order to sit down together and watch extracts from the video of the children during the preceding five weeks. This has turned out to be a great success and very popular.

Finally there is nothing more daunting or confusing for a small child than to find that having been prepared for a group experience he or she is sitting alone with a couple of equally bewildered group leaders. It is important to ensure that attendances are confirmed and that at least three or four children arrive together to attend the first session.

The first session

With young children the first group session is of crucial importance. Older participants, who dislike the first meeting, may be persuaded to return in the hopes of matters improving. Small children who do not enjoy themselves on the first occasion often resist any attempts to involve them in subsequent meetings.

It is helpful to familiarise children with the physical surroundings first. They will need to know the whereabouts of the toilet and how to reach their parent/familiar adult if they become distressed. They will also want to play with any toys present.

Once members have satisfied their curiosity about their surroundings they can be properly introduced to the grown-ups and other children in the group. Sometimes name labels are used. Various games can help children learn each other's names. One example is to have several funny hats which children put on each other's heads. The recipient of the hat says, 'Thank you, I'm Kyle' (or whatever their name is). Once the members know each other's names they can practise by saying 'Here you are, Kyle' when they put a hat on someone's head. Another idea is a game of catch, where a participant throws a ball of socks or bean bag to another child whose name the thrower remembers and calls out. The leaders will join in these games to ensure that no child is embarrassed due to possessing 'butter fingers', a poor memory or a forgettable name.

The next important part of the first session involves devising a set of group rules and some sharing of why the children are attending. The members need to know what they can expect of the group and what the group expects of them. The children should help in the task of formulating the rules and, as illustrated by the list given by the pair group, they may enjoy the inclusion of a few 'adult' rules such as 'no smoking'.

Suggested activities

The activities of the group will depend largely on its objectives. A group for neglected, understimulated children may start by encouraging children to explore different play materials such as sand, water, clay and finger paints. It will then move on to activities which require a joint effort such as a group collage or building a structure together. For these children having a meal together, sitting at a table using cutlery and saying 'Please' and 'Thank you' may be important learning experiences.

A group for those who have been subjected to physical violence will focus on helping them recognise that they should not feel guilty and ashamed. They can be invited to dress up and act out famous stories of children who have been mistreated. They can role-play self-protective behaviours. They may also need to act out angry, violent emotions, through destructive games, mock fights and throwing cushions or bean bags at hated objects. Eventually through cooperative, construction games, or a group collage perhaps, they can be shown how much more can be achieved by peaceful means.

Groups for sexual abuse survivors will need to provide outlets for angry feelings. Furthermore, their members may be very bewildered about what has happened to them because unlike physical abuse and neglect victims, there are few fairy-tales or stories about sexually abused children with whom they can identify. They may need some simple sex education in order to make sense of their experiences. But first they will need to share a vocabulary in order to communicate their experiences. In an early session the members can be encouraged to shout out their own name for the private parts of their body. They learn by this means that everybody uses 'rude' words. The exercise also gives them access to a wide range of terms to describe what has happened to them.

Abused children, whatever the nature of the mistreatment, share many negative feelings. They all have to learn to develop trust and there are games which help in this endeavour. In one game, members close their eyes and allow themselves to fall backwards in order to be caught by other group members. In the case of small children who have limitations of strength and coordination it will be advisable for the adults to take the role of catcher; dropping your partner defeats the object of the exercise!

Activities suggested in the section on individual work can be adapted to group sessions. One example, already described (see Chapter 4, p. 94), involves sketching expressions on blank faces; the children are then asked to share their drawings and say what makes them feel sad, happy, angry, ashamed or afraid. Finally, as Piaget's theories demonstrate, young children do not appreciate abstract concepts so all ideas have to be illustrated in concrete form by the use of dolls, puppets, drawings, stories and games.

Point for reflection

Cast your mind back, hopefully not too far, to a time when you joined a new group, maybe when you started a new job or training course, or became a new member of a sporting or interest club. Can you remember how you felt? Was there enthusiasm tinged with apprehension? Were you 'at home' immediately or were you made to feel as if you were in alien territory? Can you identify the factors that helped you feel more comfortable or any that caused discomfort? How important was the physical environment, or was the attitude of other people in the group more significant?

Comment: Here the purpose is to encourage you to empathise with children and adults joining a new group. Reflecting on your own experience may help you understand what makes people more or less comfortable when joining a group. This insight can be transferred to therapeutic practice. However, you need also to bear in mind that the personality and background of the individual, and circumstances causing them to join the group, will also influence their initial experience and maybe result in their experience being very different from yours.

Groups for older children and teenagers

Much of the previous section on groups for younger children will also apply to those for older ones. For example, the optimum size will still be six to eight, plus leaders (although there have been a number of successful groups with only three or four members and up to twelve). This section will therefore simply highlight some of the important features of group work with older abused children.

Planning and preparation

Older children, who have been abused for some time, will have had longer than little children to develop a mistrust of adults, longer to adapt to the victim role and longer to harbour feelings of anger, worthlessness and fear. There is likely to be considerable testing of the trustworthiness of the leaders and of the group boundaries. It is essential to have two leaders, one of whom should be experienced in group work and both of whom must be emotionally resilient. It is also essential that both workers are supervised and well supported, with both supervisor and group consultant available to give assistance.

It is again helpful to have a therapist of each sex, to present a model of adult men and women working harmoniously together and to provide an outlet for the members' feelings about women/mothers and men/fathers. When helping sexually abused girls, the male worker is likely to be subjected to periods of severe testing. In one group of four teenage girls, the male leader had to cope with cushions thrown at him, questions about his sexual prowess and 'accusations' of homosexuality when he did not respond to their sexual invitations. In another group, 'The girls were often very angry with the male therapist and expressed suspicion about his motives in running the group' (Furniss *et al.*, 1988, p. 102).

Teenagers can be shy and self-conscious. It will be difficult for them to pluck up the courage to attend the initial meeting by themselves. It may be helpful for them to come to a couple of preliminary meetings accompanied by their social worker who will stay for the first few informal gatherings. Alternatively, members can meet each other in pairs on a casual basis prior to the initial group session so that when they do arrive for the first meeting they feel they are coming with a 'friend'.

The first session

Older children, in contrast to younger ones, are likely to show more interest in their fellow group members than in their physical surroundings, although soon after their arrival they will need to know where they can put their coats and go to the toilet. But they will be curious about the other participants' names and experiences.

One useful exercise involves finding out the meanings of members' given names. This helps them to learn both each other's names and also something about themselves. It can be enhancing for a David to learn that his name means 'beloved', Kumar to hear he is a 'prince', Sanjula to discover she is 'beautiful' or Tammy to find out that she is 'perfection'. Those with unusual or less popular names may well be encouraged to learn that it has a pleasant meaning such as Beatrice being 'bringer of joy' or Cyril 'lordly'. The leaders will, however, need to ensure that they do not cause distress to those whose names have less desirable connotations such as Doreen 'sullen', Elvis 'old noise' or Cameron 'crooked nose'.

Suggested activities

Again activities will depend on the objectives of the group. A group for physically abused, violent, teenage boys may concentrate on playing snooker without coming to blows or learning to trust adults, their companions and their own abilities through an activity such as rock climbing or sailing.

Unless the objective of the group is purely social or narrowly task-focused on an issue unrelated to abuse, members should be helped to find a way to share their experiences. They can be invited to choose how to talk about the abuse to which they were subjected. They may decide to face the wall or window or try to give an account following the rules of a game like 'Just A Minute' – without repetition, hesitation or deviation.

Activities with paints, pens and paper prove useful and popular. A group collage or painting helps participants to express their feelings about themselves and the group without being alone in the spotlight. It also assists in the process of group cohesion. Discussion can be encouraged through paintings and drawings that are then described to other group members.

One suggestion is for the children to make boxes into which they put meaningful items. Memory boxes are familiar when working with children who have been bereaved. Similarly, in a group they ran for looked-after children, Coholic *et al.* (2009, p. 35) observed:

> in one group the children were all very interested in the cartoon 'Pokemon' in which the characters have special powers. Thus, the children created their own 'power boxes', and group discussion focused on what they could place in their box to help them feel more powerful, and what takes their power away.

Filling in a questionnaire is another activity that can help spark off discussions and often holds an attraction for adolescents. The objective of much group work is a change of attitudes, especially self-denigrating ones. The use of a questionnaire at one of the earliest sessions and again at the last provides a means of evaluating the effectiveness of the group and gives members an insight into their own progress.

Some of the activities, such as role-play, suggested in the section on individual work (see Chapter 4) and on groups for younger children (see above, p. 145) can prove useful in groups for older ones. This includes play and games. So many abused teenagers will have lost the opportunity to play in a happy, carefree environment. Some of the joy of being an irresponsible child can be recaptured by hold-ing the meetings in rooms with toys available or arranging parties and outings to perhaps fairs or children's films. The members should, however, have a choice in such activities because adoles-cents may well resent being treated in a juvenile fashion when they are aspiring towards adulthood.

One suggestion that will probably suit older children, although it could be used with younger ones, is to ask them to be 'advisers'. Malekoff (2008) gave the example of children whose fathers had been killed in the Twin Towers 9/11 disaster. The group was asked to advise bereavement counsellors about their experiences, what advice they would give to counsellors and what in their opinion helped them. As Malekoff (2008, p. 42) comments, 'Exercising what one has to offer is one part of what true empowerment is about.'

Putting it into practice

Think back to the children's accounts in Chapter 2 of Marie, Roy, Lloyd, Sarah, Josie and Jake. Reflecting on the content of this chapter, determine how group work would have benefited them, assuming the abuse had been discovered during their childhood. What could they have offered each other had they been in a group together?

Now, consider one of your own cases, whether from work or placement. Assuming the child or children identified in your own case have not joined in group work, could they benefit from joining in a group and what might be the possible pitfalls?

Comment: the aim of this exercise is to help you to think of the value of group work by applying the ideas to actual cases. You may find that you can identify benefits of group work but can you also identify pitfalls? For example, the children who witnessed domestic violence by their father against their mother, Roy, Marie and Sarah, may well have difficulty empathising with Lloyd, Josie and Jake, whose father was not abusive to their mother.

Harnessing modern technologies

The use of digital video cameras has proved very successful with groups. Young people in particular, despite some shyness, are eager for feedback on the way they look and behave. Re-playing a DVD film of part of a session provides uncritical, objective feedback. The members may at first express some reluctance to be filmed in which case persuasion can be tried, but a camera should not be used without the group's ultimate agreement. It is also important to clarify the legal situation and issues of disposal of the tapes or DVDs. There is the risk that if a member gives significant information to the group, which is recorded on film or digitally, there could be demands for this to be shown in court in subsequent care or criminal proceedings.

There is also the possibility of harnessing modern technology to help abused children who live in remote locations, or whose disabilities make transport to a group difficult or, for whatever reason, cannot engage in a face-to-face therapeutic group. The possibility of setting up forums or video teleconferencing could be considered. Morland *et al.* (2011) evaluated its use with six military veterans compared to seven who had direct therapy. They were living in dispersed Hawaiian islands and were suffering from post-traumatic stress disorder. The evidence was that both cohorts, including those receiving video teleconferencing, had marked improvements at the end of treatment.

This chapter and the preceding two all examined ways of working directly with children in different contexts. The next chapter explores, from the child's perspective, another intervention, although perhaps a less direct strategy: this is the provision of substitute care, in the shorter or longer term.

Further resources

Geldard, K. and Geldard, D. (2007) *Counselling Children: A Practical Introduction*, 3rd edn. London: Sage.

Geldard, K. and Geldard, D. (2001) *Working with Children in Groups*. Houndsmills, Basingstoke: Palgrave Macmillan.
The first of these books is written with the individual child–counsellor relationship in mind but the authors address group issues and many of their ideas are particularly useful when planning to run a children's group. The second book is less up-to-date but is still full of useful guidance about group work with children.

Glass, S. D. (2010) *The Practical Handbook of Group Counselling: Group Work with Children, Adolescents and Parents.* Bloomington: Trafford Publishing.

Although not specifically about child maltreatment and set in the context of North America, this is nevertheless full of guidance and suggestions for group work with children and young people which would be useful for practitioners in the UK and beyond.

Westergaard, J. (2009). *Effective Group Work with Young People.* Buckingham: Open University Press.

This focuses on young people but not necessarily those who have been abused. Rather it concentrates on personal learning and development for young people in schools in groups run by youth workers. There are however lively suggestions which would assist those running groups for abused and looked-after children.

CHAPTER 7

Perspectives of children in substitute care

CHAPTER OVERVIEW
This chapter explores substitute care, primarily from the perspective of abused children rather than that of parents, carers or practitioners. Topics covered are:

- working with diversity
- the impact of dogmas on children
- the challenges and benefits, including grief and loss, attachments, siblings, barriers to inclusion and the promotion of resilience
- strategies to help children in substitute care, including issues surrounding returning home and the benefits of kinship care

Individual, family and group work might not be available or appropriate for some abused children and insufficient for others. There still remain at least two possibilities in the stock of strategies available to those attempting to help abused children. The first is the provision of substitute care, whether temporarily during a crisis or permanently when the physical or emotional risks in the parental home are insurmountable. The second strategy is to use social support to help develop greater resilience and augment the child's sense of well-being which is explored in the next chapter.

When children die at the hands of their parents, questions are raised such as 'Why wasn't he taken to somewhere safe?' or 'Why was she allowed to go home?' The solution to child abuse seems so simple – children must be rescued from abusive parents and placed with carers who will not harm them. Unfortunately the answer is not so easy.

This chapter looks at substitute care, mostly from the child's perspective, with the term 'substitute care' covering the full range of parental alternatives, from short-term foster or residential care or boarding school to adoption. It appears that, at least in relation to temporary fostering, often the 'process appears unchild-centred, involving little preparation of the child' (Waterhouse and Brocklesby, 2001, p. 45). For this reason this chapter will not look at policy but at processes and the direct impacts of substitute care on children.

Nothing in this chapter will be unfamiliar to specialist home-finding staff. The aim is to help non-specialist workers to understand some of the issues with which children wrestle when being placed away from home. It does not aim to cover all aspects of substitute care; there are already comprehensive works on the topic, notably Sellick *et al.* (2004), Luckock and Lefevre (2008), Cocker and Allain (2008), Fahlberg (2008) and Thomas and Philpot (2009). It does not, for example, address issues, albeit vitally important ones, such as the selection, training and support for adoptive parents, foster carers and residential staff.

Working with diversity

The role of 'socio-genealogical connectedness' is persuasively outlined by Owusu-Bempah (2006, p. 114). By this he means children's sense of being an 'offshoot' of their parents' biological and social background. Always important as a facet of child development, this has particular pertinence for looked-after children. An earlier groping towards this, meant that in the 1980s there was a tendency to label children 'black' or 'white' and place them with foster carers who were similarly labelled 'black' or 'white'. My toes curled as, Bernadette, a teenager from a white Irish traveller family, was removed from her supportive residential setting, where she had settled, to an African–Caribbean foster carer, on the basis that Bernadette was from an ethnic minority therefore she was labelled 'black'. The foster carer herself was very good but the placement was deliberately undertaken with the explicit idea that it was meeting Bernadette's cultural identity, which as I continued to work with Bernadette, became obvious it did not.

Nowadays there is more awareness of the issues for dual- and multiple-heritage children and for white minorities. Owusu-Bempah (2006) explains that there is a need to enhance the child's connectedness and a sense of continuity by a child's having information about the absent parents.

There is insufficient space to discuss in detail the important issue of same-race versus trans-racial placements; Zeitlin (2002) among others provides a discerning discussion of this. There are however three important principles in such placements: continuity, sensitivity to issues of identity and respecting children's preferences.

- *Continuity*: when children are moved from their home, and therefore in a situation of loss and grieving, it is important to maintain as much that is familiar and loved as possible. There are obvious advantages of a child being placed in a home that maintains the same cultural and religious practices and patterns of daily life. This is particularly true of refugee and asylum seeking children who 'having fled a hostile country and sought sanctuary, can feel socially and psychologically bereft' (Berridge, 2001, p. 171).

- *Sensitivity to issues of identity*: there needs to be genuine sensitivity to the child's 'religious persuasion, racial origin and cultural and linguistic background' (*Children Act 1989* s.22. 5c). Substitute carers and social workers need to be responsive to the children's concerns about racism, discrimination and their cultural heritage (Banks, 2002), while not assuming that all (and only) black children have a negative self-identity (see Owusu-Bempah, 1994, 2006). Children are not simply 'black' or 'white' and particular care is required when placing dual- or multi-heritage children and those from white minorities. My own practice experience of Bernadette, portrayed above, is echoed in the literature. For example Lau (1991, pp. 110–11) described how 'an adolescent girl of mixed UK white–Hong Kong Chinese parentage' was placed in care, classified as black and consequently given an African–Caribbean social worker and foster carer with no provision to maintain her links with the Chinese community or language. Waterhouse and Brocklesby (2001, p. 42) also confirm this blinkered perspective on placing dual-heritage children: 'None of the six mixed-heritage children in the sample were placed in a foster home that reflected their particular ethnic origin – although significantly only those children placed with white carers were described as inappropriate matches'. Meanwhile one of the Jamaican origin carers in their study commented, 'Culture is ignored while the colour of the skin is a primary factor. For example, I had a Chinese child and I was ill equipped to meet his cultural needs'.

- *Respecting children's preferences*: where a trans-racial or residential placement is the only option, children's preferences in terms of diet, dress, grooming, entertainment and other activities should be met.

> ### Practice focus
>
> #### Sanjula
>
> Sanjula is a young woman with substantial learning disabilities and the only Asian person in her residential home. Her social worker visited her at the residence and found she was always wearing a tracksuit despite invariably wearing a sari when she stayed for long weekends at her parents' home. The worker asked Sanjula if she liked wearing a sari. She did but was not allowed to do so in the residential home. When the social worker raised the matter with the staff, they explained that Sanjula could not dress herself and no one else knew how to tie a sari. It seems that no one had thought to find out how to do so or to find someone who could.

Addressing diversity can also include children with disabilities. Substitute care is arguably more of an issue for children with disabilities than any other group of young people. They may experience substitute care in similar ways to all children who have a care experience but also at one extreme have long stays in specialist residential settings and on the other have respite or 'short break' care where there is an emphasis 'equally on the disabled child and the family receiving the break' (Cramer and Carlin, 2008, p. 1068).

The voice and perspectives of maltreated children with disabilities in substitute care are therefore important, although they do not come through strongly in the literature. Moreover, children with disabilities are not a homogeneous group, they are richly diverse. Lewis and Porter (2006, p. 225) researching the voices of children with disabilities and special educational needs asks how 'do we move from hearing individual children's views, to helping children to present a collective "choir" which always, and routinely, includes those with disabilities and difficulties?' I could describe particular issues for some of the children with disabilities in care with whom I have worked but the children themselves are diverse, their disabilities are also varied and their care situations differ widely. This means any general guidance may be completely inappropriate for some children and therefore provision has, as far as possible, to be customised to an individual child's specific needs.

Dogma into practice

One area where dogma appears to have imposed policies indiscriminately on children is that of substitute care. The pendulum has swung between the need to divest children of links with their families of origin to reverence for the blood-tie and back, again and again. Somehow the voice and perspectives of the children seem to have been lost as policy makers and practitioners appear to rigidly impose one set of beliefs, then swing to the alternative.

The fresh-start ideology

Pat Bastian (1994) joined a Children's Department in January 1955. Looking back forty years later she recalled 'All of us subscribed to ... the "fresh start" theory where children could be divested of their previous identity and given a new (and better) one' (p. 70). During the early twentieth century many children came into care because of illegitimacy or extreme poverty. Poor working class families were of often deemed 'unfit' and this unfitness as well as illegitimacy were both a major disgrace. The advocates of the fresh-start idea were well-intentioned and in some ways anticipated later theorists who highlighted the insidious nature of negative 'labelling'. On coming into care, children were divested of labels 'illegitimate' or 'indigent' and took on a new identity as a member of a new 'respectable' family.

This policy persisted for nearly a hundred years. It was not until the 1970s that there was a perceptible change. Then Hitchman (1960) in her book *King of the Barbareens* described how her many moves in care and attempts to give her a 'fresh start' each time had led to her life-long search to establish her identity. Bastian (1994, p. 72) recalled:

> The revelation came to me, as it did to many others, as a blindingly obvious fact ... The children who could not cope with life in whatever setting were those who did not understand who they were, why they were there and what was happening to them.

The pendulum swings: reverence for the 'blood-tie'

The 1939–45 Second World War saw the massive disruption of families throughout Europe. After the war, there was a desperate search by refugees and concentration camp survivors for blood relatives and family members. Meanwhile, the UK was reeling from the upset caused by evacuating children out of cities and from reports of the death of Dennis O'Neil who, on 9 January 1945, 'was beaten to death by his foster-father in a lonely farmhouse in Shropshire ... At the time of his death Dennis, whose stomach showed no traces of food, weighed just over 4 stone at thirteen years of age.' (O'Neill, 1981, pp. ix–xi). Then six years later came Bowlby's work on maternal deprivation and the importance of attachment to one mother figure. All these events led to an emphasis on the importance of the blood relationship and for children to remain with their birth mother, if at all feasible. The 1948 Children Act set up in the wake of the death of Dennis O'Neill stressed the importance of returning children wherever possible to their natural parents.

The pendulum swings back: rejecting the 'blood-tie'

On the 6 January 1973 another child, Maria Colwell, was killed. She was eight years old. Echoing the case of Dennis, she was 'beaten to death by her step-father in a council house in Brighton ... At the time of her death, Maria, whose stomach was empty, weighed a mere 36 pounds' (O'Neill, 1981, pp. ix–xi). She had been happily settled for nearly all her childhood with her aunt and uncle who fostered her. Then her birth mother demanded her return. With her new partner, she systematically abused and eventually killed her. The blood-tie with the natural mother prevailed over all other considerations. A report by the local authority, in whose care Maria had been, reflected after her death:

> 'The blood tie' is a term often applied to the belief held strongly by many people that there is a strong physical tie between a child and his parent by virtue of his physical inheritance and the fact of conception and child-bearing. (East Sussex County Council, 1975, p. 87)

The pendulum swinging back?

There have been some less dramatic swings in recent years between the two opposed perspectives. Concerns over revelations of abuse in care (see Biehal and Parry, 2010) have led to a belief in the need to keep children in their birth families. However, after the death of Peter Connelly (Laming, 2009) concerns about keeping children with abusive parents too long were again raised.

Messages from research

Hammond and Cooper (2011)

In-depth, individual case studies can give precious insights especially into social issues. The research by Hammond and Cooper (2011) is no exception. They undertook three interviews with 'Milly' who had herself been in care and had subsequently become a residential social worker. Milly's reflections and the themes emerging were as a result of a reflective dialogue between Milly as co-researcher and the two authors.

Milly's accounts provided the perspective of both looked-after child and service provider. She was able to compare 'then and now'. Some of her observations have worrying implications for the present UK care systems.

One of her first observations was that the residential experience is more restrictive and institutionalised nowadays. The authors speculate that this is probably due to strict safeguarding legislation and precautions. She expressed concern about the lack of preparedness of residential staff, which led to high staff turnover which, in turn, means 'affinity and subsequent trust between the young person and member of staff is lost' (p. 242) to the detriment of looked-after children.

The dilemmas and challenges of substitute care

Finding an appropriate and stable placement is far from easy but attachment theory has helped workers appreciate the damaging nature of frequent changes of carer. Phil Quinn, in his autobiographical account of 'Peter' whose single mother became seriously ill, wrote:

> So began the progression of foster homes for Peter, usually at two- or three-month intervals. He lived in several different foster homes during the two-year period following the break-up of his family... Each move became more painful than the last because each convinced the boy that no one loved him or wanted him. (Quinn, 1988, p. 47)

Point for reflection

Imagine that your home is about to be engulfed by fire or flood. All the other residents have escaped or have been rescued so there are no other people in the home. Now in escaping, apart from people, what else would you rescue and want with you. Think of three things you would try to collect up to take with you?

What did you chose. Was it the large obvious things or small objects of sentimental value? Would other people have known what the important things were to you? Was it your pet? The hamster, cat, dog, budgie? It might have been photographs of your loved ones or maybe one that reminds you of a wonderful time you had.

Comment: The reason for this exercise is to think about things that a child who has been abused might have treasured such as a picture with a star for achievement from a favourite teacher or a small toy given by 'gran' just before she died. How often when we take children into care do we ask them to make sure that they have everything they treasure, and then ensure these treasures are looked after? And what about the things they cannot take with them such as family pets or photographs that belong to other family members or large objects that cannot be easily carried? Children when they come into care lose so much and it is not just what is obvious to the adults around them.

Putting it into practice

You might be able to talk to a young person or child in your work or placement. If this is not possible try to talk, with the parents' permission, to a child that you know outside the work situation.

Draw a circle with the child in the middle and then around the child an inner circle and an outer circle. On your own, put anything and everybody that you think might be important to the child in either the inner or outer circle, depending on the degree of importance you think they are to the child. You will not show this diagram to the child, this is just for your own reflection.

Show the child a version of the diagram circle that is not filled in. Now ask the child to think of everything that is important to him or her. You might need to help the child's imagination by using a story such as a modern Ark, magic carpet or similar in or on which everything the child really treasures can be placed. Again the really important things/people are put in the inner circle and the less important ones in the outer circle.

Compare your original diagram with the child's. Are they different? Are there any things or people which you would never have imagined that child would treasure? If you were taking the child into care would he or she have had to leave some of the people/things behind and would you have known how poignant a loss that would have been?

Loss, grief and mourning

In Chapter 2, the loss and grief of abused children, whether or not they remained at home, was highlighted. When children are removed into care, at least in the early stages, their feelings of loss will be compounded. This is often not just the loss of parents, important though they are. Parker (2010) explains how profound that loss of contact with siblings and peers can be. Writing of the looked-after children she interviewed, Parker noted the grief caused by 'loss of friendships which occur as a result of placement or school moves' (p. 13) as well as separation from siblings. This can in turn lead to a loss of identity. As the reflective exercise shows there may be other significant losses of which the adults around the child have little understanding.

Attachments to 'home' and family

The loyalty and attachment many abused children show towards their parents can be explained by reference to both the Stockholm syndrome and to attachment theory. As Bowlby (1969, p. 80) observed:

> efforts to 'save' a child from his bad surroundings and to give him new standards are commonly of no avail since it is his own parents who, for good or ill, he values and with whom he is identified.

Many abused children do not want to leave their home; they simply want the abuse to stop and to be loved by their parents. Sarah, it will be recalled, did not see boarding school as an escape. Instead she looked forward to each holiday, hoping that 'this time it will be all right'. Children have a strong need to belong to their original family and many live, ever-hopeful of 'deserving' their parents' love.

Furthermore, many people in difficult situations often worry about the unknown and prefer the 'devil they know'. Both Marie and Sarah recalled being able to anticipate their father's behaviour and 'keep one step ahead of him'. Abused children will often be very fearful of an unknown new situation and will expect mistreatment and rejection. Sarah still maintains that she would not have wished to be taken into care because the task of fitting into a new family with its different mores and ways of interacting would have been too difficult for her.

Once in care, children may continue to worry about the rest of the family. Marie stated that she would have resisted being taken into care because she would have been too concerned about her mother and siblings.

Siblings

Only occasionally can more than two siblings be placed together in the same foster home, yet attachments to brothers and sisters can be stronger than those to parents. Phil Quinn (1988, p. 45) again describes, through his pseudonym Peter, his feelings when he realised he and his brothers were to be placed in separate foster homes:

> Then came the day the welfare workers arrived to take the boys to the [separate] foster homes arranged for them. Without hesitation or resistance Peter had gone with Mr White, not knowing that he was being separated from his brothers … It was not until the car began pulling away from the curb that Peter realised what was happening. Like an animal caged for the first time, he was suddenly on all fours searching out his brothers through the rear window of the car. Clawing desperately, he tore at the door trying to get out.

Serious consideration should be given to trying to recruit substitute carers who are willing to take a group of siblings. Research, some as early as 1987 by Berridge and Cleaver, indicated that foster placements are less likely to break down if siblings are placed together. Dunn's (1995, p. 345) research led her to the conclusion that 'in the face of negative life events … most siblings grew closer together and provided real support for one another'. Parker (2010) in an extensive study has highlighted the importance of siblings and peer friendships, which children can lose when then are taken into care.

Conger *et al.* (2009) have identified some of the concerns around placing the children together. These include one of the children continuing with the caring, protective role and therefore missing out on childhood. Another worry is that children may band together and not integrate with the foster carers' family. Nevertheless, Conger *et al.* (2009) conclude that the consensus of research to date is that siblings can be important attachment figures and children benefit from being placed together, especially as this mitigates against the loss of removal from home.

One perhaps over-looked group of children are foster siblings. These may be the birth or adopted children of foster carers. However, many people who foster will have more than one child and therefore there can be several unrelated foster children in the home. Bailey (2010, p. 9) highlighted this:

> Foster siblings played a significant role for many young people, and they elicited much affection, such as for Mia, whose foster sibling would shortly be returning to his birth family, and with whom she would have no further contact: 'he's important to me and I'll miss him when he goes'.

Barriers to inclusion

Few children wish to be seen as 'different' especially if this difference has negative connotations, yet there are day-to-day barriers to making 'care' an overtly positive experience and ensuring looked-after or adopted children are not excluded. First, children removed from their birth families tend to be burdened with a negative self-concept. Reviewing contemporary available literature Oswald *et al.* (2010, p. 469) concluded many foster children have 'experienced multiple forms of persistent maltreatment, often during their early development', while as early as the 1950s, Littner (1956) found that foster children often believed it was because they were bad that they had been 'rejected' by their family. Meanwhile, the involvement of the police and the use of formal legal processes and the courts, although necessary, all serve to enhance an abused child's sense that it is their misconduct that is to blame for everything that happens to them.

Foster children in particular can often find themselves singled out for different treatment.

Practice focus

Flint

Flint is eight and he has just been placed with a foster carer, Rosemary. She is a single-parent whose birth sons are now in their mid- to late-teens. Rosemary commented that she had had to get rid of the trampoline her sons had so enjoyed because it was an old one and could not be fitted with an enclosure. As a foster-child, she was told by the Local Authority, Flint could only play on trampolines with safety enclosures.

As a foster-child, Flint cannot be treated like the other local children who happily play on assorted unenclosed, rusty trampolines whose parents cheerfully take the view if their children fall off once 'they'll learn'. Additional consideration for Flint's safety is understandable because being entrusted with someone else's child requires extra care. I recall pondering life's ironies when, early in my career, long before child seats and seat belts were thought of, I was charged with taking five children aged one to six years from their home to foster carers because they were deemed neglected and at risk from hazards like unguarded fires. The six-year-old was perched on the front seat clutching her baby brother; the three others were unrestrained in the back. There was I, an inexperienced driver in an unstable heap of a car, conveying them a considerable distance along dangerous roads in dreadful weather. Matters have quite rightly improved but hopefully not so much that children in substitute care are over-protected and excluded.

Children's negative responses in care

When taken into care, children will have their own way of adapting to family or residential situations. Some may behave as well as possible, still hoping that by 'being good' they may win a little of their carers' love. Phil Quinn (1988, p. 126) using his pseudonym, Peter, describes what happened when he was eventually placed with adoptive parents, who started to beat him:

> Peter became hyper-alert to the wants and desires of his adoptive parents... He did not blame his [adoptive] mother for losing her temper with him. After all, it only confirmed what he already believed about himself – he was bad and deserved punishment.

Other children will be withdrawn and will retreat to their rooms whenever tension builds. Foster parents have also reported difficulties coping with children who are 'provocative'. The reasons for such apparently difficult behaviour are varied. Some children cannot believe that their substitute carers will not eventually mistreat them and so test the limits of their carers' patience and tolerance. Some find violence, rejection or molestation so familiar they feel insecure when given only unfamiliar kindness and protection. Others think they are so wicked that they must be punished and therefore seek punishment. Many become so used to the role of family scapegoat or seducer that they know of no other way to function.

Practice focus

Zarina

Some children must feel they cannot win. Zarina had been constantly moved from one foster home to the next. When I started to work with her she poured her drink of orange onto the table. She then put a little plastic duck on the 'pond'. She asked me to pick up a hand towel and mop up the 'pond'. The towel she explained was the 'drying machine' which dried up the pond. The duck had to constantly move to a new pond as each time it was dried up. She played this game with total absorption week after week. My concern grew as she then started to build a wall around the duck. She explained it was the only way of keeping the duck safe.

Comment: Zarina was taken into care aged two years because of neglect. She was an exceptionally pretty child. But she was rejected by her first foster carer because she had tantrums and they were disillusioned because she was not as 'angelic' as she looked. In the next home she became over-controlled and mute so was again rejected. This continued and she had seven foster carers by the time she came to me aged six years. She was rejected whether she spoke out or remained silent.

Fears of violence and rejection are such that any form of punishment may provoke an extreme response. Tom O'Neill (1981, p.75) describes another brother's feelings when very caring foster parents 'had reason to chide him. They ticked him off and sent him to bed. He went to bed and cried and cried. He cried because they didn't want him. Admittedly, it was only a temporary banishment but to him it was a real rejection.'

Abuse in care

Finally, although the majority of foster, adoptive and residential homes provide an excellent environment, there are cases where children are abused while in care. Ever since Dennis O'Neill was beaten to death by his foster father, there has been a succession of children killed by adopted and foster carers, for example, Shirley Woodcock (London Borough of Hammersmith and Fulham, 1984) died aged three at the hands of her foster carer, while Christopher Pinder (Bradford Area Review Committee, 1981) was killed by his prospective adoptive mother. Victoria Climbié (Laming, 2003) was killed by an aunt in a private fostering arrangement. More recently, three children adopted by two doctors were subjected to years of abuse (Brabbs, 2011). A mounting number of inquiry reports (e.g., Hughes, 1986; Levy and Kahan, 1991; Kirkwood, 1993; Waterhouse, 2000; Corby *et al.*, 2001; Browne, 2009) are eloquent testimony to widespread abuse in children's residential homes. However, if the figures are placed against both the number of children killed and seriously harmed while with birth and step-parents they pale into insignificance. Moreover, despite the challenges there are benefits relating to substitute care.

Benefits of substitute care

Although a few children sustain serious injuries or die at the hands of substitute carers many more would be killed by their own parents had they not been removed from home. Maria Colwell (Field-Fisher, 1974) and Jasmine Beckford (Blom-Cooper, 1985) were killed after being returned home despite the misgivings of their foster parents.

Lloyd (see Chapter 2, p. 34) virtually left home from about the age of eleven and lived as best he could. His suicide attempts and total despair in his early teens might have been avoided if he had been accommodated with foster carers or in a residential setting where he could have received counselling, comfort and had someone to turn to for help in his distress.

Some children die because their attempts to escape abuse lead them into danger. The body of eight-year-old Lester Chapman (Berkshire County Council, 1979, p. 1) was found on 26 February 1978 'Trapped in a sewage sludge at a site 50 yards from the river, about a quarter of a mile from his home. He had died of exposure, almost certainly on the bitter night on which he ran away.' Lester had been physically and emotionally abused and had run away from home on three previous occasions. Removal to a loving substitute home will usually, in similar cases, save lives.

In spite of the dangers of emotional abuse due to the vagaries of the care system, children frequently thrive when placed with substitute carers. Notwithstanding the problems of substitute care, it can provide children with significant benefits. Ward *et al.* (2005), for example, found that the children they interviewed reported negative but also positive experiences in care.

One of the best therapies for abused children is to be in an environment where they can express feelings without fearing the consequences, where they are helped to feel valued, attractive and capable. Adoptive or foster carers or residential staff can do much to provide this and make good the damage to self-esteem caused by maltreatment.

An important benefit given by substitute carers and identified in the Ward *et al.* (2005) study is that they can provide an alternative model of family life. Many foster homes show abused children that instead of violence and recrimination between adult partners there is companionship and respect. The children learn to feel safe and protected by adults. They acquire self-control and discipline through praise, encouragement and gentle correction. They begin to realise that the love of parents for their children should be unconditional. All this will help them to become better partners and parents themselves, if they choose in later life to have their own family.

Residential settings cannot provide models of family life and they are often seen as a 'last resort'. There are unquestionably problems in some residential settings as reports by Browne (2009), Hughes (1986) and Waterhouse (2000) revealed. But for some young people, who have a family and do not want a substitute one, residential care can be a positive experience. Houston (2010), for example, found that residential settings can help build resilience in young people.

Messages from research

Winter (2010)

This research captures the voice of younger children in care. Winter (2010) interviewed in depth 14 children aged four to seven years to gain their perspectives with additional interviews with their parents and social workers to provide a fuller picture of their situation. The children's time in care ranged from six months to over five years.

Winter analysed the children's perspectives and the following themes emerged:

- living with risk at home;
- removal from home;
- unresolved feelings after removal;
- not being listened to.

In terms of living with risk, the children's accounts were coherent. While negative experiences were vividly recalled so too were some positive ones and the children adopted coping strategies. Most tellingly Winter observed, 'the research interview was the first occasion where the children had explored their memories of home in any detail' (p.190). We have to question a system which appears to leave children in care with no opportunity to recount and come to terms with their experiences. All it took was someone, on this occasion a researcher willing to ask and listen.

Removal from home was recalled as traumatic 'made worse by their perception that they lacked information, explanation and a later opportunity to explore their feelings' (p.191). The children were clearly mourning losses such as Grace who longed for her brothers and sisters and other family members and Finn who missed his dogs. Winter emphasises the general significance of pets for these younger children and the poignancy of their loss.

Unsurprisingly, the children had 'feelings of sadness, guilt, anger, worry and a yearning to be re-connected with their past family lives' (p.192), which have also been constant themes in research with older children. Aine, who had been severely neglected, blamed herself for her experiences. There were some who had more positive feelings and were relieved to be away from their home.

Children felt they were not listened to and this included being ignored by their social workers. A brother and sister agreed that their social worker just talked to their father. They tried to speak to her but she would not listen.

Winter makes a number of recommendations, including the importance of social workers being trained to communicate and listen to the youngest children and changes in the system to ensure that they can put this training into practice and have time to engage with children of all ages.

One observation on Winter's (2010) research above is that responsibility for the failure to listen to and engage with young children rarely lies with social work practitioners, instead they are burdened by lack of training and constraints within the current system.

Helping children in substitute care

In the light of Winter's (2010) research above and that of others who have researched the views of children in care (e.g., Leeson, 2007; Morgan, 2007) the guidance in this section might be difficult for child protection workers to follow, due to training, time and opportunity. However, there is evidence that, given the right conditions, social workers can meet key needs of looked-after children. Selwyn *et al.* (2010, p. 706), for example, who explored the views of children in private foster care, found the 'children and young people were generally very positive about their FCA social workers'. Therefore, ideas for good practice are outlined below so that this can become something that practitioners can aim for if currently they are prevented from practising in a way they feel is important.

Preparation

Whenever possible, children coming into care should be well prepared for the changes in their situation. Ideally, before being placed they will be helped to understand why they are being removed from home and to appreciate that it is not their fault. Furthermore when they move from one substitute home to another they need to be told why. Tom O'Neill (1981, p. 61) describes the experience of his brothers:

> They had to leave this foster-home. They didn't know why. They had done nothing wrong. Why did no one tell them why they had to go? They were happy there. Could no one have soothed the hurt they were experiencing by just telling them why it had to be as it was?

Children fear the unknown. Tom O'Neill (1981, p. 66) again describes how his brother, Terry, cried out, 'Don't let them take me away, Dad' as he was carried from the foster home where he had suffered savage mistreatment and witnessed the killing of his brother, Dennis; he 'cried out because of the dire consequences that had been instilled into him of being removed'. Children can be helped to overcome this fear by being gradually introduced to their new family if circumstances allow. When children have to be removed in haste then they can at least be shown a video, photographs of, or have Skype contact with their new home.

Wherever possible the parents should also be prepared for the child's removal. If there is no partnership and the parents are angered by the actions of protective agencies, they might turn some of that anger against the child and refuse to assist, for example, in providing photographs for a life-story book.

Point for reflection

Think of a relatively recent occasion when you have been in a new location or accommodation, such as moving to new student accommodation, a holiday or conference hotel. Can you remember your feelings? What aspects made the experience more reassuring or positive? Where there any aspects which made the experience negative? Was it, for example, reassuring to have your own distinct luggage, which you packed yourself? Did you pack, or look for on arrival, any 'home comforts'?

Comment: This is similar to the exercise on joining a group in Chapter 6. The purpose of this activity is to think about the experience of children coming into care. They are likely to experience very much more emotional turmoil than you experienced. Nevertheless, the activity can help you think about some of the apparently small factors that can help alleviate homesickness, confusion and distress. An example might be having bags they identify as 'theirs' rather than their belongings packed in black bin liners and cardboard boxes.

Contact

The issue of contact, particularly in adoptions, is a controversial one and specialist workers will hopefully be able to evaluate research findings in this area. There are considerable benefits in maintaining contact between abused children and their families. First, children will worry less about their parents and siblings if they can see them at regular intervals. Second, seeing birth parents and family helps the children with their sense of identity. Third, they may feel less rejected if the parents wish to continue to see them. But contact with parents is not always positive. For example, a violent father gave the children threatening messages to pass on to their mother 'Tell the bitch I'll slit her throat'. Parents can also give the impression that they are coping well with other siblings who are still with them, so it must be the abused child who is the problem not their parenting. Contact can leave a child unsettled, not knowing if they are to remain in care or return home.

Research by Owusu-Bempah (1995) suggests that when children are not living with a parent they will do better if they have positive knowledge of the absent parent rather than negative or no information. However, information can be obtained from direct or indirect contact with the parent. In some cases a child may be better served by photographs and written information about the parent than acrimonious contact visits or ones that result in further physical, emotional or sexual abuse.

Thought needs to be given to whether contact with parents is essential or whether there are other people who are more important. Grandparents, other relatives and family friends can also make a child feel valued and less rejected by being encouraged to keep in touch, remember birthdays and perhaps give presents on special occasions. More controversial, and perhaps worthy of further exploration, is the need for children to remain in contact with previous foster carers or residential staff. Even more controversial still is the issue of pets. Maltreated children sometimes develop deep relationships with their pets who become surrogate friends, siblings and even parents. To be wrenched away from these much loved companions can be devastating and attempts need to be made to ensure pet and child remain in contact.

Practice focus

Tiffany

Tiffany was a ten-year-old girl who lived with her baby brother, Sheringham, and parents in a fairly affluent rural area. She became deeply attached to a horse in the field bordering her garden. Her father was sent to prison long term for drug dealing. Her mother who was a drug user nearly died of a drug overdose and was deemed in no fit state to care for the children. Tiffany and Sheringham were placed with separate foster carers.

While Sheringham seemed to settle well, Tiffany was profoundly distressed when she was taken into care. She was angry and resentful and for a while would turn up for therapy sessions but refused to say anything apart from bitter insults directed toward the therapist. The therapist wondered if she should continue to work with Tiffany because the child seemed so reluctant to engage but finally persuaded Tiffany to draw the people and things she loved best and was missing. What Tiffany drew was the horse. Because she had not owned the horse and it had not been part of the family, no one had realised how deeply attached she had become to it.

Subsequently, the therapist suggested that, if possible, Tiffany should be taken to visit the horse and also have riding lessons at some stables near to where the foster carers lived. Once Tiffany knew she could see her beloved horse whenever she needed to and was meanwhile developing relationships with other horses at the stables, she became very much more settled.

Another now well-accepted method of helping children to keep in touch with their family and their origins is through life-story book work (Shah and Argent, 2006; Rees and Goldberg, 2009). While working on their book they can be given answers to why they had to leave home or had several moves in care. They can be reminded of the positives in their lives such as people who loved them or achievements gained as well as being helped to understand and cope with the more negative aspects.

Messages from research

Leeson (2010)

This research returns to the theme of the capacity of social workers to engage with children in care. When thinking about contact, the relationship of looked-after children and their social worker can be seen as an important one but to maintain a positive relationship with a child in care, practitioners need to engage emotionally as well as professionally. Therefore, Leeson explored the emotional labour of caring about looked after children.

She engaged in in-depth individual interviews with seven social workers and undertook two group interviews with social work teams. When the findings were analysed a number of themes emerged.

First, in terms of experience and training, in line with other research (e.g., Handley and Doyle, 2008) Leeson found that the social workers had little training, at any stage, in direct work with children. They wanted, but found it difficult to obtain, both the skills and resources to work creatively with children, which meant that communicating with the youngest was particularly difficult. When social workers raised this, managers responded with suggestions that they use or buy in the expertise of others.

Second, generally, working conditions were poor with little emotional support. They worked under rigid administrative structures and procedures, and time pressures.

Third, there was a tendency to prioritise older children who were easier than the youngest to engage and understand.

Leeson concluded that these realities were at odds with their aspirations, which were to work creatively with children of all ages, and avoid formulaic, 'off-the-shelf' approaches.

Continuing support

It is tempting for hard-pressed social workers to remove a child from a dangerous household, breathe a sigh of relief and turn their attention to those cases where children remain in an 'at risk' situation at home. But this simple rescue is inadequate. However good the new substitute carers, the child will need help in overcoming the negative effects of mistreatment.

As well as direct work with children, the carers also need support and guidance. Most will hopefully have received training but they may need additional advice in relation to particular children. For example, Erikson's (1965) stage theory and his recognition of the importance of identity issues suggest that it is particularly important that the foster parents and residential staff say nothing derogatory about the children's family of origin within their earshot.

Another area for continuing intervention is where there are conflicts between substitute and original parents about child-rearing. This is illustrated by the case of Jasmine Beckford and her sister, Louise (Blom-Cooper, 1985, p. 109). The foster parents complained about the state in which the girls returned to them after 'access' visits to the parental home:

> There were also frequent complaints about the clothes often being dirty and smelly, and about the greasing of the children's hair. It is normal practice to grease and plait Afro-hair. The social worker felt that the girls were, in fact, returned clean and that their hair had an acceptable amount of grease for the culture involved.

Finally, it is important to keep all parties, including the children, informed of plans for the future. This can be difficult if ongoing assessment means that plans for the future remain uncertain. Nonetheless, children's feelings of powerlessness and insecurity can be moderated by ensuring that they are involved in the decisions made about their own future.

Returning home

The decision will be taken for some children to return to their original home. Factors indicating that rehabilitation may be viable include a positive change in parental attitudes towards the child, an acceptance that they, not the child, are responsible for the abuse and an ability to relate to professional helpers as partners in planning for their children's future. If problems such as overcrowding, alcohol abuse or marital violence were factors that triggered the abuse then assistance to the parents and improvement in these areas will be required before rehabilitation can be considered.

The views of the children

In any plans for rehabilitation, account must be taken of the views of the children. These always have to be taken seriously as, very often, children know what is best for themselves. Nevertheless some caution has to be exercised in the interpretation of children's verbal and non-verbal communications. Terry O'Neill's 'Don't let them take me away, dad' could so easily have been interpreted as a real desire to stay with the foster father who had killed his brother, Dennis. Sarah's crying was seen as evidence of her homesickness by the boarding-school staff. Clare Raynor (2003), who was emotionally and physically abused by her mother, describes a similar misinterpretation of her tears; as she was leaving to go to boarding school, her mother 'thought the tears were for her, that I minded going away, but in truth I wept because I *didn't* mind' (p. 88).

Other considerations

Social workers are responsible for preparing everyone for the return home. This includes the siblings who have remained at home throughout. They may resent the intrusion of the abused child and the adjustments such as losing a bedroom to themselves when rehabilitation takes place. The substitute caregivers and other professionals should also be able to appreciate the reasons for the return home decision. The child may create problems for the parents simply because both child and family may have difficulties making the necessary adjustments and because the child is anxious and insecure. The parents need to be prepared for these eventualities while the child is made fully aware of what is happening and is reintroduced at a pace which suits him or her.

Some children will be 'care leavers' in that they will have reached the age of 18 and no longer have the security of their residential home or foster carers. Increasingly, over the past few years the needs of such vulnerable young people have been recognised. Davidson (2006a, 2006b) has produced two books which will provide helpful guidance for young people especially if used alongside discussions with adults who are there to support them.

Finally, an ability to maintain changes and improvements and to cope with the adjustments required should be monitored once the child is back home. Practitioners involved need to communicate regularly with the child as well as with the parents; simply *seeing* the child is not enough.

Kinship care

Throughout history, especially when rates of mortality were greater and parents often incapacitated by ill-health, we find that kinship care was commonplace and unremarkable. In many societies it remains the norm for children whose parents are unavailable. By examining the 2001 Census data, Nandy and Selwyn (2011) estimate that in the UK there are nearly 180,000 children being looked after by relatives, with 95 per cent of these being cared for informally.

Kinship care, that is, being placed in care with a relative as foster or adoptive carer, has several benefits for children. Contact with their extended family meets children's needs for continuity and connectedness with their parents' biological and social backgrounds (Owusu-Bempah, 2006). Moreover, children's fear of the unknown is minimised, contact can be effortless and children remain within their cultural and class contexts.

Nevertheless, there is some need for caution. The case of Victoria Climbié (Laming, 2003) serves as a warning to avoid automatically assuming that all care by kinfolk is safe care. While non-relative foster carers have chosen to provide substitute care, relatives may be more reluctant. Sometimes families are riddled with acrimonious conflict and the child is likely to be used as a weapon in the warring factions. Some dual-heritage children find that the two sides of the family are deeply divided. Placing the child with one side will mean that the culture of the other part of the family, and therefore part of the child's identity, will be derided and demonised.

Another dilemma in kinship care is that because it can be viewed as 'natural', the carers may be given less support and financial help than non-relative carers. Yet often they may need more help because they may have felt obliged to offer a home when they were least equipped to do so. Yet, as Berridge (2001, p. 171) points out 'Anomalies can arise if relatives are paid a significant sum to look after a child, one that was unavailable to the birth parent.'

Final comment

In this chapter I have not covered the many issues, highlighted by epidemiological research, showing that children in the care system do not do as well educationally and on leaving care as children who do not spend time in care. This is partly because what we are now learning about early brain development means there are questions about how far children are already developmentally delayed when they come into care. Nor has there been space for a proper discussion of children with disabilities and special needs. There are suggestions for further exploration of the issues below.

Further resources

The British Association for Adoption and Fostering (BAAF) is the leading organisation in the field and produces many excellent publications. Its website is: http://www.baaf.org.uk.

Argent, H. (2008) *Ten Top Tips: Placing Siblings*. London: BAAF.

Cousins, J. (2008) *Ten Top Tips: Finding Families*. London: BAAF.
These are but two examples of wonderful series of books published by BAAF starting with the title *Ten Top Tips*. They are inexpensive and slight but absolutely full of excellent advice for practitioners. Additionally, they are useful for students because the ideas are supported by referenced evidence and scholarship.

Argent, H. (2010) *Adopting a brother or sister.* London: BAAF.
This is one of a number of books by Hedi Argent designed for children around the topic of adoption. This book helps children prepare for both the confusion and excitement of having a new brother and sister by adoption.

TACT Fostering and Adoption is one of the largest relevant organisations. It merged with Parents for Children in 2009 which specialised in finding families particularly for disabled children and those who were particularly vulnerable. TACT can be contacted on: http://www.tactcare.org.uk/index.php.

CHAPTER 8

Resilience and social support

CHAPTER OVERVIEW

This chapter looks at the reasons why some abused children can demonstrate resilience in the face of their experiences and how resilience can be promoted. It looks at:

- resilience factors which can include biological factors, locus of control and social support
- available supports including extended family members, non-family adults, friends, schools, religion and pets – these can be identified, harnessed and strengthened to help abused children.

Whether maltreated children remain at home or not they need to be helped to cope with the emotional consequences of abuse, yet therapy might not be available, possible or even sufficient. Nevertheless, promoting factors that increase resilience provides either an alternative or supplementary way of helping abused children.

We are increasingly aware of the damaging consequences of abuse, particularly in terms of brain architecture, if it starts early and continues for any length of time (Perry, 2009; Fox *et al.*, 2010). Even short periods of maltreatment in childhood or adolescence can lead to post-traumatic stress and damage to the child's sense of self-worth. Nevertheless, there are children who, despite considerable suffering, emerge into childhood without the isolation, stagnation and despair predicted in Erikson's (1965) model and indicated by later researchers (Gibb and Abela, 2007; Carpenter *et al.*, 2009; O'Dougherty-Wright *et al.*, 2009). Practitioners will be familiar with families in which distress and maltreatment was rife yet several siblings appear to be relatively unaffected and emerge into adult life as apparently valued citizens, partners and parents. It seems that children have resilience and one way of working with abused children is by strengthening this resilience indirectly by encouraging the children and their carers to harness naturally occurring protective factors.

Enhancing resilience is a particularly useful strategy in instances of emotional abuse, particularly where this is the sole form of maltreatment. This is because of the difficulty of challenging abusive carers over emotional abuse. Most physically or sexually abusive acts and physical neglect are illegal so that legal and police intervention can justifiably be used to protect children. But many types of emotionally abusive behaviour are not proscribed by law. An example is Lloyd's parents who, in rejecting him, gave him no birthday or Christmas presents when his brothers were showered with gifts. The police do not prosecute parents who choose not to give their children presents. Therefore if emotionally abusive parents will not accept voluntary intervention there seems little that can be done to help the children. Yet something needs to be offered because research shows that psychological maltreatment, even as the sole form, is one of the most damaging and insidious forms of abuse (Hart *et al.*, 1998; Moran *et al.*, 2004). One way forward is to help children by identifying and strengthening protective factors that help them cope with their experiences of maltreatment.

Resilience factors

Resilience and factors which promote it have in recent years been a matter of substantial study. In an early study Lynch and Roberts (1982) identified several factors contributing to a positive outlook for abused children, such as, the absence of perinatal problems, early intervention, the avoidance of both protracted or recurrent legal proceedings and frequent placement changes and, finally, high intelligence. However, one of the problems in identifying resilience factors is that of distinguishing cause and effect. For example, does high intelligence protect children or are abused children who have greater resilience for other reasons more likely to develop their intellectual potential?

Biological potential

Cicchetti (2010) explains that resilience is a complex, multi-layered occurrence combining biological and psychological factors. There is, for example, evidence that maltreatment has an effect on neuroendocrine regulation. However, it appears that resilient maltreated children have elevated levels of a stress-responsive adrenal steroid hormone, dehydroepiandrosterone, when compared to resilient non-abused children. This may give them the capacity to cope better with chronic stress.

A major area of study since the development of Magnetic Resonance Imaging (MRI) is the structure and functioning of the brain. We are now able to detect the impact of abuse on brain architecture. There is evidence that people with larger hippocampi are more resistant to stress. However, rather like the debate on high intelligence as a protective factor, there is a chicken and egg conundrum; it could be that adults with smaller hippocampi have been subjected to more early stress and abuse (Woon and Hedges, 2008).

Our increased understanding of brain function is also related to investigations and theories about brain plasticity. We are now aware that early chronic neglect and maltreatment can lead to abnormalities in the brain architecture. But we have also been able to observe, from patients who have brain injury through accidents, that there is a degree of plasticity in that the brain is able to heal or that other parts of the brain take over lost functions. Resilience might be attributed to those individuals born with a higher than normal degree of plasticity. Alternatively, and this is an area of considerable future interest and potential for research, positive environmental influences such as social support may promote plasticity and recovery (Cicchetti, 2010).

Locus of control and attribution theories

Among the resilience theorists, Bolger and Patterson (2003, p. 159) identify that perceived internal control is one of the domains with a 'high potential to protect children against the ill effects of maltreatment'. This is based on the theories of attribution and locus of control. Children who believe that they can control what happens to them and attribute any successes and achievements to their own abilities are likely to do better than children who believe that they have no control over events and are subjected to the vagaries of fate or more powerful people.

Loci of control and attribution theories demonstrate why it is essential to include children in decision making and maximise the control they have over their own lives. This empowerment should be applicable to all children but special efforts should be made to ensure abused children are helped to feel in control of themselves and their situation.

Social support

The resilience of children who have experienced maltreatment can be enhanced by good social support and 'buffering' factors (McLewin and Muller, 2006; Pepin and Banyard, 2006; Appleyard et al., 2007). To explore this, Doyle et al. (2010) gathered ideas of available support, when parents were absent, from 2,220 children, through a story invented by children who acted as consultants. Incidentally, the use of stories invented by children to illustrate abandonment was validated by D'Cruz and Stagnitti (2010). The following areas of social support have been identified through the literature including Doyle et al.'s (2010) study.

Potential supports for abused children

There are a number of both human and non-human supports available to young people. One way of working with abused children is to maximise access to, and the effectiveness of, these potential sources of assistance and nurture.

Supportive adult family members

One key factor in resilience is a supportive non-abusing parent (Rutter, 1979; Masten and Coatsworth, 1998). However, in some instances, especially those of emotional abuse, there is no such figure: either both parents are abusive, as in Lloyd's case; only the abusive parent is present for most of the time, or, as illustrated by Roy, Josie and Jake's account, the non-abusing parent is a co-victim. In the accounts in Chapter 2, three of the six survivors did not have much support from other family members, but Sarah, Josie and Jake showed how grandparents, aunts and uncles can have a key role.

Aunts, whether biologically related or family friends adopted as 'aunt' figures, seem to be particularly important. While they are close to the family, they are not under the same pressure as grandparents whose loyalties may be divided between their own adult children and their grandchildren. Many autobiographies of people who had difficult childhoods bear witness to the positive role of aunts, for example, writer Claire Raynor (2003) had 'Aunt Nancy' and, from a Chinese cultural background, author Adeline Yen Mah (2002) had her 'Aunt Baba'. Doyle (2001) found that of the fourteen survivors of abuse, the majority had an aunt figure who had valued and helped them and enhanced their self-esteem. In Doyle *et al.* (2010) 79 per cent and 72 per cent of children nominated grandmothers and grandfathers respectively, while 65 per cent chose aunts and 61 per cent uncles.

Messages from research

Pitcher and Arnill (2010)

Pitcher and Arnill explored how extended family members can provide help to potentially abused children, especially where the child remains at home. This was not a study of kinship care or family group conferencing but a matter of relatives 'being there' for the child. Pitcher and Arnill, echoing Doyle's (2001) study, noted the importance of aunts and uncles:

> Family members said that they found it much easier dealing with a parent who was a brother or sister, than with one who was a son or daughter. The sibling relationship is often one in which differences are expressed, and there was never the same level of dependence on them or demands made by them.

With similarities to Doyle's (1998) research, Pitcher and Arnill found that families could help the children more successfully, despite tensions and conflicts, if there was one central, wellbalanced family member. The researchers did not under-estimate the difficulties of engaging families but the outcome of their project suggests that child protection workers can have a role:

- in helping the family to fully understand what is happening;
- help at least one strong member to stand back and see objectively what has to be done;
- assist the family establish appropriate boundaries, roles and communication;
- ensure that they, as a professional, are not undermining or ignoring a family member with something to offer the child.

Siblings

As noted, it is often easier for the siblings of abusive parents to intervene to help their nieces and nephews, but what about the child's own brothers and sisters? In the accounts of Sarah and Marie we saw contrasting relationships, with Sarah rejecting her sister but Marie protecting them and finding camaraderie with her siblings helpful. In Doyle *et al.* (2010) 62 per cent of children felt a brother or sister could be a source of assistance. Gass *et al.* (2007) found affectionate sibling relationships can act as a buffer to stress, whatever the relationship between the children and their mother; a view supported by Conger *et al.*'s (2009) review. Stormshak *et al.* (2009) acknowledge some of the subversive and damaging features of sibling relationships but, nevertheless, argue that family work harnessing the potential of siblings can optimise children's social and emotional development.

Non-family supportive adults

Additional supportive adults can include non-family members such as youth leaders, voluntary workers and a variety of helping professionals including social workers and foster carers. Dogra *et al.* (2009) identify, as a key protective factor, a warm and confiding relationship with a trustworthy and reliable adult.

Practitioners can encourage other adults in children's lives to offer, in Carl Roger's (1967) terms, 'unconditional positive regard'. It might be as valuable to recruit foster aunts and uncles as it is to recruit foster carers so that children can stay at home but obtain emotional support from these alternative figures, especially in cases where the children are not in physical danger but are receiving inadequate emotional nurturing.

Messages from research

Garraway and Pistrang (2010)

Mentoring, in the context of child welfare, is where an adult, who is not a relative, provides guidance and encouragement. This may prove a form of social support which is particularly helpful for children who have been emotionally neglected.

Garraway and Pistrang (2010) evaluated a scheme in London for African–Caribbean boys aged 12 to 17 years. Each had a mentor who was a male, trained volunteer in his 30s or 40s who met with their mentee at least weekly. It is important to note that the boys were not overtly abused but instead suffered emotional distress due to having diagnoses for mental health problems including schizophrenia and ADHD. However, the transfer of the principles of the project to some abused children appears to be feasible.

Thirteen boys attended a research focus group and, of these, eight agreed to be interviewed individually. They were asked about their understanding and experiences of mentoring, for example, 'What has it been like for you, having a mentor?' In addition, five mentors took part in individual semi-structured interviews and their experiences and views on the nature of their mentoring were elicited.

There were inevitably some concerns particularly over the ending of the mentor relationships. However, the authors found that there was a wide array of substantial benefits. For example, because the volunteers tended to have had experiences similar to those of their mentees not only did the boys feel their mentor 'know where we're coming from' but the mentors found they felt their negative past experiences were now having positive benefits.

Comment: The ideas outlined by this paper could feasibly be transferred to working with abused children. For example, Lloyd, whom we met in Chapter 2 and who was unwanted and neglected by both parents was seeking a reliable role model and guide. He had few friends but mentioned that 'Bevis, a local yob turned good, taught me martial arts and showed interest in me'. Maybe a more structured relationship with a trained 'Bevis-figure' would have proved an important support and helped him to realise rather earlier that he was a worthwhile and valued young person.

Peer friendships

Another domain identified by Bolger and Patterson (2003) is peer friendship. They found that friendships in maltreated children led to a higher self-esteem, less loneliness and a feeling of greater acceptance than those without close friends. This idea of friendship is reflected in the research by Doyle (2001) who found that a key factor in helping abused children is the presence of someone who can give the child unconditional, positive regard as advocated in the theories of Carl Rogers (1967, 1980). Doyle *et al.* (2010) found a friend was chosen by 77 per cent of the child participants with only grandmothers at 79 per cent being higher. Meanwhile, Doyle (2001, 2003) established that a 'best friend' was significant. Often these were other distressed children. They could show genuine empathy and understanding and also helped the abused child to realise that maltreatment and misfortune was not 'deserved'.

Dogra *et al.* (2009) observed that adults often underestimate the support that children give each other. Nevertheless, some abused children will have difficulty making friends because their sense of basic trust has been damaged. In addition, children with certain disabilities 'may have impairments which affect their ability to make friends and many disabled children face particular barriers in establishing and maintaining friendships' (Marchant, 2001, p. 219).

The role of friendship is such that many abused children will benefit if they can be helped to forge and maintain companionship with peers. The only problem to be aware of is that peer groups engaging in high-risk behaviours can be a negative influence (Perkins and Jones, 2004). One of the results of substitute care is that it often results in children being separated from friends and siblings and, therefore, ways of enabling children to keep in touch with them could usefully be found.

School

Perkins and Jones (2004) found that a positive school climate helped enhance resilience. More specifically, Doyle (2003) explored the key role that teachers play in the lives of abused children. Even teachers only involved with a pupil for a short time can have a lasting positive impact, as in the case of Lloyd whose teacher helped him believe he was special. It is often, as in the case of Lloyd, that teachers are in a position to identify and help develop children's talents. In Doyle *et al.* (2010) 55 per cent of children chose a teacher as an important supporter.

Other education professionals can also provide key support. School nurses are not only in a position to recognise abuse but are often a source of counselling especially for adolescents. Educational psychologists can determine the cause of educational problems and suggest ways in which children can be assisted. Other people associated with schools, including classroom or lunchtime assistants, have been, and can be, the supportive adult for some children.

Religion

Parkinson (1993, p. 95) indicated that a 'firm belief and conviction can help survival' while Perkins and Jones (2004) identified 'religiosity' as a protective factor for adolescents who had been physically abused. Seidman and Pedersen (2003) also established that religious belief is a protective factor for children in adverse and oppressive circumstances. Doyle (2001) found that her interviewees identified religion and religious groups as a facet in their ability to cope with their abusive experiences. In many instances the message 'God loves you whoever you are was a powerfully reassuring one, although no particular religion appeared to have the monopoly in terms of benefits to children who have been maltreated. Doyle *et al.* (2010) discovered that 38 per cent of children suggested God/Allah and 37 per cent nominated a religious leader as sources of help, perhaps surprisingly, given the secular nature of UK society; a guardian angel was chosen by 20 per cent of the children.

There are concerns that religious 'sects', some religious practices and sexually exploiting religious leaders can damage young people (McGlone, 2004; Smith *et al.*, 2008). But it is probably safe to say that, apart from a consideration of these concerns, there has been little attention paid by social workers and other helping professionals to the spiritual needs of children unless their cultural background is strongly associated with religion. But maybe the help that can be offered by spiritual leaders and representatives within the child's community could usefully be harnessed as a source of strength.

Pets

An attachment to a pet, especially an interactive one such as a dog or cat has been shown to enhance the self-esteem of children in general (Triebenacher, 1998; Daly and Morton, 2009; Wedl and Kotrschal, 2009). Melson's (1998) study, which drew clearly on Erikson's (1965) life stage theory and ecological systems theory, demonstrated the key role of companion animals in children's development. There may be particular benefits for abused children with some disabilities. For example, contact with animals can relieve and minimise the experience of physical pain (Braun *et al.*, 2009). Animal contact can help children with attention-deficit/hyperactive disorder (ADHD) (Somerville *et al.*, 2009). Additionally, there were positive findings of dog–child relationships in a project undertaken by Burrows *et al.* (2008) with children on the autistic spectrum.

The underlying neurobiological factors are explored by Yorke (2010) especially in children exposed to trauma. Neural pathways leading to the brain's self-organisation and regulation are shaped by experiences. Positive attachments can lead to the release of neuropeptides which contribute to feelings of security in children and help build resilience to stress. Yorke (2010) hypothesises that contact with companion animals may give rise to similar chemical responses and beneficial feelings.

Doyle (2001) found that pets were another major source of support for children who were emotionally and sometimes also sexually and/or physically abused. As Bodmer (1998, p. 245) commented, 'Pets are always available and offer their affection to anyone needing it.'

Practice focus

Trevor and Chip

Trevor was an only child living with his widowed mother. His father had died when he was aged six. Subsequently his mother had become angry and abusive. She would shout at Trevor, telling him how stupid, useless, disgusting and foul he was. She would also sometimes punch and kick him. Just before his death his father had bought him Chip, a spaniel puppy who became Trevor's constant companion. His mother also directed her anger towards Chip, kicking and hitting out at him, as well as yelling obscenities. As he comforted and was comforted by Chip, Trevor began to realise that if his mother could maltreat something as lovely and affectionate as Chip then the problems were his mother's responsibility and something to do with her character or state of mind rather than Trevor's own character or behaviour.

Trevor's case shows that when pets are also mistreated by parents, children might be relieved of any sense of blame, because the children can see that their pets are clearly 'innocent' and so it must be the parents who are at fault and responsible for all the abuse, including the child's own.

As with all the other protective factors there is a negative aspect. Animals are often mistreated in abusing families because, either the abuser mistreats everyone and everything within his or her power, or the children displace their anger onto defenceless animals. In households where animals would not be safe, an alternative arrangement is to link children to a pet, which is looked after by someone else but regularly visited by the child.

Modern technologies

Further sources of assistance, which should not be underestimated, are the counsellors of telephone helplines such as the Samaritans or

ChildLine. The advantage of ChildLine is that children who are frightened and ashamed can unburden themselves to a person whom they will not meet; they can decide how much information they disclose and therefore have some control over events (ChildLine, 1998). Doyle and colleagues (2010) were surprised to find that 65 per cent of the children surveyed felt that telephone helplines were a valuable source of help for abused children. If practitioners are unable to intervene in any other way they can at least remind children of the services of telephone helplines.

The child consultants to Doyle *et al.*'s (2010) survey also suggested internet forums such as chat rooms as potential lifelines. However, only 20 per cent nominated these in contrast to the 65 per cent who chose telephone helplines. This could be because the survey participants were aged eight to thirteen; an older group of adolescents might have found the internet resources more amenable. It might also be that dedicated internet forums devised to help distressed children would be more attractive than general ones. If we think of telephone helplines, children might not have so readily accessed Samaritans but will use ChildLine, a resource specifically designed to meet their needs.

Point for reflection

Review one or more of the cases in Chapter 2, Roy, Sarah, Marie, Lloyd, Josie or Jake. Can you identify the social supports and other positive features in their lives that helped enhance their resilience? Draw an ecomap (see Figure 8.1) to demonstrate this, that is, put

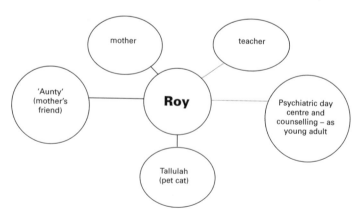

Figure 8.1   Example of ecomap: Roy

your chosen child in a circle in the middle and then draw other circles around the child. An additional refinement can be to indicate closer or more enduring relationships with more solid and thicker lines.

Putting it into practice

Having finished the reflective exercise above, do the same with one of the cases with which you are familiar through your case load at work or on placement. Are you sure that you have identified all the child's supports? Do you need to find out from the child if he or she has any other important relationships – remember Tiffany's horse? With younger children this can be a toy and with more imaginative children it might be a character from a book or film or the child's own imaginary character.

Comment: This activity should help you apply aspects of this chapter to actual cases. As will be seen in the next chapter, all six children giving their accounts in Chapter 2 had a marked degree of resilience and they all had supports of some form. Tapping into social and even non-human or imaginary life-lines can enhance, as demonstrated in Tiffany's case, any therapeutic work.

Concluding comment

Generally, while cognitive coping strategies are one aspect of resilience the other major one is social support, whether from siblings and peers, caring adults including those in schools and religious communities, and even pets. Practitioners can help children, whether in the parental home or in substitute care, to strengthen bonds with any one person or animal who can offer the child unconditional positive regard.

Further resources

Cicchetti, D. and Rogosch, F. A. (2009) 'Adaptive coping under conditions of extreme stress: Multilevel influences on the determinants of resilience in maltreated children', in Skinner, E. A and Zimmer-Gembeck, M. J. (eds) *Coping and the development of regulation. New Directions for Child and Adolescent Development.* San Francisco: Jossey-Bass.

This piece gives an intriguing insight into some of the physiological aspects of resilience, explaining the biology in more detail than could be given in this chapter. It requires some understanding of natural science but the authors expound on technical research papers with clarity.

ChildLine is a telephone helpline specifically for children. More information can be found on http://www.childline.org.uk including the number for children to call if they are distressed in any way and would like to talk to a counsellor. Information for adults about ChildLine or what to do if adults are worried about a child is available at: http://www.childline.org.uk/Pages/InformationForAdults.aspx.

Kidscape is an organisation dedicated to helping children and much of the focus of its work is to prevent sexual abuse as well as bullying in school. Its home page is: http://www.kidscape.org.uk/.

CHAPTER 9

Prevention and society

CHAPTER OVERVIEW

This chapter explores the social policy, environmental and societal issues that can contribute to the prevention of child abuse. The following topics are explored:

- primary prevention of abuse is placed in policy contexts focusing on the UK
- the importance of environmental and economic factors in relation to prevention
- social construction theory and the reconstruction of 'children' in relation to the prevention of abuse.

There are different forms and types of prevention. Hardiker *et al.* (1991) argued that there are four levels. The third and fourth (tertiary and quaternary) are about ensuring that, once harmed, children are not subjected to further harm. The prevention of further abuse was addressed in the earlier chapters on direct work with children as illustrated by Figure 4.1 (see p. 100) and protective behaviours work. Primary prevention is about ensuring that the conditions giving rise to abuse do not occur at all and secondary prevention is about identifying children and families 'at risk' and ensuring they receive targeted support. Chapter 10 looks at the long-term damage that maltreatment can cause, sometimes haunting people into adulthood and resulting in inter-generational abuse. Therefore, one of the key considerations when working with abused children is whether there can be changes in children's environments and wider society that prevent abuse from occurring in the first place. This chapter first explores the policy contexts, the immediate socio-economic environment and then the wider socio-cultural factors.

Policy contexts

The purpose of this section is not to trace the policy developments and contexts in the UK during the past few years. Other authors, notably Blewitt (2011), Parton (2009, 2011) and Rowlands (2011) do this admirably. However, as specified by the ecological model of intervention, children develop while nested within their family, which is, itself, nested within a local environment, which in turn is influenced by the wider society and culture. The wider environment is shaped by history and by the policy perspectives of powerful agencies, notably the government. This inevitably means that children, their families and professionals are ultimately influenced by history and policy, as are attempts to prevent child abuse. Therefore, some key contextual issues will be highlighted to provide an understanding of the wider issues of prevention.

Historically, most policies and procedures designed to prevent abuse have followed major incidents with the cry 'it must never happen again'. For example, after the death of Maria Colwell the subsequent report (Field-Fisher, 1974) pointed to deficits in the child protection systems; this led to the development of child protection registers, case conferences and inter-disciplinary procedures. More recently, the extreme maltreatment of Victoria Climbié (Laming, 2003) led to government initiatives such as Every Child Matters, while the 2004 Bichard Inquiry Report, which was set up in the wake of the deaths of two girls by a sexual predator, led to increased monitoring of people working with children.

Other parts of the UK have had their own issues. In Scotland, a number of inquiries into the deaths and mistreatment of children have helped in the development of law and policy and, in the wake of the death of Kennedy McFarlane and the subsequent inquiry (Hammond, 2001), there has been a wealth of child welfare initiatives (Vincent et al., 2010).

In Wales, concerns about abuse in children's homes in north Wales were raised in 1986 by social worker, Alison Taylor. Little action was taken and she was unjustly sacked. Eventually, however, evidence vindicating her allegations accumulated (Waterhouse, 2000). More recently the Welsh Assembly Government (2008) produced *All Wales Child Protection Procedures*, comprehensive guidelines on child protection in Wales.

In Northern Ireland, reports of abuse in children's homes, this time in Belfast, lead to investigations which confirmed abuse (Hughes, 1986). There were subsequent improvements in safeguarding strategies, for example, DHSSPS (2008) which sets standards for all Northern Ireland agencies and other policy revisions (Donnelly and Rose, 2011).

The various inquiries throughout the UK tended to lead to adverse publicity for the workers and agencies involved and the implementation of increased numbers of procedures as attempts were made by the governments to close any gaps in the various protection systems. Practitioners from a range of disciplines are now working against the background of 'new managerialism' and a substantial bureaucratic load. Organisations were no longer to be run by professionals but managers, preferably drawn from successful private businesses. This is explained in a powerful paper by Rogowski (2011). Practitioners who wish to work directly with abused children will encounter obstacles in the present context unless they work for organisations offering specific therapies. Yet social work used to be about using the skills of empathy, engagement and communication to engage with children and their families. Rogowski's paper is not one of despair; rather he suggests how professionals can challenge, both individually and collectively, the managerial orthodoxy and reclaim relationship-based child protection work.

Hardiker and colleagues (1991) pointed out that different forms of prevention are linked to different approaches to welfare policy. They identify four approaches:

- *Residual*: state welfare is minimal and the only prevention are strategies to avert repeat abuse in confirmed cases.
- *Institutional*: state welfare supplements family and voluntary support in cases of need. Prevention is targeted towards clear 'at risk' cases.
- *Developmental*: state welfare is available to all and social injustice is challenged. Prevention occurs because there is good support for all and so families will receive help before or as soon as difficulties arise.
- *Radical/conflict*: the victims of injustice themselves challenge society. Prevention is automatic because all formerly disempowered people will be empowered.

Practice focus

Pen Green Children's Centre, the 'developmental' approach

The Pen Green Children's Centre was established in 1983 but has grown and evolved over the years. The express philosophy of Pen Green (2011) is that:

> In every small community there should be a service for children under five and their families. This service should honour the needs of young children and celebrate their existence. It should also support families, however they are constituted within the community.

The current provision, which was originally for the 'under fives' has extended its remit to offer holiday play schemes and after-school clubs for four- to eleven-year-old children. However, the centre has remained faithful to the key philosophy that children and their families are nested within their immediate communities and support for all families with children from the community is a right and not either a privilege for the wealthy nor restricted just to 'at risk' families. There is no stigma attached to attendance at the Centre because it is open to all families within its 'reach' area.

Pen Green has a natural preventative function because it minimises isolation and supports parents who encounter difficulties. Many of the specialist groups it runs have been suggested by parents themselves who have perceived a local need.

The activities are hugely diverse from a baby nest, crèche and direct activities for children, a group for childminders, and aerobic courses and circuit training for women and men respectively. Fathers, as much as mothers, are embraced by the provision: for example, on Saturdays there is a fathers' baby massage group and on Sundays a general group where fathers can bring their young children and use the facilities perhaps to cook, paint or make things together.

Staffing is provided by trained professionals but among the staff members are trained former Centre users. Pen Green also embraces volunteers who help run some of the groups.

Overall, it is an example of extensive, high-level provision which supports rather than stigmatises families who might be facing challenges and is valued by the community it serves.

The task of primary and secondary prevention can more readily be implemented and maintained when the prevailing welfare models are 'developmental' or 'institutional'. Attempting to prevent abuse when the 'residual' model holds sway is experienced as a frustrating and dispiriting experience because workers in the statutory agencies find such activities are not viewed as a legitimate part of their workload. Meanwhile, those who are operating independently or in voluntary agencies will fare little better because although the ruling powers will countenance their preventative enterprises there will be little state assistance; by way of example in January 2011, the Pen Green Centre above was faced with a 56 per cent reduction in state funding (*Evening Telegraph*, 2011) and they have always had a continuing battle to keep services alive when the residual model of child-care policy dominates.

Messages from research

Spratt and Devaney (2009)

This study examines the responses to families with multiple problems in three countries, Australia, the USA and the UK. Children in such families are 'at risk' from emotional abuse if no other. However, short-term responses are unlikely to prove effective in preventing any abuse. Rather these families need long-term help to resolve some of their complex issues.

Australia, the USA and the UK were chosen because they share a common legal and political heritage. In total, 68 social work practitioners and managers were interviewed in order to explore their perspectives on the identification and response to families with multiple problems. The interviewees were drawn from Northern Ireland, California, Victoria and New South Wales.

The interview transcripts were analysed and several themes emerged. First, in all three countries, the interviewees tended to be very experienced and remembered working in the 1970s and 1980s. They recalled, at that time, working with families was more conducive to forming relationships and procedures were less prescriptive.

In all three countries, nowadays, there is virtue in work that is time limited. Another constraint is the restriction of the mandate with differentiation between cases requiring a child protection response and those needing family support. It appears that in all three countries, the social workers were trying to engage families particularly as a preventative measure. However, they were challenged by time constraints, limited resources and the various filtering systems.

Another constraint was that in all three countries there was a negative perception by the families of social workers which led them to resist intervention. Most tellingly in all three countries there was a view that the various procedural systems and targets are more about 'administrative achievements, they're not achievements for the family' (p. 429).

A more optimistic perspective was a growing realisation in all three countries that investigations into prevention can save resources in the long run. Nevertheless, the reactions of the public, media and politicians to high profile child deaths distorted child welfare policies and as one Californian social worker observed, 'the media, the policy leaders blame the child welfare system [this] often drives the system in turmoil to sometimes scapegoat the workers' (p. 431).

The paper highlights some of the issues and constraints on practitioners attempting to work in a preventative capacity with families with multiple problems. What is evident is that this is not just an issue in the UK but shared among child protection workers across at least parts of the world.

Environmental and economic factors

The contribution of poverty and environmental factors to child maltreatment is a complex issue and has been the subject of considerable debate (Gil, 1970; Parton, 1985). But impoverished circumstances appear to contribute to abuse (Doyle, 1997b) and therefore more adequate provision is likely to help in the prevention of abuse, particularly physical abuse and neglect.

Figures 9.1 and 9.2 illustrate two approaches to intervention and prevention. The first concentrates on the relationship between the child and the parent, usually the mother. The second includes not just the child–parent relationship but the wider family, immediate community, larger community and ultimately the widest cultural, social and legal context often encapsulated in the state, although there may be other supra-state influences such as international religions.

Therapy and support relating to abused children often focuses on the child/parent relationship, especially mother–child relations, as shown in Figure 9.1. This can be effective but it tends to put the burden on the mother or father to be extremely effective as a parent. However if, as illustrated in Figure 9.2, there is assistance and support for the children and their parents at several levels in society then the child is likely to thrive even if the parents are just about 'good enough'.

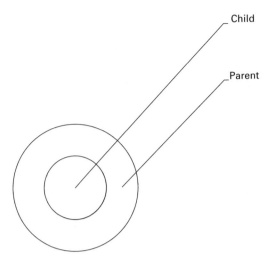

The focus here is solely on the relationship between the parent (usually the mother) and child

Figure 9.1 Helping a parent to cope with a child

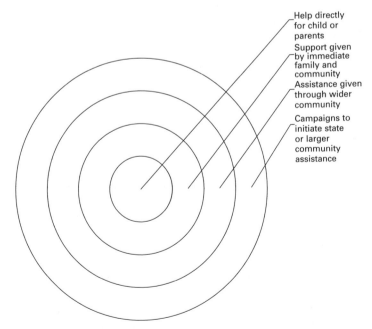

Figure 9.2 Ecological model of assistance for children and their families

The account of Becky and her children illustrates a range of environmental and economic conditions encountered by some families. The names are fictitious but the events are not.

Practice focus

Becky

Becky was in her late teens, the single mother of Kensa, her baby daughter. They lived on the fifth floor in a tower-block complex in a large city in Britain. The complex was a depressing, grey, rabbit-warren, filthy with litter and excrement. Becky's flat was damp and the community heating-scheme provided only erratic heating. The walls of her flat, as in all the others, were thin while traffic streamed past the complex, so life was noisy for the residents. There were few local amenities. Becky claimed welfare benefits but the flats were dominated by a 'protection gang'. She had to give over all her benefits to the gang, sometimes given a little money back for food. She paid the bills by borrowing from her mother or friends and sometimes by prostitution, resulting in her feeling, in her own words, 'dirty and defiled'.

Becky's physical care of Kensa was good, despite the fact that she had to hand-wash all the nappies and clothes and there was little drying space. But Becky broke Kensa's arm when the baby was three months old and, frightened of what she might do next, insisted that her daughter was taken into permanent care.

A year later, her new daughter, Nessa, was the victim of a sudden infant or 'cot' death. This was due probably to a combination of the erratic heating system that led to the baby being too warm, the advice then in vogue to lay babies face down, smoking and heavy city pollution.

By the time her third baby, Tressa, was born, Becky had been re-housed on a well-planned estate, in a detached house with a small garden near a thriving community centre and a range of facilities. She had escaped the protection gang and could manage financially because she was able to keep her own money. There were no problems with Tressa who flourished and developed well.

In the UK there are now some recognised community support programmes specifically for parents. The early decade of the twenty-first century saw the development of SureStart Centres. In contrast to the Pen Green philosophy, these tended to be sited in areas where there was a degree of socio-economic deprivation but, like Pen Green, was not targeted particularly at children who were at risk of abuse. They offered a range of activities and supports for families with children under five years such as baby massage classes, play opportunities and a toy library.

Homestart is another example of a voluntary community initiative but in contrast to SureStart the service is taken to the home of the vulnerable family rather than the parents having to make their way to a centre. Trained volunteers, usually experienced parents, visit isolated and inexperienced fellow parents who are ready to welcome support, companionship and advice. The help can be practical, for example, assisting harassed parents to understand official documents but there is also emotional support and understanding of some of the challenges of parenthood.

Point for reflection

Look at the example of Becky and imagine that she had had to stay in the tower block complex after Tressa's birth. She had all the problems of living in the block that she faced with Nessa but in addition she would experience some grief about the death of her second daughter.

How might Becky be helped to care for Tressa, assuming that for the foreseeable future a move to better accommodation was out of the question and she will have to stay in her flat?

Comment: One possibility is to work directly with Becky to help resolve her grief about the loss of Kensa and death of Nessa. There is some evidence that parents who are still morning the loss of a child or significant relationship struggle to relate to a new baby.

Second, Becky can be helped by specialists in sudden infant death to adopt strategies such as putting Tressa to sleep on her back to avoid as far as possible another 'cot death'.

Becky's isolation could be minimised and her parenting capacity could be maximised by encouraging her to join in with community facilities such as SureStart centre or 'Mums and Tots' group.

The 'protection racket' could not be resolved by Becky on her own therefore work would have to be taken with the police and a residents' group to try to disempower the criminals. However, you could initiate the suggestion with the police, act as an advocate for Becky and then encourage her to participate in schemes developed to withstand the protection racketeers.

Again, helping her to keep hold of her welfare payments would not be easy on a one-to-one basis although money advice might help. Nevertheless, there might be ways of exploring how Becky and other vulnerable parents could be paid their benefits more securely.

Do you notice anything about your own and the ideas suggested?

They are likely to follow the nests in the ecological framework, moving from the individual focus, for example, Becky's loss counselling, close relationships advice from SIDS specialists, to the immediate community focusing specifically on families, such as, SureStart. Then moving out through the ecosystems the wider communities, such as the residents' group and the local police can help and finally the state and state-allied groups such as welfare rights advocates and providers are involved.

Putting it into practice

Examine any families, which are in a similar situation to that of Becky and Tressa, that you have encountered in your work or placement:

- What help has already been given?
- Where was the help located? Was it just in the innermost nest, being directed towards the parents and child?
- Were there any extensions of support given which involved the wider nests and environment?
- Could there be any additional assistance given, and where in terms of ecological nests would this be located.

Social–cultural perspectives

The social–cultural approach to child protection does not define 'culture' simply in terms of the traditions and inheritance of a particular race or nationality but uses the term to denote the pervading values of a particular society. Social–culturalists argue that the dominant values in a society can either encourage or deter abusive behaviour. In many societies there is a level of domestic violence to partners, children and dependent older people which is condoned by the absence of any real efforts to oppose it. This means that the prevention of child abuse requires cultural and legal prohibitions against physical violence to children and a change in the negative portrayal of children and associated damaging attitudes.

Some societies endorse the physical assault of children while others do not. Zolotor and Puzla (2010) examined the 24 countries which, by 2010, had banned the corporal punishment of children. They noted that all countries with a corporal punishment ban have elected or representative government. No communist, dictatorship or absolute monarchy did so. There, therefore, appears a link between respect for the citizen and respect for the child. In contrast, Hester *et al.* (2009) reported that, in China, physical punishment is legal and seen as culturally acceptable with 74 per cent of males and 65 per cent of females endorsing it.

In relation to sexual abuse, Ennew (1986) and Kitzinger (1994) raised concerns about the use of children as sex objects. This concern about the sexualisation of children has continued and reflected in Australian (Senate, 2008) and English (Bailey, 2011) reports.

An NSPCC (2007, p. 3) briefing argued that neglect 'has received little attention until relatively recently'. Attitudes to neglect in Britain are influenced by the fear of appearing 'judgemental' or restricting parental autonomy (see Stevenson, 1996). This is in contrast to cultures in which neglect is more readily viewed as mistreatment, for example in Arab society where neglect is 'considered as a violation of the social norms about parenthood' (Haj-Yahia and Shor, 1995, p. 1216).

The vulnerability of children to neglect in the UK, where research and policy is relatively sparse and practitioners' fear of appearing 'judgemental' or intruding into families' private lives, is evident. Neurobiologists and the medical profession, notably Glaser (2000) and Perry (2009), have however recently highlighted the damaging effect of early neglect on children's brain development and this has prompted a review of social policy in relation to neglect (McSherry, 2011).

Estimates of prevalence rates for emotional abuse tend to be higher than other forms with estimates around 29 per cent in the UK (Doyle, 1998) and 30–33 per cent in the USA (Binggeli *et al.*, 2001; Pooler *et al.*, 2008; Festinger and Baker, 2010; Hart *et al.*, 2011). The widespread experience of emotional abuse can be attributed to the considerable acceptance of verbal abuse, threats and denigration towards children which is often displayed in public (Yule, 1985; Davis, 1996) and endorsed by the culture, as shown by the constant negative references to children by the British media (Ainsley-Green, 2011).

Children's rights and positive constructions of children

In terms of policy contexts, the classical work by Harding (1997) helps explain why, when governments change, the organisations within which professionals work might suddenly be disbanded or re-structured. It sheds light on why a government-commissioned report which seems full of good sense is unexpectedly not adopted. It clarifies why when practitioners know they are making progress with families, without warning their funding is cut. An understanding of social policy approaches can help to alleviate some of the frustrations of working in an area in which the state nowadays has a leading role.

Harding (1997) identified four main perspectives on child-care policy namely:

- *laissez-faire*, where state intervention is only deemed appropriate in extreme cases of abuse;
- *state paternalism* in which the state deems what is good enough parenting and acts to ensure all children have this;
- *parents' rights/modern defence* of the birth family in which birth families are deemed to be best for children and the state should support them;
- *children's rights*, where children should have similar rights to those of adults.

This last, children's rights, is not easy to define. On the one hand, it can mean that children should have full rights whereas others argue that rights merely mean being protected and being heard. However, a children's rights perspective links in with Hardiker's idea of the radical model and should be reflected in anti-oppressive practice espoused by social workers. Not only should professionals be challenging oppressions such as racism, sexism, homophobia, disablism and poverty but they should also be empowering the victims of these injustices to challenge them directly. Logically, this includes helping children to raise their voices to highlight and contest the very many oppressions to which they are subject.

The whole issue of the way children are viewed has been the subject of much research. As Graham (2011) points out it was Aries (1962) that prompted the debate about the different constructions and concepts of childhood, arguing that in medieval times in the West, only the very youngest and most dependent of infants and young children were regarded as 'children'. Similarly, Postman (1983) contended that, before the development of the printing press, the divide between children and adults was imperceptible. Anthropologists offered insights into different social constructs of childhood in different cultures, for example, Benedict (1955) pointed to cultures in which the 'child' is given the respect and dignity that Western society reserves for adults.

Hendrick (1990, 1994) traced how modern Western childhood has been constructed from different forms in the past two centuries, as either depraved or innocent, a view still reflected today. Tracing the Western concept of childhood right up to modern day, Timimi (2010) looks at the tensions created for children and childhood by free-market, individualistic ideologies and the 'McDonaldization' of childhood.

In the UK, there is evidence of a substantially negative construct of children (Ainsley-Green, 2011). They are generally seen as troublemakers on our streets, with the press referring to 'feral children'. Freeman (2010) cites a newspaper article written in 2006 by Julie Bindel in which she writes 'kids [sic] are routinely taken to proper restaurants for lunch, but I was here before it became Nappy Valley ... [the Mayor] has made it easier for the little monsters to follow me around London by giving school children free bus passes'. Rewrite this as a younger adult complaining about older people substituting 'pensioners' and 'older adults' for 'kids' and 'school children' and the grossly discriminatory attitude becomes clear.

Children are also too often seen as objects and referred to as 'it'. Authors of social science books often refer to a child as 'it' yet when writing about adults of unknown gender will use alternative strategies. Next to me, as I write, there is a book published in 2006 and in the title are the words '...for Social Work'. In the index there are sections on 'values' and 'discrimination' and yet throughout the child is an 'it', for example, 'it has to make an attachment to its mother' and it is 'important that the child is supported at this stage of its life so that it does not develop a sense of inferiority' (p. 82). I have refrained from mentioning the author because he or she is far from being the only one to refer to the child in this way and rather than condemn individual authors, my intention is to highlight just how far children are objectified by society and treated as objects of study by researchers and academics. It is, therefore, unsurprising that, at times, practitioners treat a child – inappropriately in the view of

Butler-Sloss (1988, p. 245) – as 'an object of concern' rather than a fellow human being.

One of the reasons for raising concern when children are objectified is that if we recall the precursors of abuse in Figure 1.1 (see p. 6) the 'objectification of victims' is a major contributory factor. The Jews in Nazi Germany were featured as 'rats'. African slaves were traditionally viewed as sub-human. Where a group in society is regarded as not fully human or an object then it is far easier for their abuse to be justified. Part of the task of social workers and other child protection practitioners is to challenge the objectification of children in all its forms. Hart (1988) writing about the prevention of emotional abuse urged a 'positive ideology' of children. One way to protect all children is to press for them to be valued and respected in society.

Further resources

Ayre, P. and Preston-Shoot, M. (eds) (2010) *Children's Services at the Crossroads*. Lyme Regis: Russell House Publishing.
This is an engaging exploration of child-care policy and includes chapters examining policy in Wales and Scotland. Taken as a whole, the book seems to address the question 'how did we get into this mess?'

Lonne, B., Parton, N., Thomson, J. and Harries, M. (2009) *Reforming Child Protection*. Abingdon, Oxon: Routledge.
This provides a context for understanding present systems and argues for fundamental changes. It looks beyond the UK to embrace lessons from a range of cultures.

Stafford, A., Vincent, S. and Parton, N. (eds) (2010) *Child Protection Reform Across the UK*. Edinburgh: Dunedin Academic Press.
This is a slim volume but replete with absorbing chapters written by a range of specialists in child protection and social policy. It looks at policy throughout the UK.

The National Children's Bureau is an excellent source of information on children's issues generally especially in relation to policy, legislation and new initiatives for children's welfare. Its website is: www.ncb.org.uk

More information about:

Homestart can be obtained from: http://www.home-start.org.uk/
about/what_we_do.

KidsAid is available at http://www.kidsaid.org.uk.

The Pen Green Children's Centre, Corby, can be found at:
http://www.pengreen.org.

CHAPTER 10

The effects of abuse: the later years

CHAPTER OVERVIEW

This chapter looks at the prospects for abused children in later life:

- the first section examines some of the evidence that exists about the long-term effects of abuse
- this is followed by accounts of the early adulthood and present situations of Marie, Lloyd, Sarah, Roy, Josie and Jake
- the penultimate section examines ways in which social workers can help adults who were abused as children

Evidence of long-term effects

There have been numerous research studies, some of which will be discussed below, that have explored the long-term effects of abuse on children. There are, however, difficulties in collecting and interpreting data which can, if not recognised, give rise to faulty assumptions.

Theoretically, it should be possible to compare the development of abused children with non-abused children, tracking them as they grow up. In such 'prospective' research, there are problems choosing a reliable control group. Josie, Jake, Roy and Sarah would almost certainly have found themselves in a control group of apparently non-abused children with which the group of abused children would have been matched and compared. Researchers usually have to rely on the subjective assessment of the participants to determine who was and who was not abused and there is evidence of retrospective under-reporting of abuse (Dube *et al.*, 2004; Kendall-Tackett and Becker-Blease, 2004). With the passage of time, abuse can be seen as a minor problem or justifiable chastisement. Sometimes adults simply forget what happened. For example, Williams (1994) asked survivors about their sexual maltreatment, twenty years after it was documented. Over a third had forgotten most or all of the abuse. Conversely, some studies have shown an apparently 'false memory' (see Wisdom *et al.*, 2004) but this may be because no childhood is totally free of emotional pain and the memory can elaborate and augment adverse events to explain distress in adulthood.

Another factor is the difficulty of separating out the negative long-term effects directly attributable to what is constructed as 'child abuse' from those which are due to other difficulties, such as, a significant bereavement or violence in the community. Morrison's (1993) description of his uneasy childhood is attributable not so much to abuse as to a mismatch between an ebullient parent's temperament and his son's more reticent one.

Negative consequences of abuse

For a number of children, death is the ultimate negative consequence. For other children, there is the burden of multiple disability. One baby, Michelle, was sixteen-days old when she was picked up by the feet by her father and her head smashed against the floor. She was rushed to a specialist hospital and her life saved. However, five years later she was severely mentally and physically disabled, only able to make a small range of noises and unable to control her body.

Other children have to live with disfiguring scars from cuts, burns and scalding. But many more have emotional scars which do not show so readily. Emotional and behavioural difficulties, which have been recorded in follow-up studies of abused children, are summarised in a study by Davidson *et al.* (2010).

Sixty-five per cent of people who were diagnosed as 'non-organic failure-to-thrive' were found to have substantial problems especially in terms of poor social relationships and substance misuse in a fifteen-year follow-up study (Iwaniec, 2006). Walker (1992) described how personality development can be impaired to the extent that people demonstrate multiple-personality disorder. In relation to sexual abuse, eating disorders and psychiatric problems have been noted (Roberts *et al.*, 2004). Up to 81 per cent of women requiring treatment for drug misuse had a history of abuse and neglect (Min *et al.*, 2007).

In more recent years, researchers and practitioners have been interested in evidence that victims of abuse, especially where there may have been the use of terror and violence, sometimes suffer from post-traumatic stress, discussed briefly in relation to children in Chapter 3 (see p. 58). Adults may show an avoidance of anything connected with the abusive events. This might also be manifest as a general lack of responsiveness to any association with the abuse, or the inability to recall events. Second, there might be a continual re-experiencing of the traumatic incidents, including flashbacks and persistent distressing dreams. Third, there might be increased arousal. With adults this is likely to occur when memories return or if they are in a situation that re-creates past abusive experiences. They may have difficulties sleeping, relaxing and concentrating, and hence become irritable. They often display a phobia of apparently innocuous situations, which seems irrational until the associations with past abuse are recognised.

Generational cycle of abuse

One of the consequences of abuse, which gives rise to considerable concern, is the idea of a cycle of abuse from one generation to the next, with people abused as children growing up to be abusers themselves. Herzberger (1993) argued that there is no sound foundation for these theories. It is also evident that children who have been abused know the warning signs and can protect their own children. On the other hand there are sound reasons why abuse in childhood should lead to abusive parenting. A feature of the Stockholm syndrome is that abuse victims interpret parental behaviour as strong, courageous and justified, a model which they grow up to emulate. Behavioural theories suggest violence is learnt and 'families, through their use of violence, teach that violence is an acceptable form of expression or problem solving' (Gelles and Strauss, 1979, p. 542). Children who have been neglected may not know how to cope with household demands and become neglecting parents. Sexual abuse victims may protect their self-image by convincing themselves that there is nothing wrong in sexual relationships between adults and children.

Finally, it perhaps comes as no surprise that Hitler's father was:

> a drunkard and a tyrant ... in Hitler's case the love for his young mother and the hate for his old father assumed morbid proportions ... which drove him to love and to hate and compelled him

to save or destroy people and peoples who really 'stand for' his mother and his father (Erikson, 1965, pp. 319–20).

Children who do well

By no means all abused children grow up to be severely damaged or dangerous. Although some may have social difficulties and private sorrows, others become happy, well-adjusted individuals who provide excellent care for their own offspring (Rutter, 1996).

In a follow-up study of abused children and their siblings, Lynch and Roberts (1982) noted that 37 per cent appeared to have no particular problems, they could enjoy themselves and were self-confident. They were also healthy, neurologically intact, well grown, intellectually normal and had no discernible behaviour disturbances. They could form good relationships with both adults and children.

There is also increasing interest not just in the damage caused by maltreatment to the developing brain but the plasticity of the brain and possible therapy to improve and repair it (Giza *et al.*, 2009; Johnson, 2009; Thompson *et al.*, 2009; Kolb *et al.*, 2011). Twardosz and Lutzker (2010, p. 64) note 'research with humans provides consistent support for brain plasticity in response to experience throughout life' and they argue that, because of this, adults, and particularly parents abused as children, may well be able to learn positive behaviours. There is, therefore, evidence that even as adults, victims can be helped, despite having been repeatedly abused as children and despite having no consistent caring figure for much of their early life. Phil Quinn for example found 'salvation' in the form of acceptance by a group of motor-bikers 'Satan's Saints' (Quinn, 1988). In the following accounts it will be seen that Marie, Lloyd, Sarah, Roy, Josie and Jake were all given significant help in their adult lives.

Marie's account continued (see Chapter 2, p. 24, for childhood narrative)

Marie was married early to a man who was violent and sexually abusive. She returned to her parents' home only to be molested by her father. She realised how inappropriate her father's attitude to his children was when, on one occasion during this period, he was trying to kiss her, using considerable force. As Marie resisted, he shouted, 'What's the matter? You're a woman and I'm a man.' Marie responded with, 'No, you're my father and I'm your daughter.'

While back with her parents Marie formed a relationship with Glen, a young friend of her father. He was gentle and trustworthy, never showing any anger or swearing. He felt that he was sexually impotent so theirs was a platonic friendship. Marie was able to receive a cuddle from him without feeling dirty and defiled. Glen showed her that not all men were violent and demanding like her father and her first husband.

Marie liked Glen but never loved him. After a while she was able to move on to a relationship demanding more commitment. Her second husband, Luke, was gentle and caring like Glen but she loved him and was able to have a satisfactory sexual relationship with him. Glen remained in the background for a while and told her, 'I'll always be in the bank for you emotionally.' Marie realised that she was now strong enough to help her husband when he needed support.

The couple had a number of children and when one daughter was molested, Marie immediately sought help for her. Neither parent was responsible for the incident, their daughter was able to tell them what had happened, and they went to great lengths to ensure that all their children were protected in future.

At the time, Marie was attending a self-help group for adults who had been abused as children. She found that the support of its members was important to her and they helped her put events into perspective. She also received help during this critical period from a very gentle, caring male social worker who referred her to a psychotherapist. She benefited from the counselling she was given but did not need such intensive help for long. Eventually, she became a 'senior member' of the self-help group giving assistance to newer members who were at a more vulnerable and painful stage of the healing process.

Marie views her father with a mixture of anger and pity. He is an old man now. When the family visits her parents she ensures that none of her children are left alone with him. Pauline, her elder sister, still has emotional difficulties and cannot communicate with her husband; she will attack him even if he has only one drink. Linda married a violent man who broke her arm and then found solace in relationships with women. Marie's brother, Barry, followed their father into the Services but he was convicted of causing grievous bodily harm and given a dishonourable discharge. He is still very violent and in Marie's words 'mixed up and not coping with adult life'.

Marie herself is still sometimes affected by her experiences. She acknowledges that she is a 'worrier'. She 'worries for others' and becomes anxious about potential problems before they arrive. Nevertheless she is determined that her father, having destroyed her childhood, will not destroy her future. She is a tall, elegant woman who dresses smartly and has an air of confidence mixed with a warm, generous manner. Asked what helped her survive those unhappy earlier years, Marie replied that humour had been her salvation; she would always try to see the funny side of any situation.

Lloyd's account continued (see Chapter 2, p. 33, for childhood narrative)

Lloyd was on a generally downward spiral of drink and drugs when at the age of twenty-one he met a group of 'born-again' Christians. He stayed with them for about five years. He found in the group there was total acceptance, 'however bad I was I was accepted as part of a family'. The reality of what he was doing to himself hit home. He received counselling and the counsellor suggested his experiences were for a purpose. The counsellor also helped him to come to terms with the sexual abuse and understand why it happened and that it was not his fault. He found that he could use his experiences to counsel other abandoned and distressed people. The acceptance of the group and the sense of being of some value to others increased his self-esteem. He eventually left the religious group because he wanted to extend his counselling work and became professionally qualified.

He has now married and has three step-children. He has made a conscious choice not to be abusive. He has to check out with his wife about how to respond to the children because he is not sure how to be a good father figure: for example, he did not realise that when the children fell over they needed to be picked up and comforted.

Lloyd occasionally visits his original family. His brothers have fared less well. They are unable to find jobs and have become involved in drugs. While Lloyd is very optimistic about his own future, he is left wondering about the effects on siblings of witnessing abuse rather than being directly abused themselves.

Sarah's account continued (see Chapter 2, p. 35, for childhood narrative)

Having left home, Sarah went to live with her aunt and uncle until she felt ready for greater independence. They did not try to stop her leaving; they appreciated the fact that she needed to move on. Living in digs she met a woman who accepted her and hearing of her experiences commented, 'It isn't fair, why should it have happened to you.' This helped Sarah realise that she was not to blame for what had occurred and there was nothing bad about her, she had not deserved such maltreatment. She learnt about friendship from that woman and was able, through her, to make other friends. Sarah explained, 'I reached out a little, it worked so I reached out a little further.'

Sarah then married Mark, a kindly, mild-mannered man. She acknowledges that she almost married a man like her father in the form of the boyfriend to whom she became engaged when she was seventeen. She realised when she had recovered from the broken engagement that she did not want to marry a bully. Mark is very similar to her grandfather who, as described by Sarah, was 'the one good man who could love in a giving way, who loved me for myself and who, with his wife, could offer me a safe family'. Sarah's grandparents also loved each other so she had faith that a loving relationship was possible.

Sarah knows that it has taken her a long time to work through her feelings of worthlessness. She started the work herself. She raised her own family and completed a teacher training course. She reached a position of strength but recognised that she could become inappropriately angry. Furthermore, she would dwell on the deaths of people to whom she was close. She had a profound sense of loss and was stuck in the anger of that loss; in Sarah's words 'It was beginning to explode'. She knew the anger was inappropriate so she sought help from a counsellor.

She still had problems over body image and general worth. In therapy she recalled, amid intense pain, the incident when her father called her a 'pregnant cow'. The counsellor made her realise that what her father had shouted on the beach that day was untrue, emphasising, 'That was a lie, a vicious lie.' Sarah rejoiced in the realisation of the fact that her father was not always right and she was able to lay her burden of anger down.

Sarah also had to cope with a difficult period when a head of department, Mrs A, took a dislike to her and made her life a misery. Sarah realised that the woman felt threatened by her apparent strength and efficiency; therefore, she told Mrs A about her childhood in an attempt to demonstrate her vulnerability. After this revelation, Mrs A became increasingly vindictive. Perplexed, Sarah went to a colleague for help. The colleague observed that Mrs A was probably even more threatened now because she knew Sarah had the strength to survive such a testing childhood.

Despite the influence of Mrs A, Sarah's teaching abilities were recognised and she now has a successful career. Barbara lives abroad and there is still only a distant, superficial relationship between the two sisters. Their parents divorced and their father emigrated. Sarah has no contact with him. Her mother, while still married, tried to throw herself out of a window, but once divorced could cope no better alone and turned more and more to drink. She eventually died and was lying dead for a fortnight before anyone found her body.

Sarah is a vivacious, attractive woman with a happy marriage, grown-up children, and a fulfilling career. She can readily be described as a warm person with a bright, cheerful expression in her eyes. When asked what helped her survive she, like Marie, mentioned humour. She recalled how stupid her father looked having an erection in his dressing-gown. She has retained her sense of humour. Sarah also had a much loved dog and was able to escape the house by taking him for long walks. The countryside around was very beautiful and this sustained her. She felt the mountains belonged to her and used to 'fill up on the beauty of the mountains'. She found that she was and is creative with considerable artistic gifts. She managed to win a prize and knew that this was a talent her father could not deny her.

Sarah is now free of the burden of abuse. She once pointed to a photograph of herself as a little girl saying, 'How could my father have done that to me, I was a lovely child.' She is aware that some of the children she teaches are being abused. She is not sorry that she was abused because she can use her experiences to help others.

Roy's account continued (see Chapter 2, p. 39, for childhood narrative)

Roy emerged into adulthood still battling with anorexia nervosa. He continued to eat very little and would do everything to expend energy such as running round a huge park six times a day.

However, the help given to him by staff and fellow patients at the day centre was doing much to restore his self-esteem. As he was recovering from anorexia, he met his wife who further enhanced his feeling of worth. His mother-in-law, who is a social worker, understood his needs and was, and still is, very supportive. He has three children in whom he delights. Roy's father will not leave Roy or his family alone. But, due to his past violence and his liking for young girls, they will not let him have contact with the grandchildren. He kept pestering them and one day attacked Roy's wife in front of the children in a shopping centre because she would not let him see his grandchildren. He was not charged with assault because there were no visible injuries but they did get an injunction to ensure that he could not come into contact with the family. This appears to have worked because he has stopped pestering them.

Roy is tall and slim but not thin and is happy to eat with the family. There is no sign of the anorexia. He is optimistic about the future and feels he has found a niche in life working with young people. Although his job is poorly paid and they are struggling financially, the home is comfortable. Roy finds he has to work at his marriage as he is not always sure of the best way of overcoming problems. However, there is no question of domestic or emotional violence towards his wife or children. He is an attractive, thoughtful person who is committed to his family.

Josie and Jake's accounts continued (see Chapter 2, pp. 41, 44, for childhood narratives)

Josie

Although for both Josie and Jake, their paternal grandparents' illness and decline had been the cause of some heartbreak, it caused their aunt Debbie and uncle Mark to enter their lives. Debbie was their father's older sister and Mark, her husband. They had lived some considerable distance away so had been rare visitors during the children's earlier years. However, when the grandparents' health failed, Debbie visited as much as possible to help out. Although not fully aware of the situation, Debbie began to realise that Josie was burdened with heavy family responsibilities and began to take an interest in her niece. She encouraged Josie to think about being independent. Jodie started to earn some money babysitting and then, with the emotional support of her aunt, uncle and father, managed to obtain a job as an assistant at a children's nursery. She was sponsored to undertake a part-time foundation degree in early childhood studies and is hoping to top this up to a full honours degree and gain the Early Years Professional Status award.

Working at the nursery, she made friends with colleagues of her own age and recently she has moved out of the family home and into a flat shared with two colleagues. She is still very concerned about her family and feels responsible for the well-being of her parents and Jake. For her, the events of childhood are still a recent memory. She is not sure how easily she will be able to break free of her family. She would love to travel but believes she has to stay not too far from her parents in case they need her. Nevertheless, she has a job she loves and is gaining enhanced self-esteem through both her work and her qualifications. She has not yet had a serious boyfriend and is very wary of marriage but she has a good group of friends and enjoys a social life.

Jake

Jake is still young, although in early adulthood. He left school as soon as he was sixteen and only managed three GCSEs at grade C. He admired Mark who is a paramedic. Eventually, after a couple of holidays with them he moved in with Debbie and Mark. This might have seemed a risky prospect because they live on the edge of a large city and there was the temptation of gang membership. However, Jake is no longer interested in belonging to a gang or in lighting fires.

For a while after moving in with his aunt and uncle, Jake became depressed. He spent his days in bed not wanting to eat, wash himself, exercise or do anything. Mark, as a paramedic, had some understanding of the situation and persuaded Jake to see his GP. He was given anti-depressants but also saw a counsellor.

He has trained as a tree-surgeon, and perhaps inheriting his father's creativity and love of gardening, he is thinking of becoming a landscape architect. Meanwhile, recognising his fascination with fires has made him wonder if he should apply to become a fire officer. His main problem, however, is that he does not relate well to people of his own age so he is not sure how far he could give the type of total commitment to the team demanded of a fire officer. Jake is aware that he has quite a lot of anger inside him, so encouraged by Mark who is himself a judo enthusiast, Jake is learning to express controlled and largely defensive aggression through martial arts.

Point for reflection

Now that you know the outcomes for Roy, Lloyd, Marie, Sarah, Josie and Jake, are there any additional supports or assistance that helped enhance their resilience? Identify any key factors in adulthood that you think was particularly helpful.

Comment: This is to help you think more broadly about resilience factors and to recognise that social support and other forms of help can be continued or introduced in adulthood to positive effect.

Helping adult survivors

The phrase 'adult survivor' is used in this section to refer to those abused children who reach independent adulthood. Not all do; some are killed, some commit suicide, some die of preventable diseases – sexually transmitted or as a result of neglect. Others are permanently damaged in such a way that, mentally and emotionally, they remain like dependent children.

As illustrated by the accounts of Marie, Lloyd, Sarah, Roy, Josie and Jake it is never too late to attempt to release an adult survivor from the negative feelings and inaccurate perspectives which imprison them. Men and women who were abused over fifty years ago have sought and received assistance. If abused people are not helped during childhood, they may have to live with a lot of pain but need not be condemned to life-long misery. Those involved in child welfare may well have skills that could also help 'grown-up' abused children.

The following sections examine ways of helping adult survivors although, because this book is about working with children, there will be only a brief overview. As with children, practitioners know that survivors can come from a range of ethnic and cultural groups, have varying degrees of ability, disability and diverse capabilities, they will have different sexual orientations and be of both genders and a broad age span. This means care has to be taken to ensure that all intervention is sensitive to this diversity.

Helping the individual

Adults sometimes carry a heavier burden than children because negative feelings arising from the abuse may have been reinforced over time. They will have an increased number of painful incidents to remember if, like Marie and Sarah, the abuse continued into their late teens or early twenties. One of the most constructive initial steps is to encourage the survivor to recall, when ready to do so, as much of his or her early life as possible. Having described events, it is easier to view them from a more accurate perspective. Sarah describes how during counselling she was able to recognise that her father had lied about her. Having been relived and reassessed, such incidents can be left behind and the survivor can move on. However, no one should be forced to recall distressing events (see Evert and Bijkerk, 1987). If someone prefers never to talk about the past but deals with feelings in the present, they are entitled to do so and there is no failure in either that person or their helper if past events are not discussed.

As Sarah and Jake recognised, anger may need to be dealt with. Often in the wake of recall comes long-suppressed anger. Frequently it is directed towards the survivor, him or herself. Sometimes it is targeted at society in general or a particular group in society such as men or authority figures such as the police. Occasionally it is turned against the therapist – 'you can't know what it felt like'. 'I bet you are enjoying this, hearing the juicy details'. Survivors need to be helped to express anger against the perpetrators of the abuse and those who failed to protect them. They then need to move on to make sense of events, directing their anger into constructive rather than destructive channels. Anger made Marie, Roy and Sarah determined that even though their fathers had ruined their childhoods they were not going to spoil their future. Anger has spurred people into helping abused children, setting up schemes to prevent abuse or supporting other adults abused during childhood.

All survivors share a sense of loss. They have lost their only opportunity to be carefree, cared-for children. They need to work through this loss in the same way that bereaved people have to complete the task of mourning. They, like those who are grieving, can be helped to come to terms with what has happened by acknowledging their losses and expressing their feelings, doubts and fears.

Survivors are likely to be most comfortable if they are able to reach a stage when they can look back at themselves as children and can imagine cuddling and comforting their child-self. One useful exercise involves the survivors looking at a photograph of themselves when young and describing how they feel about the child they see. Once the mourning and healing process is complete, they will be able to express largely positive emotions about their child-self.

One issue that survivors like Roy have to face is how best to protect their children from possible abuse by their own parents. It is not always easy, as Roy's case illustrates, to keep grandparents away from their grandchildren.

Another related issue with which survivors have to contend, are the theories about the generational 'cycle of abuse'. The survivor accounts above show that abused children do not necessarily become abusive adults. One survivor articulated the issue for all experiencing childhood maltreatment, 'People who have not suffered abuse as children probably do not have to think about whether they will abuse their own or not. But we have a choice to make. We can make a conscious decision not to be like our own parents.'

Group therapy

Groups for adult survivors can vary from relatively short-term projects run by professional workers to open-ended self-help groups. Adults, unlike young children, can take on responsibility for running their own group. One model is that of a self-help group started by experienced group workers who are already skilled in assisting the victims of various situations. These 'facilitators' set up the group in response to a perceived demand. They make the initial practical arrangements such as finding meeting rooms and organising refreshments.

Facilitators also help in the healing process, preventing the group from becoming stuck in a mood of despair or destructive anger. As one or two survivors work through their problems, they take over the responsibility for both practical arrangements and for assisting newer or more vulnerable members. Eventually, the facilitators withdraw from group sessions, remaining in the background as advisers in case the members need guidance.

The main benefit of group therapy is that it alleviates the sense of isolation that so many survivors experience. This is particularly important for sexually abused men because much of the publicity is directed towards physical abuse and sexually victimised girls.

Group work always requires careful preparation. Facilitators need to think and talk through all the problems that they can anticipate. If they themselves were abused as children, how will they respond when asked about their own experiences? Are they using the group as a therapeutic tool for themselves? If they were not abused, how will they reply to the accusation of failing to understand what it is like to be abused? What action if any should the facilitators take if they learn that a member is now abusing a child? What will they do if a member appears to be suicidal? As with children's groups it is important that several members should turn up for the first session and some potential members will be parents, therefore, a crèche may be necessary.

Activities can help to promote or direct discussion. However, adults, more than children, may well want to talk at length because they have much to talk about. There should be few rules but it is helpful if members agree to finish promptly. There is a tendency for people to put off bringing up difficult subjects till the last possible moment. This can place other members who have to leave on time in a dilemma, unable to stay any longer but wanting to support the distressed member. In a case of severe distress, a facilitator may have to spend some time after the main session assisting the member with the immediate crisis and helping him or her bring it to the group on another occasion.

Putting it into practice

Recall some of the activities suggested in Chapters 5, 6 and 7 for working directly with children. Could you adapt any of the exercises for use with any adult survivors with whom you are working?

For example, could the 'castle' exercise be adapted for adults to help them recognise people, strategies and agencies who could help them when they feel threatened by memories or people from their past, or incidents or people who recreate their experiences of abuse?

Comment: The purpose of this exercise is to show that practitioners' repertoire of ways of intervening and helping people therapeutically, can be enhanced by adapting activities, designed for one group, to meet the needs of another.

Further resources

Courtois, C. (2010) *Healing the Incest Wound: Adult Survivors in Therapy*, 2nd edn. New York: W. W. Norton & Company.
This is a second edition of a classic book which addresses the issues of adults sexually abused as children. The thirteenth chapter explores group work with survivors.

Knight, C. (2009) *Working with Adult Survivors of Childhood Trauma.* Belmont, CA: Thomas Brooks/Cole Publishing.
Although this describes therapeutic intervention in the USA, there is useful guidance in relation to both individual and group work with adult survivors.

The Ann Craft Trust's website is: www.anncrafttrust.org
The Trust offers information and advice services on aspects of sexual abuse and exploitation of adults as well as children with learning difficulties.

SupportLine can be contacted on: http://www.supportline.org.uk
It offers sympathetic guidance on its web pages for all survivors of childhood abuse including a section dedicated to male survivors. The services also include telephone and email support.

CHAPTER 11

Valuing child protection practitioners

> **CHAPTER OVERVIEW**
> The chapter looks at the value of those who work on the front line of child protection work and explores:
>
> - stress, 'burnout' and practitioner resilience and optimism
> - team work, inter-agency working and coping with case conferences, courts and the media
> - supervision, support and training

This chapter returns to one of the themes of the first chapter; the importance of the child protection practitioners. It explores further how they can best be equipped to undertake one of the most demanding jobs in existence.

Let us consider the perceptive comments of Radford (2010, p. 12) as he concluded his inquiry into the death by neglect of Khyra Ishaq:

> Dealing with safeguarding enquiries and assessments can be a stressful process for workers, particularly when attempting to undertake work with aggressive and highly resistant adults... In addition, the availability of quality supervision and support are paramount to ensure an objective and child focused response are maintained.

The observations above highlight many of the challenges faced by professionals including stress, facing aggression and the need for front-line staff to have support and guidance. This chapter therefore looks at some of the pressures faced by child protection practitioners and ways in which these pressures can be managed.

Sport-governing bodies and coaches recognise that whatever 'rules of the game' or regulations they devise, ultimately it will be the fitness, training, dedication and skills of the individual athletes or team members that produce the results. Great sports coaches can make a huge difference but if their teams are tired, injured and unfit they cannot produce great results. Why, one is left to wonder, do governments and some commentators repeatedly believe that practice will improve by implementing more and more policies and procedural rules, without paying attention to the health, training, skills and fitness of front-line staff?

Messages from research

Healy *et al.* (2009)

As indicated above, one of the problems is that policy and procedures need people to implement them on the front line. However, if these staff are difficult to recruit and retain, whatever the merits of the policies, intervention will be weak and ineffective. The research below highlights a significant problem and advances some solutions.

Healy *et al.* (2009) examined the front-line staff working with child protection in Australia, Sweden and the UK. They undertook semi-structured interviews with 58 workers from both government and non-government child protection organisations.

The researchers established that turnover among front-line child protection staff is considerable. A number of factors led to the high turnover in all three countries: a concentration of inexperienced workers at the front line; disincentives such as stress, lack of professional development and support, a culture of blame, and low rewards; and finally the availability of ways out of front-line child protection work into management, administration, non-statutory settings or an exit from child welfare altogether.

The authors' recommendations included good supervision so that complicated cases could be identified and a 'referral pathway' which would enable the most complex and demanding cases to be passed up to experienced practitioners. These strategies, the authors proposed, plus a proper career structure, good remuneration and publicly demonstrated support for their staff by employers would hopefully lead to better retention of front-line child protection workers.

Understanding stress, compassion fatigue and burnout

One notable omission from most public inquiries and serious case reviews into the abuse of children is the contextualisation of the case in terms of the workloads of front-line staff. Although the reports demonstrate oversights and missed opportunities, the fact that the workers might have been concentrating on doing excellent work and preventing abuse in other families is rarely examined. Sometimes there are comments on work overload and staff shortages, and occasionally broad figures are given. For example, London NHS (2009, p. 7) commissioned to address the 'Baby P' case recorded that one of the hospitals involved 'treated more than 46,000 inpatients, 16,000 day-patients, 200,000 outpatients and 157,000 people in the accident and emergency and walk-in centres'. If the caseloads of key social workers, health visitors and other staff were given it might be easier to understand the very real and often extreme pressures under which most child protection professionals work.

Practice focus

Mike

For once, the pseudonym 'Mike' refers to a social worker and not a child. But it is a case example, which has implications for vulnerable children and their families. 'Mike' has given me permission to relay the incident which occurred in late 2011.

Mike is a qualified, able, experienced and dedicated social worker in a local authority child protection team. He is working with a family of eight children who are deemed 'at risk'. Two are already in care. The case conference recommended, and the local authority decided, that four of the remaining children would be accommodated and the other two would be subject to a child protection plan. Mike had to fill in a lengthy form for each child. All the children had the same background information therefore Mike wrote a background summary and attached the same one to each form, providing separate details of each child on the rest of the form. He submitted the forms. They were sent back to him, not to amend, but to fill in again from scratch with a detailed separate background report for each child. He had to spend a day thinking of a slightly different form of words for each of the six background reports and complete the forms in their entirety again.

The original forms would have served the needs and interests of each child perfectly well and would have made no difference to any decisions made. This is typical of bureaucratic waste of time, which has nothing to do with the welfare of children and only leads to unnecessary stress and frustration for front-line workers. Moreover, Mike has no voice. There is nowhere that he can complain about this type of needless work pressure.

The pressures are such that practitioners have to prioritise cases. This means that they have the constant worry about what would happen if one of those seemingly less serious cases unexpectedly 'blew up'. Reading through inquiry reports such as Laming (2003), there is the niggling feeling 'there but for the grace'; how could those workers have imagined the suffering to which Victoria was subject?

Child protection professionals have to think the unthinkable, imagine the unimaginable, believe the unbelievable. But what is the psychological impact of having to do so? It can, without support and adequate resources, result in undue stress, compassion fatigue, secondary post-traumatic stress, vicarious victimisation and burnout.

Stress: the terms stress, compassion fatigue and burnout are sometimes used interchangeably. Obsessions with semantic distinctions are unhelpful; nevertheless, there are subtle differences between the concepts which are worth exploring. Stress can be positive as well as negative. For many front-line professionals it is the challenge of child protection work that motivates them. A moderate level of stress can be invigorating, while coping with it can provide a sense of achievement. It is when stress becomes so great or so interminable that there is little relief from it that it starts to damage both the physical and psychological well-being of the individual.

Compassion fatigue: in recent years there has been more attention paid to compassion fatigue especially amongst social work and other caring services staff (Figley, 2002; Adams *et al.*, 2008; Harr and Moorre, 2011). It is part of the stress profile, with its damaging physiological processes and psychological distress but there is also a moral dimension (Forster, 2009). The teaching of ethics and values is now high on the training curriculum for many care professionals. This means that they become sensitive to the tensions between conflicting values such as the right to self-determination versus the duty of care. They struggle when the law and the practitioner's belief in what is ethical may clash, for example, trying to give consistent support to a traveller family when the family is moved because they have breached planning permission.

The result of compassion fatigue is a reduced capacity to empathise with service users. This leads the practitioner to feel less motivated to help. It can give rise to denigration of clients or patients: 'people who keep winging like that don't deserve help', 'why am I bothering with them when they bring it on themselves'.

It also leads to self-denigration as the worker reflects on the dissonance between the generosity they should be feeling and the grudging emotions they harbour. Bourassa and Clements (2010) discuss various therapies and ways of helping professionals with compassion fatigue.

Secondary post-traumatic stress: this is the same as direct post-traumatic stress but applies to those who are not directly traumatised but are working with those who are and hearing the stories or witnessing the fringes of the events. This can be illustrated by my experiences when, as a young history student, I cheerfully but naively went along with friends who were helping at a London night-shelter for multiple drug users. The reality and horror of what I experienced for the first time hit me like a body blow – limbs and breasts amputated because veins had collapsed, dirty needles, blood, bleak stories of lives of rejection, sobbing, the stench of drugs, disinfectant and vomit – all gave me nightmares and flashbacks. I felt compelled to return to help but dreaded doing so. After a user grabbed my arm threatening to inject 'heaven-knows-what', I became jumpy and hyper-vigilant. I saw my friends coping, so I coped; I continued helping out, I became a social worker. But still, even now, I do not feel comfortable in substance-user facilities, the flashbacks return and I am again jumpy and hyper-vigilant.

Vicarious victimisation: this is another term which is associated with the stress spectrum. One of the key requirements is for helping professionals to empathise with the people with whom they work. They are expected to feel the distress of families so that they can fully appreciate the suffering of others and through this avoid minimising or misreading the situation. However, empathising with a Victoria Climbié, a Khyra Ishaq or a Peter Connelly is literally 'insufferable'. The possible pain borne by the child victims of abuse can be unbearable. This can help explain why so often child protection workers find it easier to empathise with parents; their distress is considerable but not as poignant as that of helpless children. It can also explain why some child protection workers collude with adults who blame the child: 'she's so provocative', 'he's impossible to control'. It is always easier to cope with distress if in some ways victims have brought misfortune on themselves. When practitioners are able to empathise with the child, vicarious victimisation can result in a sense of powerlessness which can lead to apathy and despair.

Another feature of vicarious victimisation is that workers may be readily intimidated by the adult abusers. The child victim has been disempowered. If practitioners identify with the child there is the danger that they too will experience disempowerment. Yet these are the people who should be challenging the abusers. Empathy means standing with the child but protection means positioning ourselves in front of the child. It is hugely difficult to be in two places at one.

Burnout: Many workers find that they can only engage in direct, front-line work for a limited time before becoming 'burnt out'. This is the draining of emotion because of repeated over-demand on limited emotional resources. Signs of burnout can be detected in relation to practitioners themselves, to service users and to colleagues.

- *The self*: there is increasing exhaustion and somatic symptoms such as lingering colds, general aches and pains. A deep reluctance to go to work sets in. Tasks are put off and there is the hope that services users will not turn up or, when home visiting, the family is out. Ferguson (2011, p. 41) refers to the 'quiet knock', hoping parents will not hear and not answer the door. This results in dissatisfaction with one's own performance and feelings of guilt and self-denigration.
- *Service users*: negative attitudes to service users multiply, including insensitivity, intolerance and dehumanisation of them. This is why the use of 'it' to refer to a child can be so perilous; this general cultural and societal objectification can lead to children being the first service users to be dehumanised by burnt out professionals.
- *Colleagues*: profound cynicism develops and attitudes to colleagues become negative. Unable to trust fellow workers, they increase the pressure on themselves by insisting 'I'll have to do it myself'. Bright new colleagues or eager students are a particular source of frustration. The burnt out worker harbours resentment against them and greets their suggestions with 'It won't work', 'We've tried it all before' or 'They'll learn.' Unable any longer to summon up energy and initiative, their reliance on rules becomes obsessive. They insist on everything being done 'by the book'. These attitudes can also spill over into their private lives with growing resentment of partners, offspring, friends and neighbours.

It is a sad fact that the better and more committed practitioners are more likely to become burnt out. A new worker arrives eager and enthusiastic, so busy colleagues are only too happy to divest some of their more irksome tasks onto the shoulders of their new keen colleague. The newcomers work with fervour and, at first, start to have good results, therefore are given more work. After a while, the resources to meet the work demands become inadequate. They are given tasks beyond their training, skill and ability or they simply have insufficient time to do a good job. Their successes rapidly diminish and they become frustrated as little progress is made. Despite stagnation they have to work very hard and begin to feel drained, exhausted and frustrated. Perceptions of clients start to change and there is the gradual withdrawal of emotional involvement. Empathetic and generous practitioners recognise with dismay their hardening attitudes and feel incompetent and inadequate. But they also look for others to blame including politicians, society, management, colleagues, services users and even their own family.

Presenteeism

A symptom of a dysfunctional organisation is absenteeism. This is when burnt out or alienated staff repeatedly take days off work for minor reasons. It can result in more pressure on remaining colleagues who become resentful and frustrated. Consequently, some managers try to build a culture where taking one or two days off work for ostensibly minor coughs and colds is discouraged. Presenteeism is where workers appear at work despite suffering from tiredness, colds, flu-like illnesses and temporary but debilitating conditions, such as, migraine, back ache or wrist strain. Johns (2010) noticed it is more common in contexts where professionals have dependent clients. The professional who is present, but suffering from colds and other contagious conditions, will spread their illnesses among colleagues and possibly to people who are more physically vulnerable. When tired or coping with headaches, practitioners may make serious mistakes, be inefficient, short-tempered and their generally gloomy demeanour might alienate others. Unable to rest, they might eventually end up with serious chronic conditions, resulting in lengthy sick leave which means that teams can be depleted long term by colleagues needing lengthy absences, thereby putting huge pressure on remaining practitioners; as Dew (2011, p. 1) asserts, presenteeism 'increases morbidity, including musculoskeletal pain, fatigue, depression, and serious coronary events'.

Arguably therefore presenteeism is more harmful to an organisation than absenteesm but few managers and organisations appreciate this. Admasachew and Dawson (2011, p. 31) surveyed 156,951 NHS workers and concluded 'our analysis clearly indicates that presenteeism is negatively associated with engagement'. The ability to take time off without feeling guilty or condemned is important to the well-being of staff, colleagues, service users and the organisation.

Bullying at work

One reason for stress, burnout and presenteeism can be bullying at work either by managers, peers or subordinate staff; this can have a downward spiral effect. A colleague starts to suggest a fellow worker is useless, lazy, a waste of space. The victim, desperate to prove the suggestion untrue starts to double check his work to make sure it is perfect, leaving him with less time for the essentials. He feels pressurised to volunteer for extra work to show he is not 'lazy', so now he is having to work harder and has less time for self-care. Exhausted, he makes a few mistakes which the bully pounces on and exposes. The victim is provoked into double checking even more rigorously and accepting the most challenging of tasks to prove he is worthwhile. It is easy to see that the end result is a self-fulfilling prophecy, an exhausted, inefficient demoralised practitioner.

It is important to hold on to the realisation that the cause of the problem is the bully and not the victim. Sometimes it is possible to find colleagues who have been bullied by the same person and take a united stand. However, many workplace bullies are very skilful at dividing and ruling. The advice then is the usual one, to keep detailed records of what is happening and follow the organisational complaints procedures when enough evidence has been accumulated.

Practitioner resilience and optimism

Despite all the stress, burnout, fatigue, pressures and constant worries, it is remarkable how many child protection workers remain fully engaged in direct work for considerable periods of time. Many of the most active front-line workers eventually move into training, management or less pressured non-statutory work. Nevertheless, they have often devoted some twenty years or more to direct child protection services and appear to have thrived on the experiences. It is clear that many find ways of coping and developing resilience. Wendt *et al.* (2010) identified factors such as the ability to maintain boundaries, which enabled practitioners to survive, and thrive by enjoying the challenge, having confidence and having or being a role model.

Radley and Figley (2007) argue that in contrast to compassion fatigue, compassion satisfaction can be a feature of social work. They explain that there are four major contributors to compassion fatigue: poor self-care; previous unresolved trauma; inability or refusal to control work stressors; and a lack of satisfaction for the work. Therefore, logically, avoiding these contributors should ensure compassion satisfaction.

In terms of self-care, advice abounds about how to remain healthy. There are the well-publicised strategies of healthy food, plenty of exercise and rest and avoidance of over-indulgence of cigarettes, alcohol and various other legal and illegal substances. Taking time out and annual leave without feeling guilty also helps. Trial and error will show you what suits you individually. For example, my own strategy was to have sporadic adrenalin rushes through a penchant for risky sports. Shepherding my children, novice skiers, down a long, sheer, ice drop when I had inadvertently thought an advanced skiers' black run was a blue, beginners' one, gave me an adrenalin rush which kept me going for the next couple of years.

The problem of unresolved trauma is another area where advice abounds. The previous chapter suggested how survivors of abuse might be helped. Some professionals, such as psychotherapists, are sometimes expected to seek counselling however happy they think their earlier life was to ensure that there are no unresolved conflicts. For anyone who is a survivor it might be advisable to ensure that help is sought well away from employers or if associated with them that confidentiality is assured. Remember in Sarah's up-dated story in the last chapter the reaction of Sarah's head of department, Mrs A, when Sarah told her she had been a victim of abuse?

The third of Radford and Figley's factors is inability or refusal to control work stressors. One function of supervision or simply talking to colleagues is to identify work stressors and then examine how they can be ameliorated before exhaustion sets in, by which time they will have become insurmountable.

The fourth contributor is a lack of satisfaction yet child protection work should be intrinsically rewarding and satisfying. Clearly the problem is huge but practitioners can emulate the child picking up starfish and throwing them back in the sea when they were stranded above the tide line and dying. An adult approaches the child and says 'Why bother to do that, there are too many, what you're doing will make no difference'. The child picks up the nearest starfish saying 'Yes it will, it will make a difference to that one' and gently tosses it into the sea. As we saw from the last chapter, small positive interventions can make a difference, being remembered by abused children and sustaining them into adulthood. Even if not all cases work out well, the benefits to the few who are helped are hugely important for that few.

When working with children and families, practitioners are exhorted to recognise and build on strengths. Weaknesses and limitations, particularly when they are creating not solving problems, have to be acknowledged. However, most work with children and families is not just managing weaknesses but recognising and building on strengths. The same is true for ourselves. There are considerable difficulties, and keeping a 'stiff upper lip' and pretending stresses are not present will ultimately take its toll. Nevertheless, practitioners have knowledge and abilities on which they can build. Child protection work has rewarding challenges. It is important to hang on to the memories of instances when distressed parents and children were clearly helped.

Point for reflection

Try simply to undertake a SLOT analysis (see p. 114) on yourself:

- What are your strengths and how can you maintain and build on these?
- What are your limitations and is there anything you can do to address at least some of them?
- What opportunities are there, how do you capitalise on them and do you need to find out about more opportunities?
- What are the threats and how can you prepare for and minimise the impact of these? In terms of threats, are they really worth worrying about? Can you turn them into opportunities? For example, your closest and most supportive colleague is leaving. Is there any possibility of you and your colleague becoming ' work buddies'. It is sometimes useful to have a trusted person who is not in your workplace but understands your job with whom to share experiences and exchange support. Also is there any task for which your colleague was responsible which you would like? Is there a chance you could make a bid for it?

Collins (2007) emphasised the importance of optimism as a coping mechanism. Although inquiry reports and serious case reviews often reveal parents whose behaviour is truly offensive, for most protection workers, the majority of parents with whom they work welcome help because they do not want to harm their children and many are determined not to be as abusive as their own parents. Preventing or relieving the suffering of the next generation is arguably one of the most valuable contributions to human welfare.

Putting it into practice

Support is an important feature of coping with stress. Think about who supports you. It is important to have more than one person available. Make yourself a table similar to the one outlined below and have a go at filling in the cells.

	In your work situation	In your private life
Who gives you practical help?		
Who gives you emotional support?		
Who can you rely on for good advice?		
Who will give you honest feedback?		
Who is fun to be with?		
Who makes you feel good about yourself?		
Who can you share some of your bleakest experiences with?		
Who can you share some of your bleakest thoughts with?		
Who can you share your anger with?		
Who can you share your achievements with?		

You can also think about:

- what do you do for fun
- what do you do to keep yourself physically healthy
- what do you do to 'switch off' from the stresses of work

Comment: your aim is to be able to identify several strong supports, with a different set of people in your work and in your private life. If your answers are rather thin or you seem to be filling in the same person each time then it is worth trying to extend your range of supports.

Teams and team-working

Burnout can quickly pervade a team, sucking even the most able workers into the downward spiral. As Cousins (2010, p. 285) observes, it can start with one member of staff being given a less challenging workload: 'allowances are made and the rest of the team is forced to carry an additional workload'. Other over-stretched team members have an increased workload. They become stressed and tired, with a supressed antagonism to the colleague who has the lighter load. Their frustration and pessimism grows and before long the entire team is tired, unenthusiastic, cynical, working purely 'by the book' and negative about their abilities, their clients, their managers and their organisation alike.

There are, however, many teams who appear to cope with the pressures and remain resilient. Having experienced, throughout my career, both buoyant and burnout teams, I was left wondering why, given that they often faced very similar circumstances, some were hugely positive and others were bordering on the pathological. I have no answer, but I can offer a description of a current buoyant team. This is admittedly anecdotal but the team seemed to 'work' and thus I share my observations with you.

The bouncing team

This is a description of a genuine team which seems to have taken reorganisation and massive workloads in its stride. This is not to romanticise the team. There were divisions and difficulties. Recently, for example, one supervisor was off sick for longer than expected after a relatively minor fall; the length of her recovery was possibly due to underlying exhaustion. However, the team seemed to cope with a long list of challenges: reorganisation, rapid expansion meaning that several new staff had to be absorbed quickly, massive workloads, physical moves including 'camping' in mobiles and covering for sick colleagues. Despite everything, the team members kept 'bouncing back' and overall morale remained remarkably high. Interestingly, this was a multi-disciplinary team in the sense that, although members all had the same employer and line-managers, the 'team' embraced administrators plus field staff whose original training had been in social work, health, education, early years or psychology.

How did the team manage this bounce? It seems that relatively small, inexpensive ideas worked well. First, there was considerable mutual care and support. Sick leave was sympathetically acknowledged with cards and when relatively lengthy, flowers. There was a give and take about covering each other in domestic emergencies. Everyone's birthday or other special day was remembered.

The enjoyment of staff meetings was maximised. These were well-organised and chaired to ensure that they were not perceived as a 'waste of time'. Additionally, members contributed tasty nibbles such as chocolates, cakes and fruit which catered for dietary and cultural needs. If a lunch-time meeting was organised, even more exotic delicacies appeared. There was also time for humour. For example, although a multi-cultural team, all in some way celebrated Christmas, so at the start of an early January meeting each was asked to contribute a brief description of the most 'naff' present they had received. Another strategy was to have an agenda item 'what have we done/are doing well?' to ensure time for positive perspectives.

The team had a social life of its own. At Christmas and other times of year there was a social team get-together. Account was taken of culture, income and other needs and preferences when finding suitable activities and venues; a great value local Balti restaurant ended up being a favourite.

One observation is that the 'bouncing team' shared a lot of humour; jokes and laughter was a consistent feature. The topic of humour in child protection work is explored in some detail by Gilgun and Sharma (2011). They conclude that humour which might cause harm needs to be avoided and not everyone has the same sense of humour. However, humour can be used to gain relief from anxiety and frustration and lead to creative problem solving.

Multi-professional and inter-agency working

Munro (2010, p. 1138), reflecting on how child protection agencies can improve performance, writes:

> in a systems approach, there is also recognition of the need to dig deeper to understand why practitioners break rules rather than just focus on ensuring compliance through more control and monitoring. Practitioners can break rules for good reason. … In child protection, where inter-agency working is so crucial, senior managers need to recognise that those at the front line

have more knowledge than they do about how the behaviour of their subsystem is interacting with that of other subsystems.

There are different terms used with the prefix inter- or multi-followed by 'agency' or 'professional'. Here the terms are used interchangeably to denote functioning across organisational barriers. Working 'cheek by jowl' with other professionals, in the same building, with the same remit and with the same line-management tends to cause few difficulties. But the problems intensify as the barriers increase, therefore, they are likely to be substantial if practitioners are separated by geography, line-management, professional identity and remit.

Problems of inter-agency working

Inquiries and serious case reviews exhort practitioners to communicate more effectively between agencies. However, practitioners rarely fail to communicate because they think there is no need. Instead there are substantial obstacles to inter-agency communication. All professions develop their own language in order to converse effectively within their profession. For example, part of the task of medical, nursing and allied profession students is to learn a very precise language. Moreover, often values are basically the same between helping professions but are expressed in different ways. The different professions will prize some values more than others. Doctors, for instance, are particularly concerned about confidentiality. This is understandable because much of their technical language has a significantly different meaning in the vernacular, for example 'anorexia' which medically simply means a loss of appetite, in the vernacular is synonymous with an eating disorder indicative of a mental health problem.

Smith (2009) outlines other areas of potential conflict in multi-professional or inter-agency practice. He identified potential problems which could be structural, policy, organisational, procedural or professional and personal. In terms of structure, professions have different priorities, such as child protection, which might be prominent for children's services social workers, whereas for education or health professionals it might be more marginal.

Relating to policy, differences in priorities will be reflected in policies and these can clash. For example, to ensure the smooth running of a school, teachers may press for a strategy of exclusion of particularly disruptive pupils, whereas the social worker will be under pressure to ensure continuity of education for looked-after children. Therefore if the disruptive child is in foster care there will be the potential for conflict.

Benefits of inter-agency working

Smith (2009) also identifies the very many benefits of joint working. These include a potential for increased efficiency particularly if practitioners use common information – collection instruments such as the Common Assessment Framework (Children's Workforce Development Council, 2009) – so that facts can be collected once and then shared.

The services should hopefully be more responsive and holistic so that where children and families have complex needs, they can have a team of professionals working together to provide for all of their needs including social, health and educational.

Collaboration can lead to more creative and innovative practice with services being more user-centred. For example, in Northampton, a charity, KidsAid, works with social workers, health professionals and specialist therapists to provide play therapy services for children often based in schools with the willing cooperation of the education professionals.

Case conferences and court proceedings

The most formal inter-agency information sharing and recommendation or decision-making forums are case conferences with associated review conferences and courts, particularly the family court. All can, however, create challenges for child protection workers. This section, while not covering all aspects of case conferences and court proceedings, will look at some key ways of withstanding the pressures.

Case conferences

The key forum in which the pieces of the jigsaw of knowledge about risks can be matched together is the case conference. Here, once there has been an incident of abuse or mounting concerns, the relevant professionals will gather in a meeting to share information about one or several children and their family. The case conference system can be criticised because often conferences are time-consuming and unwieldy. However, anyone who worked in child protection before procedures and case conferences were established in the UK in the wake of the Maria Colwell public inquiry will know that, despite any inadequacies, case conferences are better than having no formal systems for sharing information.

Not only are all the professionals with knowledge about the children and the family invited but so are the parents and sometimes the children. In reality, few children especially younger ones attend. It is unquestionably appropriate that parents are aware of decisions made about their children and the reasons for those decisions. However, child protection workers have to be aware who holds what power if the parents are present and the children are not. When parents are present then they can appeal to the gathered professionals for sympathy and understanding in a way that their children are unable to do. An example is the murder of Child H. The Serious Case Review (Salford Children Safeguarding Board, 2010) noted overall 'the children were not at the centre of all agency assessments and interventions' (p. 9) and the 'decisions made in the early Child Protection Review Conference in 2003 and May 2009 were fundamentally flawed and not based on an accurate understanding of the level of risk, the capacity for Adult A to change or the true impact on the children' (p. 11). Child H was aged 12 when she was killed and yet her voice, views and wishes seem to have been absent.

Given the frequent absence of the child, practitioners working directly with abused children may well be one of the few sources of advocacy for them in case conferences and reviews. In order to maximise your contribution, there are some points to think about if this is a new experience for you.

First, preparation is essential. Ensure you have collated all necessary information and in a clear order. If required to write a report in advance, ensure that you are succinct but accurate, avoiding sweeping generalisations but instead painting a factual picture of events and observations. Try to locate the venue beforehand, checking travel times, parking or public transport facilities and, if in a large complex, try to find the actual room in advance. Wear dignified but comfortable clothes on the day.

Second, during the conference you will probably be invited to give your report orally or it will have been read by members and you will be asked to summarise or address key issues in it. Do so clearly, looking up at the chair and around at the other conference members, acknowledging the parents and children when you mention them, if they are present. Ensure you provide essential information in good time. It's best not to emulate the professional who, as we were getting up to leave, suddenly asked if it was relevant to mention that the mother, who had suffered severe postnatal depression after the birth of all her previous children, was again pregnant.

After the conference, you should receive the minutes of the meeting. Check them and ensure that any mistakes are rectified. Agencies are not bound by the recommendations of the conference but if you cannot follow them it is important to let the chair person know.

Ideally, practitioners should have the opportunity to take part in a role-play conference before having to cope with the real thing: but these do not appear to be a common feature of social work and other professional qualifying courses. However, I act as independent chair to one for 'early years' students at the University of Northampton. Attendance is compulsory and the students are assessed on their professionalism, oral presentation and a written reflection. Two students role play family members and the assessment of their presentation is adjusted to ensure they are not disadvantaged. Consistent feedback from the student group is that the experience is nerve-wracking but extremely good preparation for the 'real thing' and it heightens their awareness of the difficulties facing parents while demonstrating the need to keep the welfare of the child central (see Lumsden, 2009; Taylor *et al.*, 2008)

Courts and legal forums

This section cannot cover all aspects of preparation and presentation in court but there are thankfully nowadays some excellent guides such as Seymour and Seymour (2011) and Davis (2007) which address issues, such as, what to do if you arrive in court and find you know one of the magistrates personally.

In addition to reading useful and supportive guides, inexperienced practitioners can help themselves by becoming as conversant with court proceedings as possible before having to act as a witness in care proceedings. In terms of courts, familiarity will hopefully breed confidence rather than contempt. The general public can attend most criminal proceedings and coroners' courts. The latter in particular has some similarities to family courts in that there is less formality although within clear legal procedures. Witnesses give evidence on oath and interested parties can have legal representation with the result that witnesses might be subject to some hostile questioning. Therefore a morning spent attending inquests can be well spent.

As with case conferences, good preparation for court is the key; if possible, visit the court beforehand to check on travel time, parking, facilities and accessible refreshments. On the day wear smart but comfortable and unremarkable clothes. Importantly, decide well beforehand whether you plan to take the oath or simply 'affirm'. If you choose to take the oath and you use a sacred text other than the Bible then it is worth contacting the court to make sure your particular text is present or can be obtained for you. Similarly, if you have a disability which requires additional facilities it is worth checking they are available beforehand.

As mentioned, this section cannot cover all the ways of coping with nerves or with cross-examination; the books by Davis (2007) Seymour and Seymour (2011) do so brilliantly. However, one point specific to people who work with abused children is the possibility of personal questions. A local solicitor was fond of asking us if we had been abused as children. Several professional witnesses found this line of questioning distressing. The first point to remember is that such questioning means that the cross-examining lawyer is struggling. It indicates that he or she cannot find weaknesses in your evidence and so is now having to try to discredit you by suggesting an over-identification with the victims on the basis that you might be a co-victim. Second, you are there as a professional, therefore, it is worth querying the relevance of any personal questions. If the solicitor tries to justify the question on the basis of over-identification then you can remind the court that you are a qualified professional and that in common with all professionals, including lawyers, you are trained to avoid unbalanced empathy.

Do remember that you can both control and depersonalise proceedings by using court-room conventions to your advantage, for example, although you can look at the lawyers when they are asking you questions, you look at the judge or bench of magistrates to give your reply. This helps to avoid an undignified or unnerving encounter with the lawyer. Also unwinding slowly to turn back to address the bench can give you vital seconds to collect your thoughts.

Putting it into practice

Decide whether you want to give the oath as a witness in court or affirm. Find and print out the oath or affirmation onto a piece of card. If you are taking the oath then find a small book to act as your Bible or other sacred text. Now practise giving your oath or affirmation aloud, clearly and accurately. In court, this will normally be the first time you address the court and first impressions count. A clear, confident voice will indicate a self-assured, professionally competent witness. Then practise briefly looking round to check that the chair you think you are sitting down on is actually there. It's surprising how often dropped holy books and missed chairs have thwarted colleagues' attempts to appear poised and dignified.

Working with the media

Munro (2011, p. 107) comments, 'In the review's analysis of why previous reforms have not had their intended success, unmanaged anxiety about being blamed was identified as a significant factor in encouraging a process-driven compliance culture'. Laming (2009, p. 45) acknowledges "Public vilification of social workers has a negative effect on staff and has serious implications for the effectiveness, status and morale of the children's workforce as a whole. There has been a long-term appetite in the media to portray social workers in ways that are negative and undermining.'

An interesting paper by Urh (2011) might seem far removed from UK social work but it throws light on the reason for the often 'negative and undermining' media portrayal of social workers. It is about working with Roma families in Slovenia. Urh points out that social workers in Slovenia who choose to work with the Roma, a term used as a 'label for someone who is poor, dirty, untidy, and also naughty' (p. 474) are viewed negatively. She adds the 'main idea of pollution is the fact that everything in contact with dirt can become dirty' (p. 479). This is a harsh sentence but it captures a truth about working with stigmatised groups. Child abuse is seen by society, and conveyed through the media, as a deep stain on society. Those who abuse the 'innocent' are seen as truly monstrous and have no place in any decent society. Alternatively, there is the view that maltreated children must have in some way deserved their treatment or have become troublesome outsiders as a result of abuse. Either way, those attempting to work with abused children and their families are perceived as defiled and contemptible because of their connection with those deemed 'defiling' and 'deserving of contempt'.

Messages from research

Kuijvenhoven and Kortleven (2010)

Written policy and procedures have abounded in recent years and this is not just in the UK. Often these follow child deaths and Kuijvenhoven and Kortleven (2010) explain that inquiries have been recently introduced into the Netherlands. They compare the differences between UK and Dutch inquiries.

They note that 'Dutch and British investigations show many similarities in the problems they reveal and the solutions they offer, they differ considerably with respect to the allocation of responsibility. British inquiry reports tend to name and blame professionals', whereas the Dutch reports avoid doing so.

The authors suggest that the inquiries might be unduly influenced by the media which in the UK 'do not hesitate to single out individual professionals ... firmly illustrated in the Baby Peter case, in which The Sun successfully campaigned to sack various practitioners and senior managers' (p.1166), whereas the Dutch media is considerably less hostile towards individual child protection workers.

The various news media is the link between child protection work and the public. A responsible and sincere investigative journalist can reveal abuses as shown by the Winterbourne View case (House of Commons, 2011). Good, positive information will inform and advise the public. Silence will be filled with any number of inaccurate imaginings. Front-line practitioners need to be trained to handle the media and use it as a potentially beneficial partner.

Supervision, mentoring and support

Effective supervision is essential for those working in the field of child protection. As one student reflected:

It is important to be able to step back and reflect and not be blinkered. Supervision enabled me to view situations from a different perspective, and to realise that my original perspective could sometimes be naïve and often plainly wrong. (Watson *et al.*, 2002, p. 161)

Walton (2002) points out that there are usually two tasks in supervision, a managerial one and a mentoring one. The use of power distinguishes these two components. In the first, the supervisor has the greater power, whereas in mentoring 'power is mainly with the person being mentored and the purpose of the relationship is to encourage their professional development. Mutual trust is important in both relationships' (p. 565). Some supervisors are unable to share their power and so only the managerial function is fulfilled. Yet Laming (2009, p. 33) observed:

> Regular, high-quality, organised supervision is critical, as are routine opportunities for peer-learning and discussion. Currently, not enough time is dedicated to this and individuals are carrying too much personal responsibility, with no outlet for the sometimes severe emotional and psychological stresses that staff involved in child protection often face.

Bradley *et al.* (2010) explored supervision for child welfare workers in England, South Africa and Sweden. They noted that, with the rise not only in the UK but elsewhere of 'new managerialism', supervision in child protection has been based on ideas from market economies. These 'have been evidenced within the social professions in the recent past by high levels of accountability linked to performance management, efficiency measures and the rise in importance of the consumer in service provision' (p. 774).

There can be concerns about the knowledge and ability of supervisors, as Bradley *et al.* (2010, p. 786) acknowledge the 'educative function of supervision is likely to be less strong if the supervisor has not received the right level of training'. However, for those who are able practitioners there is a different problem, Cousins (2010, p. 284) highlights the 'sense of guilt the supervisor may feel due to leaving behind direct practice with clients and becoming a manager, removed from "proper" client work'.

Chen and Scannapieco (2010) found that a belief that they had the ability to achieve tasks could keep child welfare staff motivated and dedicated to their job. Nevertheless, effective supervision could help in the motivation and retention of practitioners who doubted their abilities. This means that the various difficulties with supervision need to be overcome and this is an area for innovation with ideas perhaps from other countries or professions. For example, Bradley *et al.* (2010) found that in Sweden there was group supervision sometimes using psychologists as supervisors. In the UK and throughout the world the medical profession uses the model of the most experienced practitioners, consultants and senior GPs, supervising junior staff.

Training issues

Repeatedly commentators (for example, Handley and Doyle, 2008; Lefevre *et al.*, 2008; Leeson, 2010; Munro, 2011) have noted how training, at qualifying and even post-qualifying level, poorly equips social workers to work with abused children. Compared to 'early years' professionals, teachers, psychologists and child nurses or health visitors, social workers' knowledge of child development is rudimentary and they are not taught to communicate with young children.

Handley and Doyle's (2008) research showed that some social workers, especially in specialist children's organisations like Cafcass and the NSPCC, had in-service training which had substantially enhanced their skills. One recommendation is for employers to give their staff two or three weeks leave to spend time in a well-run day care setting for young children.

Messages from research

Balen and Masson (2008)

Balen and Masson (2008) are experienced social workers now involved in social work training. In this delightfully engaging paper they sought to explore issues of education, training and practice in relation to child protection in the wake of the case of Victoria Climbié. Both had undertaken a similar exploration of these issues some ten years earlier, so this gave them an additional perspective on the current situation. For the present paper they identified 16 recent papers commenting on social work training and practice related to the death of Victoria and the subsequent Laming (2003) report. Examining the 16 papers they highlighted four key themes:

- the nature and purpose of public inquiries;
- resources and constraints, notably pressures and shortages of staff and resources;
- organisational factors;
- individual factors, including 'turning a blind eye, not seeing the child' (p.124).

The authors conclude in 'our view, current social work education and training continue to be framed by notions of competence and specialist knowledge, rather than by opportunities to develop openness to the exploration of feelings and the management of uncertainty and anxiety, as well as the capacity to contribute to the reflective organisational cultures' (p.128). They then suggest training strategies for front-line social work and health students, which could address some of the difficulties identified. These include:

- the direct use of inquiry reports;
- critical reflection workshops;
- role plays and simulations.

Balen and Masson acknowledge that there are major constraints because of the pressures of high student to staff ratios, the need to meet requirements for quality assurance and research assessment exercises, shrinking budgets and an ever-expanding curriculum with ever-contracting physical space for teaching. Nevertheless, without engaging in critical reflection of training and promoting suggestions to improve areas of deficit, as Balen and Masson do here, child protection training will remain less effective than it might be.

The value of working with abused children

Many social workers, other professionals and volunteers striving to help the victims of child abuse may wonder from time to time whether their intervention is effective. It is not unreasonable to assume that people who have been exposed to years of mistreatment will need at least as many years of consistent affection and care in order to be released from the negative effects of abuse.

Nevertheless, from the accounts given by Marie, Lloyd, Sarah and Roy it is clear that short-term intervention can create positive change in the courses of victims' lives. All four had, as adults, counselling, psychotherapy or the support of a self-help group. Furthermore, in their teenage years or early twenties they all had someone special to give them direct help. For Marie, Glen opened her eyes to the fact that not all men are violent and demanding. Many male social workers give their clients similar assistance, showing sensitivity and caring but not expecting any sexual favours. For Lloyd, members of a religious group and a counsellor gave him unconditional positive regard. Sarah's female friend whom she met in lodgings has her counterpart in those helping professionals who recognise the injustice of abuse and who prove trustworthy helpers. Roy was assisted by hospital staff and fellow patients.

Many of the survivors' acquaintances – Glen, Lloyd's counsellor, Sarah's fellow lodger, other day centre patients for Roy – were only involved for a relatively short time. Yet, they all played a vital part in the lives of the five. They did much to undo the damage caused by close family members over many years. It is therefore quite possible that through properly focused individual, family or group work, assistance given by committed child protection workers will be effective in helping the victims of child abuse.

Further resources

Donnellan, H. and Jack, G. (2009) *The Survival Guide for Newly Qualified Child and Family Social Workers: Hitting the Ground Running.* London: Jessica Kingsley Publishers.
This is a valuable book designed for newly qualified workers but the guidance around issues such as coping with stress, understanding the organisation and using supervision would also be of benefit to students and already qualified workers, especially anyone transferring from adult services into child and family work.

Ferguson, H. (2011) *Child Protection Practice.* Basingstoke: Palgrave Macmillan.
This reflects intimate knowledge and understanding of child protection practice including those small but essential practice details, for example, knocking hard enough on the door when visiting for the family to hear.

Godden, J. (2012) *BASW England research on supervision in social work, with particular reference to supervision practice in multi disciplinary teams: England Document.* Birmingham: BASW.
This is an absorbing report about supervision based on theory and recent research. There are recommendations, such as, the value of specialist, peer and informal supervision.

Thompson, N. (2009) *People Skills*, 3rd edn. Basingstoke: Palgrave Macmillan.
This is but one of Thompson's excellent series of books on a range of social work topics. The early chapters in this book cover issues such as time-management, coping with stress and beating the bully. Later chapters look at issues of intervention such as handling conflict, anti-discriminatory practice and being systematic.

For those interested in issues affecting the Roma community, see http://www.errc.org.

The Department of Education website https://www.education.gov.uk/ publications/standard/publicationDetail/Page1/DFES-Safeguarding is where the 'Working Together 2011' document and other related important government safeguarding documents can be accessed.

Bibliography

Abel, G. G., Becker, J. V. and Mittleman, M. (1987) 'Self-reported sex crimes of non-incarcerated paraphiliacs', *Journal of Interpersonal Violence*, 2(1) pp. 3–25.

Adams, R. E., Figley, C. R. and Boscarino, J. A. (2008) 'The compassion fatigue scale: its use with social workers following urban disaster', *Research on Social Work Practice*, 18, pp. 238–50.

Admasachew, L. and Dawson, J. (2011) 'The association between presenteeism and engagement of National Health Service staff', *Journal of Health Services Research & Policy*, 16 (Suppl 1), pp. 29–33.

Aguilera, D. (1998) *Crisis Intervention Theory and Methodology*, 8th edn. St Louis, MO: Mosby.

Ahmad, B. (1989) 'Protecting black children from abuse', *Social Work Today*, 8 June p. 24.

Ainsley-Green, A. (2011) Keynote address to KidsAid Inaugural Conference, St Andrew's Hospital, Northampton, 29 September.

Alderson, P. and Morrow, V. (2011) *The Ethics of Research with Children and Young People: A Practical Handbook*. London: Sage.

Algate, J., Jones, D., Rose, W. and Jeffrey, C. (eds) (2006) *The Developing World of the Child*. London: Jessica Kingsley.

Allen, B. (2011a) 'The use and abuse of attachment theory in clinical practice with maltreated children, Part I: Diagnosis and assessment', *Trauma Violence Abuse*, 12(1), pp. 3–12.

Allen, B. (2011b) 'The use and abuse of attachment theory in clinical practice with maltreated children, Part II: Treatment', *Trauma Violence Abuse*, 12(1), pp. 13–22.

Allen, N. E., Wolf, A. M., Bybee, D. I. and Sullivan, C. M. (2003) 'Diversity of children's immediate coping responses to witnessing domestic violence', *Journal of Emotional Abuse*, 3, pp. 123–47.

Angelou, M. (1984) *I Know Why the Cage Bird Sings* London: Virago.

Appleyard, K., Egeland, B. and Sroufe, L. A. (2007) 'Direct social support for young high risk children: Relations with behavioural and emotional outcomes across time', *Journal of Abnormal Child Psychology*, 35, pp. 443–57.

Argent, H. (2008) *Ten Top Tips: Placing Siblings*. London: BAAF.

Argent, H. (2010) *Adopting a Brother or Sister*. London: BAAF.

Argyle, M. (1988) *Bodily Communication*. London: Methuen.

Aries, P. (1962) *Centuries of Childhood* (trans. R. Baldick). London: Jonathan Cape.

Ayre, P. and Preston-Shoot, M. (eds) (2010) *Children's Services at the Crossroads*. Lyme Regis: Russell House Publishing.

Bahn, C. (1980) 'Hostage takers, the taken and the context: discussion', *Annals of the New York Academy of Sciences*, 347, pp. 129–36.

Bailey, H. (2010) *The relationships and supports that matter to children looked after (CLA) in long term voluntary accommodation (Children Act 1989, s. 20)*. London: Children's Workforce Development Council.

Bailey, R. (2011) *Letting Children be Children: Report of an Independent Review of the Commercialisation and Sexualisation of Childhood*. Norwich: The Stationery Office.

Balen, R. and Masson, H. (2008) 'The Victoria Climbié case: social work education for practice in children and families' work before and since', *Child & Family Social Work*, 13, pp. 121–32.

Bandura, A. (1973) *Aggression: A Social Learning Theory*. Englewood Cliffs, NJ: Prentice Hall.

Banks, N. (2002) 'What is a positive black identity', in Dwivedi, K.N. (ed.) *Meeting the Needs of Ethnic Minority Children*, 2nd edn. London: Jessica Kingsley.

Bannister, A. (2002) 'Group work in child protection agencies', in Wilson, K. and James, A. (eds) *The Child Protection Handbook*, 2nd edn. Edinburgh: Ballière Tindall.

Barker, D. J. (1990) 'The fetal and infant origins of adult disease', *BMJ*, 301, p. 1111.

Bastian, P. (1994) 'Family care in the United Kingdom', in Gottesman, M. (ed.) *Recent Changes and New Trends in Extrafamilial Child Care: An International Perspective*. London: FICE.

Beckett, C. (2007) *Child Protection: An Introduction*, 2nd edn. London: Sage.

Bell, M. and Wilson, K. (2006) 'Children's views of family group conferences', *British Journal of Social Work*, 36, pp. 671–81.

Ben (Anonymous) (1991) *Things in my Head*. Dublin: Blendale Publishing.

Benedict, R. (1955) 'Continuities and discontinuities in cultural conditioning – 1938', in Mead, M. and Wolfenstein, M. (eds) *Childhood in Contemporary Cultures*. Chicago: University of Chicago Press.

Benson, J. F. (2010) *Working More Creatively with Groups*, 3rd edn. Abingdon: Routledge.

Bentovim, A. (2002) 'Working with Abusive Families', in Wilson, K. and James, A. (eds) *The Child Protection Handbook*, 2nd edn. Edinburgh: Ballière Tindall.

Bentovim, A., Cox, A., Miller, L. B. and Pizzey, S. (eds) (2009) *Safeguarding Children Living with Trauma and Family Violence*. London: Jessica Kingsley.

Berger, R. and Lahad, M. (2010) 'A Safe Place: ways in which nature, play and creativity can help children cope with stress and crisis – establishing the kindergarten as a safe haven where children can develop resiliency', *Early Child Development and Care*, 180(7), pp. 889–900.

Berkshire County Council (1979) *Lester Chapman Inquiry Report*. Reading: Berkshire County Council.

Berridge, D. (2001) 'Foster families', in Foley, P., Roche, J. and Tucker, S. (eds) *Children in Society*. Basingstoke: Palgrave Macmillan.

Berridge, D. and Cleaver, H. (1987) *Foster Home Breakdown*. Oxford: Blackwell.

Bettleheim, B. (1979) *Surviving and Other Essays*. London: Thames & Hudson.

Bichard, M. (2004) *An inquiry into child protection procedure in Humberside Police and Cambridgeshire Constabulary in the light of the recent trial of Ian Huntley for the murder of Jessica Chapman and Holly Wells*. London: The Stationery Office.

Biehal, N. and Parry, E, (2010) *Maltreatment and Allegations of Maltreatment in Foster Care. A Review of the Evidence*. York: University of York.

Bindel, J. (2006) *The Guardian*, 18 August. p. 35.

Binggeli, N. J., Hart, S. N. and Brassard, M. R. (2001) *Psychological maltreatment of children: The APSAC study guides 4*. Thousand Oaks: Sage Publications.

Blakey, C., Collinge, M. and Jones, D. N. (1986) 'The one-way screen', *Community Care*, 25 September, pp. 16–17.

Blewitt, J. (2011) 'Reflections on the impact of the *Children Act 1989*: child care policy, the knowledge base and the evolving role of social work', *Journal of Children's Services*, 6(1), pp. 34–44.

Bloch, D. (1979) *So the Witch Won't Eat Me: Fantasy and the Child's Fear of Infanticide*. London: Burnett Books.

Blom-Cooper, L. (1985) *A Child in Trust: the report of the panel of inquiry into the circumstances surrounding the death of Jasmine Beckford*. London: London Borough of Brent.

Bodmer, N. M. (1998) 'Impact of pet ownership on the well-being of adolescents with few familial resources', in Wilson, C. C. and Turner, D. C. (eds) *Companion Animals in Human Health*. Thousand Oaks: Sage.

Bolger, K. E. and Patterson, C. J. (2003) 'Sequelae of child maltreatment', in Luthar, S. S. (ed.) *Resilience and Vulnerability*. Cambridge: Cambridge University Press.

Bourassa, D. B. and Clements, J. (2010) 'Supporting ourselves: Groupwork interventions for compassion fatigue', *Groupwork*, 20(2), pp. 7–23.

Bowlby, J. (1951) *Maternal Care and Mental Health: Report to the World Health Organisation*. New York: Shocken Books.

Bowlby, J. with Ainsworth, M. (1969) *Child Care and the Growth of Love*. Harmondsworth: Pelican.

Bowlby, J. (1980) *A Secure Base*. London: Routledge.

Brabbs, C. (2011) *Serious case review ce001: Child B, Child C, Child D. Executive Summary*. Cheshire East: Cheshire East Safegarding Children's Board.

Bradford Area Review Committee (1981) *Child Abuse Enquiry Sub-Committee Report Concerning Christopher Pinder/Daniel Frankland born 19.12.79 died 8.7.80*. Bradford: Bradford Area Review Committee.

Bradley, G. (1992) 'Stress and time management workshops for qualifying social Workers', *Social Work Education*, 11(1), pp. 5–16.

Bradley, G., Engelbrecht, E. and Höjer, S. (2010) 'Supervision: A force for change? Three stories told', *International Social Work*, 53, pp. 773–90.

Braun, C., Stangler, T., Narveson, J. and Pettingell, S. (2009) 'Animal-assisted therapy as a pain relief intervention for children', *Complementary Therapies in Clinical Practice*, 15, pp. 105–9

Bridge Child Care Consultancy Services (1991) 'Sukina: An evaluation of circumstances surrounding her death', London: BCCCS.

Bridge Child Care Consultancy Services (1993) *Paul: Death by Neglect*. London: BCCCS.

Bronfenbrenner, U. (1979) *The Ecology of Human Development: Experiments by Nature and Design*. Cambridge, MA: Harvard University Press.

Brown, R. (2000) *Group Processes: Dynamics Within and Between Groups*. Oxford: Blackwell.

Browne, K. (2002) 'Child abuse: defining, understanding and intervening', in Wilson, K. and James, A. (eds) *The Child Protection Handbook*, 2nd edn. Edinburgh: Ballière Tindall.

Browne, K. (2009) *The Risk of Harm to Young Children in Institutional Care*. London: The Save the Children Fund.

Burke, P. (2010) 'Brothers and sisters of disabled children: the experience of disability by association', *British Journal of Social Work*, 40, pp. 1681–99.

Burrows, J., Adams, C. L. and Spiers, K. E. (2008) 'Sentinels of safety: service dogs ensure safety and enhance freedom and well-being for families with autistic children', *Qualitative Health Research*, 18(12), pp. 1642–9.

Butler-Sloss, E. (1988) *Report of the Inquiry into Child Abuse in Cleveland 1987*. London: HMSO

Calder, M. C. (ed.) (2008) *Contemporary Risk Assessment in Safeguarding Children*. Lyme Regis: Russell House Publishing.

Calder, M. C. and Hackett. S. (eds) (2002) *Assessment in Child Care: Using and Developing Frameworks for Practice*. Lyme Regis: Russell House Publishing.

Cameronchild, J. (1987) 'An autobiography of violence', *Child Abuse and Neglect*, 2, pp. 139–49.

Carpenter, F. (1974) 'Mother's face and the newborn', *New Scientist*, 21 March, pp. 742–4.

Carpenter, L. L., Tyrjam, A. R., Ross, N. S., Khoury, L., Anderson, G. M. and Price, L. H. (2009) 'Effect of child emotional abuse and age on cortisol responsivity in adulthood', *Journal of Biological Psychiatry*, 66, pp. 69–75.

Carrión, V. G., Haas, B. W., Garrett, A., Song, S. and Reiss, A. L. (2010) 'Reduced hippocampal activity in youth with post-traumatic stress symptoms: An fMRI study', *Journal of Pediatric Psychology*, 35(5), pp. 559–69.

Chambers, H., Amos, J., Allison, S. and Roeger, L. (2006) 'Parent and Child Therapy: An attachment-based intervention for children with challenging behaviour problems', *Australia and New Zealand Journal of Family Therapy*, 27(2), pp. 68–74.

Chen, S-Y. and Scannapieco, M. (2010) 'The influence of job satisfaction on child welfare worker's desire to stay: An examination of the interaction effect of self-efficacy and supportive supervision', *Children and Youth Services Review*, 32, pp. 482–6.

ChildLine (1998) *I Know You're Not a Doctor But ...* London: ChildLine.

Children Act 1989. London: HMSO.

Children's Workforce Development Council (2009) *The Common Assessment Framework for Children and Young People: A Guide for Practitioners.* Leeds: CWDC.

Chodoff, P. (1981) 'Survivors of the Nazi Holocaust', *Children Today*, Sept–Oct, pp. 2–5.

Choi, J., Bumseok, J., Rohan, M. L., Polcari, A. M. and Teicher, M. H. (2009) 'Preliminary evidence for white matter tract abnormalities in young adults exposed to parental verbal abuse', *Biological Psychiatry*, 65, pp. 227–34.

Christensen, P. and James, A. (eds) (2008) *Research with Children: Perspectives and Practices*, 2nd edn. Abingdon, Oxon: Routledge.

Cicchetti, D. (2010) 'Resilience under conditions of extreme stress: a multilevel perspective', *World Psychiatry*, 9, pp. 145–54.

Cicchetti, D. and Rogosch, F. A. (2009) 'Adaptive coping under conditions of extreme stress: Multilevel influences on the determinants of resilience in maltreated children', in Skinner, E. A and Zimmer-Gembeck, M. J. (eds) *Coping and the development of regulation. New Directions for Child and Adolescent Development.* San Francisco: Jossey-Bass, pp. 47–59.

Clark, A. and Moss, P. (2011) *Listening to Young Children: The Mosaic Approach*, 2nd edn. London: National Children's Bureau Enterprises.

Clark, B. C., Thatcher, D. L. and Martin, C. S. (2010) 'Child abuse and other traumatic experiences, alcohol use disorders, and health problems in adolescence and young adulthood', *Journal of Pediatric Psychology*, 35(5), pp. 499–510.

Cleaver, H., Cawson, P., Gorin, S. and Walker, S. (eds) (2009) *Safeguarding Children*. Chichester: John Wiley & Sons.

Cocker, C. and Allain, L. (2008) *Social Work with Looked After Children*. Exeter: Learning Matters.

Cohen, A. J., Mannarino, A. P., Zhitova, A. C. and Capone, M. E. (2003) 'Treating child abuse related posttraumatic stress and comorbid substance abuse in adolescents', *Child Abuse and Neglect*, 27, pp. 1345–65.

Coholic, D., Lougheed, S. and Lebreton, J. (2009) 'The helpfulness of holistic arts-based group work with children living in foster care', *Social Work With Groups*, 32(1–2), pp. 29–46.

Cole, P. M., Woolger, C., Power, T. G. and Smith, K. D. (1992) 'Parenting difficultiesamong adult survivors of father-daughter incest', *Child Abuse and Neglect*, 16(2), pp. 239–50.

Collins, S. (2007) 'Social workers, resilience, positive emotions and optimism', *Practice*, 19(4), pp. 255–69.

Compton, M. (2002) 'Individual work with children', in Wilson, K and James, A. (eds) *The Child Protection Handbook*, 2nd edn. Edinburgh: Harcourt Publishers.

Conger, K. J., Stocker, C. and McGuire, S. (2009) 'Sibling socialization: The effects of stressful life events and experiences', in Kramer, L. and Conger, K. J. (eds) *Siblings as agents of socialization. New Directions for Child and Adolescent Development, 126*. San Francisco: Jossey-Bass, pp. 45–60.

Cooper, A. (2005) 'Surface and depth in the Victoria Climbié Inquiry Report', *Child & Family Social Work*, 10, pp. 1–9.

Corby, B. (2000) *Child Abuse: Towards a Knowledge Base*, 2nd edn. Buckingham: Open University Press.

Corby, B., Doig, A. and Roberts, V. (2001) *Public Inquiries into Abuse of Children in Residential Care*. London: Jessica Kingsley.

Corey, G. (2010) *The Theory and Practice of Group Counselling*, 8th edn. Belmont, CA: Brooks/Cole.

Coulshed, V. and Orme, J. (2006) *Social Work Practice*, 4th edn. Basingstoke: Palgrave Macmillan.

Courtois, C. (2010) *Healing the Incest Wound: Adult Survivors in Therapy*, 2nd edn. New York: W. W. Norton & Company.

Cousins, C. (2010) '"Treat me don't beat me": exploring supervisory games and their effect on poor performance management', *Practice*, 22(5), pp. 281–92.

Cousins, J (2008) *Ten Top Tips: Finding Families*. London: BAAF.

Cowen, E. L. (1994) 'The enhancement of psychological wellness: Challenges and opportunities', *American Journal of Community Psychology*, 22, pp. 149–79.

Cramer, H. and Carlin, J. (2008) 'Family-based short breaks (respite) for disabled children: results from the fourth national survey', *British Journal of Social Work*, 38, pp. 1060–75.

Daly, B. and Morton, L. L. (2009) 'Empathic differences in adults as a function of childhood and adult pet ownership and pet type', *Anthrozoös*, 22(4), pp. 371–82.

Daniel, B., Wassell, S. and Gilligan, R. (2010) *Child Development for Child Care and Protection Workers*, 2nd edn. London: Jessica Kingsley.

Davidson, G., Devaney, J. and Spratt. T. (2010) 'The impact of adversity in childhood on outcomes in adulthood: research lessons and limitations', *Journal of Social Work*, 10, pp. 369–90.

Davidson, R. (2006a) *Getting Sorted*. London: BAAF.

Davidson, R. (2006b) *Getting More Sorted*. London: BAAF.

Davis, L. (2007) *See You in Court: A Social Worker's Guide to Presenting Evidence in Care Proceedings*. London: Jessica Kingsley.

Davis, L. and Duckett, N. (2008) *Proactive Child Protection and Social Work*. Exeter: Learning Matters.

Davis, P. (1996) 'Threats of corporal punishment as verbal aggression: a naturalistic study', *Child Abuse and Neglect*, 20(4), pp. 289–304.

Dawood, N. J. (translator) (1990) *The Koran*. Harmondsworth: Penguin.

D'Cruz, H. and Stagnitti, K. (2010) 'When parents love and don't love their children: some children's stories', *Child & Family Social Work*, 15, pp. 216–25.

De Bellis, M. D., Hooper, S. R., Woolley, D. P. and Shenk, C. E. (2010) 'Demographic, maltreatment, and neurobiological correlates of PTSD symptoms in children and adolescents', *Journal of Pediatric Psychology*, 35(5), pp. 570–7.

Denham, A. (1981) *Malcolm Page*. Essex: Essex County Council and Essex Area Health Authority.

Department for Children, Schools and Families (DCSF) (2010) *Working Together to Safeguard Children*. Nottingham: DCSF Publications.

Department of Health (2000) *Framework for the assessment of children in need and their families*. London: The Stationery Office.

Derby Safeguarding Board (2009) *Serious Case Review Child H Executive Summary*. Derby: Derby Safeguarding Board.

Dew, K. (2011) 'Pressure to work through periods of short term sickness', *British Medical Journal*, 341, d3446.

DHSSPS (2008) *Standards for Child Protection Services*. Belfast: Department of Health, Social Services & Public Safety.

Dingwall, R., Eekelaar, J. and Murray, T. (1983) *The Protection of Children: State Intervention and Family Life*. Oxford: Blackwell.

Dogra, N., Parkin, A., Gale, G. and Frake, C. (2009) *A Multi-disciplinary Handbook in Child and Adolescent Mental Health for Front-line Professionals*, 2nd edn. London: Jessica Kingsley.

Dominelli, L. and McLeod, E. (1989) *Feminist Social Work*. Basingstoke: Macmillan.

Donnellan, H. and Jack, G. (2009) *The Survival Guide for Newly Qualified Child and Family Social Workers: Hitting the Ground Running*. London: Jessica Kingsley Publishers.

Donnelly, C. and Rose, R. (2011) 'Navigating Children (NI) Order 1995 applications through the courts: revised Best Practice Guidance', *Child Care in Practice*, 17(1), pp. 87–93.

Doyle, C. (1985) *The Imprisoned Child: Aspects of Rescuing the Severely Abused Child*, London: NSPCC Occasional Paper no. 3.

Doyle, C. (1986) 'Management sensitivity in CSA training', *Child Abuse Review*, 1, pp. 8–9.

Doyle, C (1991) 'Caring for the Workers', *Child Abuse Review*, 5(3), pp. 25–7.

Doyle, C. (1997a) 'Terror and the Stockholm syndrome: the relevance for abused children', in Bates, J., Pugh, R. G. and Thompson, N. (eds) *Protecting Children: Challenges and Change*. Aldershot: Arena.

Doyle, C. (1997b) 'Emotional abuse of children: issues for intervention', *Child Abuse Review*, 6, pp. 330–42.

Doyle, C. (1998) 'Emotional abuse of children: issues for intervention'. PhD Thesis, University of Leicester.

Doyle, C. (2001) 'Surviving and coping with emotional abuse in childhood', *Clinical Child Psychology and Psychiatry*, 6(3), pp. 387–402.

Doyle, C. (2002) 'Palliative factors in psychological maltreatment of children', Research report for the British Academy.

Doyle, C. (2003) 'Child emotional abuse: the role of educational professionals', *Educational and Child Psychology*, 20(1), pp. 8–21.

Doyle, C., Timms, C. D. and Sheehan, E. (2010) 'Potential sources of support for children who have been emotionally abused by parents', *Vulnerable Children and Youth Studies*, 5(3), pp. 230–43.

Dube, S. R., Williamson, D. F., Thompson, T., Felitti, V. J. and Anda, R. F. (2004) 'Assessing the reliability of retrospective reports of adverse childhood experiences among adult HMO members attending a primary care clinic', *Child Abuse and Neglect*, 28, pp. 729–38.

Dunn, J. (1995) 'Studying relationships and social understanding', in Barnes, P. (ed.) *Personal, Social and Emotional Development of Children*. Oxford: Blackwell.

Dwivedi, K.N. (ed.) (2000) *Post-traumatic Stress Disorder in Children and Adolescents*. London: Whurr.

Dwork, D. (1991) *Children with a Star: Jewish Youth in Nazi Germany*. New Haven: Yale University Press.

East Sussex County Council (1975) *Children at risk*. Lewes: East Sussex County Council.

Ennew, J. (1986) *The Sexual Exploitation of Children*. Cambridge: Polity Press.

Erikson, E. H. (1965) *Childhood and Society*, 2nd edn. Harmondsworth: Penguin.

Evening Telegraph (2011) 'Pen Green centre says £1.1m budget cut will decimate services', available from: http://www.northantset.co.uk / news/education/ pen_green_centre_says_1_1m_budget_cut_will_deci-mate_services_1_2332797. Accessed 03/10/11.

Evert, E. and Bijkerk, I. (1987) *When You're Ready*. Walnut Creek, CA: Launch Press.

Fahlberg, V. (2008) *A Child's Journey through Placement*. London: BAAF.

Farrell, A. (ed.) (2005) *Ethical Research with Children*. Maidenhead: Open University Press/McGraw Hill.

Ferguson, H. (2005) 'Working with violence, the emotions and the psycho-social dynamics of child protection: reflections on the Victoria Climbié case', *Social Work Education*, 24(7), pp. 781–95.

Ferguson, H. (2010) 'The understanding systemic caseworker: the chang-ing nature and meanings of working with children and families', in Ayre, P. and Preston-Shoot, M. (eds) *Children's Services at the Crossroads*. Lyme Regis: Russell House Publishing, pp. 28–37.

Ferguson, H. (2011) *Child Protection Practice*. Basingstoke: Palgrave Macmillan.

Festinger, T and Baker, A. (2010) 'Prevalence of recalled childhood emotional abuse among child welfare staff and related well-being factors', *Children and Youth Services Review*, 32, pp. 520–6.

Field-Fisher, T. G. F. (1974) *Report of the Committee of enquiry into the care and supervision provided in relation to Maria Colwell*. London: HMSO.

Figley, C. (ed.) (2002) *Treating Compassion Fatigue*. New York: Brunner-Routledge.

Finkelhor, D. (1984) *Child Sexual Abuse: New Theory and Research*. New York: The Free Press.

Finkelhor, D., Ormrod, R., Turner, H. and Holt, M. (2009) 'Pathways to poly-victimization', *Child Maltreatment*, 14(4), pp. 316–29.

Forrester, D. (2010) 'Playing with fire or rediscovering fire? The perils and potential for evidence based practice in social work', in Ayre, P. and Preston-Shoot, M. (eds) *Children's Services at the Crossroads*. Lyme Regis: Russell House Publishing, pp. 115–26.

Forster, D. (2009) 'Rethinking compassion fatigue as moral stress', *Journal of Ethics in Mental Health*, 4(1), pp. 1–4.

Foucault, M. (1980) *Power/knowledge* (papers edited and translated by C. Gordon). Brighton: Harvester.

Fox, S. E., Levitt, P. and Nelson, C. A. (2010) 'How the timing and qual-ity of early experiences influence the development of brain architec-ture', *Child Development*, 81(1), pp. 28–40.

Fraiberg, S. (1952) 'Some aspects of casework with children. 1. Understanding the child client', *Social Casework*, 33(9), November.

Freeman, M. (2010) 'The human rights of children', *Current Legal Problems*, 63(1), pp. 1–44.

Furniss, T., Bigley-Miller, L. and Van Elburg, A. (1988) 'Goal-orientated group work for sexually abused adolescent girls', *British Journal of Psychiatry*, 152, pp. 97–108.

Garraway, H. and Pistrang, N. (2010) 'Brother from another mother: Mentoring for African-Caribbean adolescent boys', *Journal of Adolescence*, 33(5), pp. 719–29

Gass, K., Jenkins, J. and Dunn, J. (2007) 'Are sibling relationships protective? A longitudinal study', *Journal of Child Psychology and Psychiatry*, 48(2), pp. 167–75.

Geiger, B. (1996) *Fathers as Primary Caregivers*. Westport: Greenwood Press.

Geldard, K. and Geldard, D. (2001) *Working with Children in Groups*. Basingstoke: Palgrave Macmillan.

Geldard, K. and Geldard, D. (2007) *Counselling Children: A Practical Introduction*, 3rd edn. London: Sage.

Gelles, R. J. and Strauss, M. A. (1979) 'Family experience and public support of the death penalty', in Gil, D. G. (ed.) *Child Abuse and Violence*. New York: AMS Press.

Gibb, B. E. and Abela, J. R. Z. (2007) 'Emotional abuse, verbal victimization, and the development of children's negative inferential styles and depressive symptoms', *Cognitive Therapy & Research*, 32, pp. 161–76.

Gil, D. G. (1970) *Violence against Children, Physical Child Abuse in the United States*. Cambridge MA:, Harvard University Press.

Gilgun, J. F. and Sharma, A. (2011) 'The uses of humour in case management with high-risk children and their families', *British Journal of Social Work Advance Access*, 1–18, doi:10.1093/bjsw/bcr070.

Gittins, D. (1993) *The Family in Question*, 2nd edn. London: Macmillan.

Giza, C. D., Kolb, B., Harris, N. G., Asarnow, R. F. and Prins, M. I. (2009) 'Hitting a moving target: Basic mechanisms of recovery from acquired developmental brain injury', *Developmental Neurorehabilitation*, 12(5), pp. 255–68.

Glaser, D. (2000) 'Child abuse and neglect and the brain: a review', *Journal of Child Psychology and Psychiatry*, 41, pp. 97–116.

Glass, S. D. (2010) *The Practical Handbook of Group Counselling: Group Work with Children, Adolescents and Parents*. Bloomington: Trafford Publishing.

Godden, J. (2012) *BASW/CoSW England research on supervision in social work, with particular reference to supervision practice in multi disciplinary teams: England Document*. Birmingham: BASW/CoSW.

Goldberg, A. P., Tobin, J., Daigneau, J., Griffith, R. T., Reinert, S. E. and Jenny. C. (2009) 'Bruising frequency and patterns in children with physical disabilities', *Pediatrics*, 124, pp. 604–9.

Gonsiorek, J. C., Bera, W. H. and Le Tourneau, D. (1994) *Male Sexual Abuse*. London: Sage.

Goodsell, T. L. and Meldrum, J. T. (2010) 'Nurturing fathers: a qualitative examination of child-father attachment', *Early Child Development and Care*, 180(1–2), pp. 249–62.

Graham, M. (2011) 'Changing paradigms and conditions of childhood: implications for the social professions and social work', *British Journal of Social Work Advance Access*, doi:10.1093/bjsw/bcr033.

Greene, S. and Hogan, D. (2005) *Researching Children's Experience*. London: Sage.

Greig, A. D., Taylor, J. and MacKay, T. (2007) *Doing Research with Children*, 2nd edn. London: Sage.

Gunner, M. and Quevedo, K. (2007) 'The neurobiology of stress and development', *Annual Review of Psychology*, 58, pp. 145–73.

Haj-Yahia, M. and Shor, R. (1995) 'Child maltreatment as perceived by Arab students of social science in the West Bank', *Child Abuse and Neglect*, 19(10), pp. 1209–20.

Hammond, H. (2001) *Child protection inquiry into the circumstances surrounding the death of Kennedy McFarlane*. Edinburgh: Dumfries & Galloway Child Protection Committee.

Hammond, S. P. and Cooper, N. (2011) 'From looked after children to looking after children: Insight from an unusual perspective', *International Social Work*, 54, pp. 238–45.

Handy, C. (1985) *Understanding Organisations*, 3rd edn. Harmondsworth: Penguin.

Handley, G. and Doyle, C. (2008) 'Giving young children a voice in legal proceedings', paper presented to the XVIIth ISPCAN International Congress. Hong Kong, 7–10 September.

Hardiker, P., Exton, K. and Barker, M. (1991) 'The social policy contexts of child care', *British Journal of Social Work*, 21, pp. 341–59.

Harding, L. (1997) *Perspectives in Child Care Policy*, 2nd edn. Burnt Mill, Harlow: Longman.

Harr, C. and Moorre, B. (2011) 'Compassion fatigue among social work students in field placements', *Journal of Teaching in Social Work*, 31(3), pp. 350–63.

Hart, S. N. (1988) 'Psychological maltreatment: emphasis on prevention', *School Psychology International*, 9, pp. 243–55.

Hart, S. N., Binggeli, N. J. and Brassard, M. R. (1998) 'Evidence for the effects of psychological maltreatment', *Journal of Emotional Abuse* 1(1), pp. 27–58.

Hart, S. N., Brassard, M. R., Davidson, H. A., Rivelis, E., Diaz, V. and Binggeli, N. J. (2011) 'Psychological maltreatment', in Myers, J. E. B. (ed.) *The APSAC handbook on child maltreatment*, 3rd edn. Thousand Oaks: Sage Publications, pp. 125–44.

Healy, K., Meagre, G. and Cullin, J. (2009) 'Retaining novices to become expert child protection practitioners: creating career pathways in direct practice', *British Journal of Social Work*, 39(2), pp. 299–317.

Helm, D. (2010) *Making Sense of Child and Family Assessment*. London: Jessica Kingsley.

Hendrick, H. (1990) 'Constructions and reconstructions of British childhood: an interpretative survey, 1800 to the present', in James, A. and Prout, A. (eds) *Constructing and Reconstructing Childhood*. London: The Falmer Press.

Hendrick, H. (1994) *Child Welfare: England 1872–1989*. London: Routledge.

Hennum, N. (2011) 'Controlling children's lives: covert messages in child protection service reports', *Child & Family Social Work*, 16, pp. 336–44.

Hester, M., Pearson, C. and Harwin, N. (2007) *Making an Impact; Children and Domestic Violence*, 2nd edn. London: Jessica Kingsley Publishers.

Hester, M., He, J. and Tian, L. (2009) 'Girls' and boys' experiences and perceptions of parental discipline and punishment while growing up in China and England', *Child Abuse Review*, 18(6), pp. 401–13.

Herzberger, S. (1993) 'The cyclical pattern of child abuse: a study of research methodology', in Renzetti, C. M. and Lee, R. M. (eds) *Researching Sensitive Topics*. Newbury Park, CA: Sage.

Hildebrand, J. (1988) 'The use of groupwork in treating child sexual abuse', in Bentovim, A., Elton, A., Hildebrand, J., Tranter, M. and Vizard, E. (eds) *Child Sexual Abuse within the Family: Assessment and Treatment*. London: Wright.

Hindmann, J. (1983) *A Very Touching Book*. Durkes, Oregon: McClure-Hindmann.

Hitchman, J. (1960) *The King of the Barbareens*. London: Putman.

Holland, S. (2010) *Child and Family Assessment in Social Work Practice*, 2nd edn. London: Sage.

Hoover, K. and Donovan, T. (1995) *The Elements Of Social Scientific Thinking*, 6th edn. New York: St Martin's Press.

Hothersall, S. J. (2008) *Social work with children, young people and their families in Scotland*, 2nd edn. Exeter: Learning Matters.

House of Commons (2011) Parliamentary business: Tuesday 7 June, Winterbourne View Care Home. Available from: http://www.publications.parliament.uk/pa/cm201011/cmhansrd/cm110607/debtext/1106 07-0001.htm#11060729000001 accessed 06/10/11.

Houston, S. (2010) 'Building resilience in a children's home: results from an action research project', *Child & Family Social Work*, 15, pp. 357–68.

Howarth, J. (ed.) (2009) *The Child's World: The Comprehensive Guide to Assessing Child in Need*. London: Jessica Kingsley.

Howe, D. (1995) *Attachment Theory for Social Work Practice*. London: Macmillan.

Howe, D. (2005) *Child Abuse and Neglect: Development and Intervention*. Basingstoke: Palgrave Macmillan.

Howe, D., Brandon, M., Hinings, D. and Schofield, G. (1999) *Attachment Theory, Child Maltreatment and Family Support*. Basingstoke: Palgrave Macmillan.

Howitt, D. and Owusu-Bempah, J. (1994) *The Racism of Psychology: Time for Change*. Hemel Hempstead: Harvester Wheatsheaf.

Hughes, L. and Owen, H. (eds) (2009) *Good Practice in Safeguarding Children*. London: Jessica Kingsley.

Hughes, W. H. (1986) *Report of the Inquiry into Children's Homes and Hostels*. Belfast: HMSO.

Humphreys, C. and Stanley, N. (2006) *Domestic Violence and Child Protection*. London: Jessica Kingsley.

Humphries, C., Thiara, R. K., Skamballis, A. and Mullender, A. (2006a) *Talking to My Mum: A Picture Workbook for Workers, Mothers and Children Affected by Domestic Abuse*. London: Jessica Kingsley.

Humphries, C., Thiara, R. K., Skamballis, A. and Mullender, A. (2006b) *Talking about Domestic Abuse: A Photo Activity Workbook to Develop Communication between Mothers and Young People*. London: Jessica Kingsley.

Iwaniec, D. (2006) *The Emotionally Abused and Neglected Child: Identification, Assessment and Intervention*. Chichester: John Wiley & Sons.

Jacob, M. (2003) *Sigmund Freud*, 2nd edn. London: Sage.

Jenkins, A. (ed.) (2006) *The Poems of Gerard Manley Hopkins: A Sourcebook*. Abingdon, Oxon: Routledge.

Jennings, S. (1999) *Introduction to Developmental Playtherapy*. London: Jessica Kingsley.

Johns, G. (2010) 'Presenteeism in the workplace: a review and research agenda', *Journal of Organizational Behavior*, 31, pp. 519–42.

Johnson, M. V. (2009) 'Plasticity in the developing brain: implications for rehabilitation', *Developmental Disabilities Research Reviews*, 15, pp. 94–101.

Kendall-Tackett, K. and Becker-Blease, K. (2004) 'Importance of retrospective findings in child maltreatment research', *Child Abuse and Neglect*, 28, pp. 723–7.

Kennedy, D. (2006) *The Well of Being: Childhood, Subjectivity, and Education*. Albany: State University of New York Press.

Kennedy, M. (1990) 'The Deaf child who is sexually abused – is there a need for a dual specialist?', *Child Abuse Review* 4(2), pp. 3–6.

Kennedy, M. (2002) 'Disability and child abuse', in Wilson, K. and James, A. (eds) *The Child Protection Handbook*, 2nd edn. Edinburgh: Harcourt Publishers.

Kirkwood, A. (1993) *The Leicestershire Inquiry 1992*. Leicestershire: Leicestershire County Council.

Kitzinger, J. (1994) 'Challenging sexual violence against girls: a social awareness approach', *Child Abuse Review* 3(4), pp. 246–58.

Knight, C. (2009) *Working with Adult Survivors of Childhood Trauma*. Belmont, CA: Thomas Brooks/Cole Publishing.

Kolb, B., Mychasiuk, R.,Williams, P. and Gibb, R. (2011) 'Brain plasticity and recovery from early cortical injury', *Developmental Medicine & Child Neurology*, supplement s4, pp. 4–8.

Kriz, K. and Skivenes, M. (2010) 'Lost in translation: how child welfare workers in Norway and England experience language difficulties when working with minority ethnic families', *British Journal of Social Work*, 40, pp. 1353–67.

Kubler-Ross, E. (1970) *On Death and Dying*. London: Tavistock.

Kuijvenhoven, T. and Kortleven, W. J. (2010) 'Inquiries into fatal child abuse in the Netherlands: a source of improvement?', *British Journal of Social Work*, 40(4), pp. 1152–73.

Lahad, M. (1992) 'Story making and assessment method for coping with stress: Six part story and BASIC Ph', *Dramatherapy: Theory and Practice*, 2. London: Routledge.

Lahad, M. (2002) *Creative Supervision*. London: Jessica Kingsley.

Lamb, M. E. (ed.) (1987) *The Father's Role: Cross-cultural Perspectives*. Hillsdale, NY: Lawrence Erlbaum.

Laming, H. (2003) *The Victoria Climbié Inquiry*. London: Stationery Office.

Laming, H. (2009) *The Protection of Children in England: A Progress Report*. London: Stationery Office.

Lau, A. (1991) 'Cultural and ethnic perspectives on significant harm: its assessment and treatment', in Adcock, M., White, R. and Hollows, A. (eds) *Significant Harm*. London: Significant Publications.

Lau, A. (2002) 'Family therapy and ethnic minorities', in Dwivedi, N. (ed.) *Meeting the Needs of Ethnic Minority Children*, 2nd edn. London: Jessica Kingsley.

Leeson, C. (2007) 'My life in care: experiences of nonparticipation in decision making processes', *Child & Family SocialWork*, 12, pp. 268–77.

Leeson, C. (2010) 'The emotional labour of caring about looked-after children', *Child & Family Social Work*, 15, pp. 483–91.

Lefevre, M., Tanner, K. and Luckock, B. (2008) 'Developing social work students' communication skills with children and young people: a model for the qualifying level curriculum', *Child & Family Social Work*, 13, pp. 166–76.

Levy, A. and Kahan, B. (1991) *The Pindown Experience and the Protection of Children*. Staffordshire: Staffordshire County Council.

Lewis, A. (2011) 'Disabled children's "voice" and experience', in Ruebain, D. and Haines, S. (eds) *Education, Disability and Social Policy*. Bristol: The Policy Press, pp. 89–104.

Lewis, A. and Porter, J. (2006) 'Research and Pupil Voice', available from http://eprints.bham.ac.uk/281/1/Lewis_(16).pdf (accessed 01/10/11).

Lindon, J. (2008) *Safeguarding Children and Young People*, 3rd edn. Abingdon, Oxon: Hodder & Stoughton.

Lindsay, T. and Orton, S. (2011) *Groupwork Practice in Social Work*. Exeter: Learning Matters.

Littner, N. (1956) *Some Traumatic Effects of Separation and Placement*. New York: Child Welfare League of America.

London Borough of Hammersmith and Fulham (1984) *Report on the Death of Shirley Woodcock*. London: London Borough of Hammersmith and Fulham.

London Borough of Hillingdon (1986) *Report of the Review Panel into the Death of Heidi Koseda*. London: London Borough of Hillingdon.

London NHS (2009) *Baby P post-death incident review: Executive summary and recommendations*. London: London NHS.

Lonne, B., Parton, N., Thomson, J. and Harries, M. (2009) *Reforming Child Protection*. Abingdon, Oxon: Routledge.

Lowenstein, L. (ed.) (2010) *Creative Family Therapy Techniques*. Toronto: Champion Press.

Luckock, B. and Lefevre, M. (eds) (2008) *Direct work – social work with children and young people in care*. London: BAAF.

Lumsden, E. (2009) 'Joined-up thinking in practice: an exploration of professional collaboration', in Waller, T. (ed.) *An Introduction to Early Childhood*, 2nd edn. London: Sage, pp. 152–66.

Lynch, R. and Garrett, P. M. (2010) ' "More than Words": touch practices in child and family social work', *Child & Family Social Work*, 15, pp. 389–98.

Lynch, M. A. and Roberts, J. (1982) *Consequences of Child Abuse*. London: Academic Press.

MacFarlane, A. (1977) *The Psychology of Childbirth*. London: Fontana/Open Books.

MacLeod, M. and Saraga, E. (1988) 'Challenging the orthodoxy: towards a feminist theory and practice', *Feminist Review*, 28, pp. 16–55.

Maitra, B. and Miller, A. (2002) 'Children, Families and Therapists', in Dwivedi, N. (ed.) *Meeting the Needs of Ethnic Minority Children*, 2nd edn. London: Jessica Kingsley.

Malekoff, A. (2008) 'Transforming trauma and empowering children and adolescents in the aftermath of disaster through group work', *Social Work with Groups*, 31(1), pp. 29–52.

March, S., Spence, S. and Donovan, C. L. (2009) 'The efficacy of an internet-based cognitive-behavioral therapy intervention for child anxiety disorders', *Journal of Pediatric Psychology*, 34(5), pp. 474–87.

Marchant, R. (2001) 'Working with disabled children', in Foley, P., Roche, J. and Tucker, S. (eds) *Children in Society*. Basingstoke: Palgrave Macmillan.

Mascaro, J. (translator) (1962) *The Bhagavad Gita*. Harmondsworth: Penguin.

Margolin, G. and Vickerman, K. A. (2007) 'Posttraumatic stress in children and adolescents exposed to family violence: I. overview and issues', *Professional Psychology: Research and Practice*, 38(6), pp. 613–19.

Maslow, A. H. (1970) *Motivation and Personality*, 2nd edn. New York: Harper Row.

Masson, J., McGovern, D., Pick, K. and Oakley, M. W. (2007) *Protecting Powers*. Chichester: John Wiley and Sons.

Masten, A. S. and Coatsworth, J. D. (1998) 'The development of competence in favorable and unfavorable environments: Lessons from research on successful children', *American Psychologist*, 53, pp. 205–20.

Masten, C. L., Guyer, A. E., Hodgdon, H. B., McClure, E. B., Charney, D. S., Ernst, M., Kaufman, J., Pine, D. S. and Monk, C. S. (2008) 'Recognition of facial emotions among maltreated children with high rates of post-traumatic stress disorder', *Child Abuse and Neglect*, 32, pp. 139–53.

McGlone, G. J. (2004) 'The pedophile and the pious', *Journal of Aggression, Maltreatment and Trauma*, 8, pp. 115–31.

McKnight, R. (1972) 'Group work with children', in Holgate, E. (ed.) *Communicating with Children: Collected Papers*. London: Longman.

McLewin, L. A. and Muller, R. T. (2006) 'Attachment and social support in the prediction of psychopathology among young adults with and without a history of physical maltreatment', *Child Abuse & Neglect*, 30, pp. 171–91.

McSherry, D. (2011) 'Lest we forget: remembering the consequences of child neglect: a clarion call to "feisty advocates"', *Child Care in Practice*, 17(2), pp. 103–13.

Melson, G. F. (1998) 'The role of companion animals in human development', in Wilson, C. C. and Turner, D. C. (eds) *Companion Animals in Human Health*. Thousand Oaks: Sage.

Mills, M. and Melhuish, E. (1974) 'Recognition of mother's voice in early infancy', *Nature*, 252, pp. 123–4.

Min, M., Farkas, K., Minnes, S. and Singer, L. T. (2007) 'Impact of childhood abuse and neglect on substance abuse and psychological distress in adulthood', *Journal of Traumatic Stress*, 20(5), pp. 833–44.

Monckton, W. (1945) *Report by Sir Walter Monckton on the circumstances which led to the boarding out of Dennis and Terence O'Neill at Bank Farm, Miserley and the steps taken to supervise their welfare.* Cmnd 6636, London: HMSO.

Moran, P. B., Vuchinich, S. and Hall, N. K (2004) 'Associations between types of maltreatment and substance use during adolescence', *Child Abuse and Neglect*, 28, pp. 565–74.

Morgan, R. (2007) *Children's Messages on Care*. London: Commission for Social Care Inspection.

Morland, L. A., Hynes, A. K., Mackintosh, M-A., Resick, P. A. and Chard, K. M. (2011) 'Group cognitive processing therapy delivered to veterans via telehealth: a pilot cohort', *Journal of Traumatic Stress*, 24(4), pp. 465–9.

Morris, K. (2011) 'Thinking family? The complexities for family engagement in care and protection', *British Journal of Social Work Advanced Access* doi:10.1093/bjsw/bcr116.

Morrison, B. (1993) *And When Did You Last See Your Father?* London: Granta Books.

Mullender, A., Hague, G., Imam, U., Kelly, L., Malos, E. and Regan, L. (2002) *Children's Perspectives on Domestic Violence*. London: Sage.

Muller, U., Carpendale, J. I. M. and Smith, L. (eds) (2009) *Cambridge Companion to Piaget*. Cambridge: Cambridge University Press.

Munro, E. (2008) *Effective Child Protection*, 2nd edn. London: Sage.

Munro, E. (2010) 'Learning to reduce risk in child protection', *British Journal of Social Work*, 40, pp. 1135–51.

Munro, E. (2011) *The Munro Review of Child Protection: Final Report*. Norwich: The Stationery Office.

Nandy, S and Selwyn, J. (2011) *Spotlight on Kinship Care*. Bristol: University of Bristol.

Nicoletto, S. F. and Rinaldi, A. (2011) 'In the womb's shadow', *European Molecular Biology Organization Reports*, 12(1), pp. 30–4.

Norfolk County Council (1975) *Report of the Review Body Appointed to Enquire into the Case of Stephen Meurs*. Norwich: Norfolk County Council.

NSPCC (2007) Child protection research briefing: Child neglect. London: NSPCC, available from: www.nspcc.org.uk/inform, accessed 30/08/11.

O'Dougherty-Wright, M., Crawford, E. and Del Castillo, D. (2009) 'Childhood emotional maltreatment and later psychological distress among college students: The mediating role of maladaptive schemas', *Child Abuse & Neglect*, 33, pp. 59–68.

O'Neill, T. (1981) *A Place Called Hope. Caring for Children in Distress*. Oxford: Basil Blackwell.

Orchard, B. and Fuller, R. C. (eds) (1966) *The Holy Bible*. London: Catholic Truth Society.

O'Shaughnessy, R., Collins, C. and Fatimilehin, I. (2010) 'Building Bridges in Liverpool: exploring the use of family group conferences for black and minority ethnic children and their families', *British Journal of Social Work*, 40, pp. 2034–49.

Oswald, S. H., Heil, K. and Goldbeck, L. (2010) 'History of maltreatment and mental health problems in foster children: a review of the literature', *Journal of Pediatric Psychology*, 35(5), pp. 462–72.

Owusu-Bempah, K. (1994) 'Race, self-identity and social work', *British Journal of Social Work*. 24, pp. 123–36.

Owusu-Bempah, K. (1995) 'Information about the absent parent as a factor in the well-being of children of single-parent families', *International Social Work*, 38, pp. 253–75.

Owusu-Bempah K. (2003) 'Political correctness: in the interest of the child?', *Educational and Child Psychology*, 20, pp. 53–63.

Owusu-Bempah, K. (2006) 'Socio-genealogical connectedness: knowledge and identity', in Algate, J., Jones, D., Rose, W. and Jeffery, C. (eds) *The Developing World of the Child*. London: Jessica Kingley, pp. 112–21.

Parker E. (2010) 'The meaning and significance of sibling and peer relationships for young people looked after on behalf of local authorities'. Thesis submitted for the Degree of PhD at the University of Warwick. Available from: http://wrap. warwick.ac.uk/3920/1/WRAP_THESIS_Parker_2010.pdf, accessed 03/10/2011.

Parker, J. and Bradley, G. (2010) *Social Work Practice: Assessment, Planning, Intervention and Review*, 3rd edn. Exeter: Learning Matters.

Parkinson, F (1993) *Post-Traumatic Stress*. London: Sheldon.

Parton, C. and Manby, M. (2009) 'The contribution of group work programmes to early intervention and improving children's emotional well-being', *Pastoral Care in Education*, 27(1), pp. 5–19.

Parton, N. (1985) *The Politics of Child Abuse*. London: Macmillan.

Parton, N. (2009) 'From Seebohm to *Think Family*: reflections on 40 years of policy change of statutory children's social work in England', *Child & Family Social Work*, 14, pp. 68–78.

Parton, N. (2011) 'Child protection and safeguarding in England: changing and competing conceptions of risk and their implications for social work', *British Journal of Social Work*, 41, pp. 854–75.

Pen Green (2011) Pen Green Centre for Children and Families. Available from http://www.pengreen.org/pengreencenter.php. Accessed 29/09/2011.

Pepin, E. N. and Banyard, V. L. (2006) 'Social support: A mediator between child maltreatment and developmental outcomes', *Journal of Youth & Adolescence*, 35, pp. 617–30.

Perkins, D. F. and Jones, D. R. (2004) 'Risk behaviours and resiliency within physically abused children', *Child Abuse and Neglect*, 28, pp. 547–64.

Perry, B. D. (2009) 'Examining child maltreatment through a neurodevelopmental lens: clinical applications of the neurosequential model of therapeutics', *Journal of Loss and Trauma*, 14, pp. 240–55.

Phillips, M. (2002) 'Issues of ethnicity and culture', in Wilson, K. and James, A. (eds) *The Child Protection Handbook*, 2nd edn. Edinburgh: Harcourt Publishers.

Philpot, T. (1995) 'Uncertain ground', *Community Care*, issue 1067, 11–17 May, p. 1.

Pitcher, D. and Arnill, M. (2010) ' "Allowed to be there": the wider family and child protection', *Practice*, 22(1), pp. 17–31.

Plymouth Safeguarding Children Board (2010) *Serious Case Review Overview Report, Executive Summary in respect of Nursery Z.* Plymouth: PSCB.

Pollack, S. D. and Tolley-Schell, S. A. (2003) 'Selective attention to facial expression in physically abused children', *Journal of Abnormal Psychology*, 112(3), pp. 323–38.

Pooler, D. K., Siebert, D. C., Faul, A. C. and Huber, R. (2008) 'Personal history and professional impairment: implications for social workers and their employers', *Administration in Social Work* 32(2), pp. 69–85.

Postman, N. (1983) *The Disappearance of Childhood.* London: W H Allen.

Preston-Shoot, M. (2007) *Effective Group Work*, 2nd edn. Basingstoke: Palgrave Macmillan.

Preston-Shoot, M. and Ayre, P. (2010) 'For my next trick: illusion in children's policy and practice', in Ayre, P. and Preston-Shoot, M. (eds) *Children's Services at the Crossroads.* Lyme Regis: Russell House Publishing, pp. 127–32.

Quinn, P. (1988) *Cry Out!* Eastbourne: Kingsway.

Radford, J. (2010) *Serious case review under Chapter VIII 'Working Together to Safeguard Children' in respect of the death of a child*, Case Number 14. Birmingham: Birmingham Safeguarding Board.

Radford, L., Corral, S., Bradley, C., Fisher, H., Bassett, C., Howat, N. and Collishaw, S. (2010) *Child abuse and neglect in the UK today.* London: NSPCC.

Radley, M. and Figley, C. (2007) 'The social psychology of compassion', *Clinical Social Work Journal*, 35, pp. 207–14.

Raynor, C. (2003) *How Did I Get Here From There?* London: Virago Press.

Rees, J. and Goldberg, J. (2009) *Life Story Books for Adopted Children: A Family Friendly Approach.* London: Jessica Kingsley.

Roberts, R., O'Connor, T., Dunn, J. and Golding, J. (2004) 'The effects of child sexual abuse in later life: mental health parenting and adjustment of offspring', *Child Abuse and Neglect*, 28, pp. 535–46.

Rogers, C. R. (1967) *On Becoming a Person.* London: Constable.

Rogers, C. R. (1980) *A Way of Being.* Boston, MA: Houghton Mifflin.

Rogowski, S. (2011) 'Managers, managerialism and social work with children and families: the deformation of a profession?', *Practice*, 23(3), pp. 157–67.

Rose, R. and Philpot, T. (2005) *The Child's Own Story: Life Story Work with Traumatized Children.* London: Jessica Kingsley.

Rothbaum, B. O. (2009) 'Using virtual reality to help our patients in the real world', *Depression and Anxiety*, 26, pp. 209–11.

Rouf, K. (1991a) *Black Girls Speak Out.* London: The Children's Society.

Rouf, K. (1991b) *Into Pandora's Box.* London: The Children's Society.

Rowan, A. B., Foy, D. W., Rodriguez, N. and Ryan, S. (1994)

'Posttraumatic stress disorder in a clinical sample of adults sexually abused as children', *Child Abuse and Neglect*, 18(1), pp. 51–62.

Rowlands, J. (2011) 'Need, well-being and outcomes: the development of policy-thinking for children's services 1989–2004', *Child & Family Social Work*, 16, pp. 255–65.

Rutter, M. (1979) 'Protective factors in children's response to stress and disadvantage', in J. S. Bruner and A. Garden (eds) *Primary Prevention of Psychopathology Vol 3*. Hanover, New Hampshire: University Press of New England.

Rutter, M. (1981) *Maternal Deprivation Reassessed*, 2nd edn. Harmondsworth: Penguin.

Rutter, M. (1996) 'Childhood resilience in the face of adversity', paper presented to 11th International Conference on Child Abuse and Neglect. University College, Dublin, August.

Ryan, G. (1989) 'Victim to victimiser: rethinking victim treatment', *Journal of Violence*, 4(3), pp. 325–41.

Ryan, T. and Walker, R. (2007) *Life Story Work: A Practical Guide to Helping Children Understand Their Past*, 3rd edn. London: BAAF.

Rymaszewska, J. and Philpot, T. (2006) *Reaching the Vulnerable Child*. London: Jessica Kingsley.

Salford Safeguarding Board (2010) *Serious case review: Child H, executive summary*. Salford: Salford Safeguarding Board.

Sedley, S. (1987) *Whose Child? The Report of the Panel Appointed to Inquire into the Death of Tyra Henry*. London: Borough of Lambeth.

Seidman, E. and Pedersen, S. (2003) 'Holistic contextual perspectives on risk, protection and competence among low-income urban adolescents', in Luthar, S. S. (ed.) *Resilience and Vulnerability*. Cambridge: Cambridge University Press.

Seligman, M. E. P. (1975) *Helplessness. On Depression, Development and Death*. San Francisco: W. H. Freeman.

Sellick, C., Thoburn, J. and Philpot, T. (2004) *What works in adoption and foster care?* Ilford: Barnados.

Selwyn, J., Saunders, H. and Farmer, E. (2010) 'The views of children and young people on being cared for by an independent foster-care provider', *British Journal Social Work*, 40, pp. 696–713.

Senate (2008) *Sexualisation of Children in the Contemporary Media*. Brisbane: Commonwealth of Australia.

Seymour, C. and Seymour, R. (2011) *Courtroom and Report Writing Skills for Social Workers*, 2nd edn. Exeter: Learning Matters.

Shah, S. and Argent, H. (2006) *Life Story Work – What It Is and What It Means: A Guide for Children and Young People*. London: BAAF.

Skinner, S. and Kimmel, E. (1984) *The Anti-Colouring Book*. London: Scholastic Books.

Smith, M. J. (1998) *Social Science in Question*. London: Sage.

Smith, M. L., Rengifo, A. F. and Vollman, B. K. (2008) 'Trajectories of abuse and disclosure: child sexual abuse by catholic priests', *Criminal Justice & Behavior*, 35, pp. 570–82.

Smith, R. (2009) 'Interprofessional learning and multi-professional practice for PQ', in Higham, P. (ed.) *Post-Qualifying Social Work Practice*. London: Sage Publications, pp. 135–47.

Solzhenitsyn, A. (1974) *The Gulag Archipelago 1918–56*. London: Collins/Fontana.

Somerville, J. W., Swanson, A. M., Robertson, R. L., Arnett, M. A. and MacLin, O. H. (2009) 'Handling a dog by children with attention-deficit/hyperactivity disorder: calming or exciting?', *North American Journal of Psychology*, 11(1), pp. 111–20.

Sperry, L. (2012) *Family Assessment*, 2nd edn. Abingdon, Oxon: Routledge.

Spratt, T. and Devaney, J. (2009) 'Identifying families with multiple problems: perspectives of practitioners and managers in three nations', *British Journal of Social Work*, 39, pp. 418–34.

Stafford, A., Vincent, S. and Parton, N. (eds) (2010) *Child Protection Reform Across the UK*. Edinburgh: Dunedin Academic Press.

Stalker, K., Lister, P. G., Lerpiniere, J. and McArthur, K. (2010) *Child protection and the needs and rights of disabled children and young people: A scoping study*. Strathclyde: University of Strathclyde.

Sterne, A. and Poole, L. (2010) *Domestic Violence and Children*. Abingdon, Oxon: Routledge.

Stevenson, O. (1996) 'Emotional abuse and neglect: a time for reappraisal', *Child And Family Social Work*, 1(1), pp. 13–18.

Stormshak, E. A., Bullock, B. M. and Falkenstein, C. A. (2009) 'Harnessing the power of sibling relationships as a tool for optimizing social–emotional development', in L. Kramer and K. J. Conger (eds) *Siblings as agents of socialization. New Directions for Child and Adolescent Development*, 126. San Francisco: Jossey-Bass, pp. 61–77.

Strenz, T. (1980) 'The Stockholm Syndrome: law enforcement, policy and ego defenses of the hostage', *Annals of the New York Academy of Sciences*, 347, pp. 137–50.

Sunderland, M. (2000) *Using Story Telling as a Therapeutic Tool with Children*. Bicester: Speechmark.

Sunderland, M. and Armstrong, N. (2001) *The Frog Who Longed for the Moon to Smile*. Bicester: Winslow.

Sunderland, M. and Armstrong, N. (2008) *Draw on Your Emotions*. Bicester: Speechmark Publishing.

Summit, R. C. (1983) 'The child sexual abuse accommodation syndrome', *Child Abuse and Neglect*, 7, pp. 177–93.

Symonds, M. (1980) 'Victim responses to terror', *Annals of the New York Academy of Sciences*, 347, pp. 129–36.

Taylor, I., Whiting, R. and Sharland, E. (2008) *Knowledge Review*.

Southampton: Higher Education Academy Subject Centre of Social Policy and Social Work.

Thomas, B. (2009) *Creative Coping Skills for Children*. London: Jessica Kingsley.

Thomas, M. and Philpot, N. (2009) *Fostering a Child's Recovery: Family Placement for Traumatised Children*. London: Jessica Kingsley.

Thompson, K., Biddle, K. R., Robinson-Long, M., Poger, J., Wang, J., Yang, Q. X. and Eslinger, P. J. (2009) 'Cerebral plasticity and recovery of function after childhood prefrontal cortex damage', *Developmental Neurorehabilitation*, 12(5), pp. 298–312.

Thompson, N. (2009) *People Skills*, 3rd edn. Basingstoke: Palgrave Macmillan.

Thompson, N. (2011) *Crisis Intervention*. Lyme Regis: Russell House Publishing

Timimi, S. (2010) 'The McDonaldization of childhood: children's mental health in neo-liberal market cultures', *Transcultural Psychiatry*, 47(5), pp. 686–706.

Tisdall, K., Davis, J. and Gallagher, M. (eds) (2009) *Researching with Children and Young People*. London: Sage.

Tomoda, A., Sheu, Y-S., Rabi, K., Suzuki, H., Navalta, C. P., Polcari, A. and Teicher, M. H. (2011) 'Exposure to parental verbal abuse is associated with increased gray matter volume superior temporal gyrus', *NeuroImage*, 54, S280–S286.

Triebenacher, S. L. (1998) 'The relationship between attachment to companion animals and self-esteem: a developmental perspective', in Wilson, C. C. and Turner, D. C. (eds) *Companion Animals in Human Health*. Thousand Oaks: Sage.

Tsujimoto, S. (2008) 'The prefrontal cortex: functional neural development during early childhood', *Neuroscientist*, 14, pp. 345–58.

Tuckman, B. (1965) 'Developing sequences in small groups', *Psychological Bulletin*, 63, pp. 384–99.

Tuckman, B. and Jensen, M. (1977) 'Stages in small group development revisited', *Group Organizational Studies*, 2, pp. 419–27.

Turney, D., Platt, D., Selwyn, J. and Farmer, E. (2012) *Improving Child and Family Assessments: Turning Research into Practice*. London: Jessica Kingsley Publishers.

Twardosz, S. and Lutzker, J. R. (2010) 'Child maltreatment and the developing brain: A review of neuroscience perspectives', *Aggression and Violent Behavior*, 15, pp. 59–68.

Urh, S. (2011) 'Ethnic sensitivity: a challenge for social work', *International Social Work*, 54(4), pp. 471–84.

Vincent, S. (2009) *Learning from Child Deaths and Serious Abuse in Scotland*. Edinburgh: Dunedin Academic Press.

Vincent, S., Daniel, B. and Jackson, S. (2010) 'Where now for "child protection" in Scotland?', *Child Abuse Review*, 19(6), pp. 438–56.

Vizard, E. (1987) 'Self esteem and personal safety', in *ACPP Newsletter*, 9(2), pp. 16–22.

Vygotsky, L. S. (1978) *Mind in Society*. Cambridge, MA: Harvard University Press.

Wade, J., Biehal, N., Farrelly, N. and Sinclair, I. (2011) *Caring for Abused and Neglected Children*. London: Jessica Kingsley Publishers.

Walker, M. (1992) *Surviving Secrets*. Buckingham: Open University Press.

Walton, P. (2002) 'Safeguarding and promoting children's welfare: a question of competence?', in Wilson, K. and James, A. (eds) *The Child Protection Handbook*, 2nd edn. Edinburgh: Harcourt Publishers.

Wanlass, J., Moreno, J. K. and Thomson, H. M. (2006) 'Group therapy for abused and neglected youth: therapeutic and child advocacy challenges', *The Journal for Specialists in Group Work*, 31(4), pp. 311–26.

Ward, H., Skuse, T. and Munro, E. (2005) ' "The best of times, the worst of times": young people's views of care and accommodation', *Adoption & Fostering*, 29(1), pp. 8–17.

Washington, K. T. (2008) 'Attachment and alternatives: theory in child welfare research', *Advances in Social Work*, 9(1), pp. 8–16.

Waterhouse, R. (2000) *Lost in Care: report of the tribunal of inquiry into the abuse of children in care in the former county council areas of Gwynedd and Clwyd since 1974*. Norwich: The Stationery Office.

Waterhouse, S. and Brocklesby, E. (2001) 'Placement choice in temporary foster care', *Adoption and Fostering*, 25(3), pp. 39–46.

Waters, E., Vaughan, B. E., Posada, G. and Kondo-Ikemura, K. (eds) (1995) 'Caregiving, Cultural and Cognitive Perspectives on Secure-Base Behavior and Working Models', *Monographs of the Society for Research in Child Development*, 60, pp. 27–48.

Watson, F., Burrows, H. and Player, C. (2002) *Integrating Theory and Practice in Social Work Education*. London: Jessica Kingsley.

Wechsler-Zimring, A. and Kearney, C. A. (2011) 'Posttraumatic stress and related symptoms among neglected and physically and sexually maltreated adolescents', *Journal of Traumatic Stress*, 24(5), pp. 601–4.

Wedl, M. and Kotrschal, K. (2009) 'Social and individual components of animal contact in preschool children', *Anthrozoos*, 22(4), pp. 333–96.

Welsh Assembly Government (2008) *All Wales Child Protection Procedures*. Cardiff: Welsh Assembly Government.

Wendt, S., Tuckey, M. R. and Prosser, B. (2011) 'Thriving, not just surviving, in emotionally demanding fields of practice', *Health and Social Care in the Community*, 19(3), pp. 317–25.

Westergaard, J. (2009) *Effective Group Work with Young People*. Buckingham: Open University Press.

Wiffin, J. (2012) *Mastering Assessment in Child and Family Social Work*. London: Jessica Kingsley.

Williams, L. M. (1994) 'Recall of childhood trauma: a prospective study of women's memories of child sexual abuse', *Journal of Consulting and Clinical Psychology*, 62, pp. 1167–76.

Wilson, K. and James, A. (eds) (2007) *The Child Protection Handbook*. 3rd edn. London: Ballière Tindall.

Winter, K. (2010) 'The perspectives of young children in care about their circumstances and implications for social work practice', *Child & Family Social Work*, 15, pp. 186–95.

Wisdom. C. S., Raphael, K. G. and DuMont, K. A. (2004) 'The case for prospective longitudinal studies in child maltreatment research', *Child Abuse and Neglect*, 28, pp. 715–22.

Woodhead, M. and Faulkner, D. (2008) 'Subject, object or participants: dilemmas of psychological research with children', in Christensen, P. and James, A. (eds) *Research with Children: Perspectives and Practices*, 2nd edn. Abingdon, Oxon: Routledge, pp. 10–39.

Woon, F. L. and Hedges, D. W. (2008) 'Hippocampal and amygdala volumes in children and adults with childhood maltreatment-related posttraumatic stress disorder: a meta-analysis', *Hippocampus*, 18, pp. 729–36.

Worsham, N. L and Goodvin, R. (2007) 'The Bee Kind Garden: A qualitative description of work with maltreated children', *Clinical Child Psychology and Psychiatry*, 12, pp. 261–79.

Yen Mah, A. (2002) *Chinese Cinderella*. Harlow, Essex: Longman.

Yorke, J. (2010) 'The significance of human–animal relationships as modulators of trauma effects in children: a developmental neurobiological perspective', *Early Child Development and Care*, 180(5), pp. 559–70.

Yule, V. C. (1985) 'Why are Parents Tough on Children?', *New Society*, 27 September, pp. 444–6.

Zeitlin, H. (2002) 'Adoption of children from minority groups', in Dwivedi, N. (ed.) *Meeting the Needs of Ethnic Minority Children*, 2nd edn. London: Jessica Kingsley.

Zolotor, A. J. and Puzla, M. E. (2010) 'Bans against corporal punishment: a systematic review of the laws, changes in attitudes and behaviours', *Child Abuse Review*, 19(4), pp. 229–47.

Index